Jenny Hartley was among the first intake of students at the University of Kent in 1965, where she read English and American Literature. She went on to complete a Ph.D at the University of Essex on Victorian women novelists. She currently works as a part-time Senior Lecturer at the Roehampton Institute of Higher Education, where she teaches courses on women writers, images of women, and the literature of war. She lives in London with her husband and two sons.

CONTENTS

xi

ABBREVIATIONS

AFS	Auxiliary Fire Service
ARP	Air Raid Precautions
ATS	Auxiliary Territorial Service
BEF	British Expeditionary Force
BUF	British Union of Fascists
CO	Commanding Officer
ENSA	Entertainments National Service Association
FANY	First Aid Nursing Yeomanry
LDV	Local Defence Volunteers (later Home Guard)
MT	Motor Transport
NAAFI	Navy, Army and Airforce Institutes (operated canteens)
POW	Prisoner of War
WAAF	Women's Auxiliary Air Force
WLA	Women's Land Army
WRNS	Women's Royal Naval Service (known as Wrens)
WVS	Women's Voluntary Service

[. . .]   indicates a cut made by the editor

Small changes in spelling and punctuation have been made for the sake of consistency

INTRODUCTION

Journalism has become the eyes of modern writing.
> DIANA TRILLING, *HARPER'S MAGAZINE*, MAY 1944.

The act of keeping the record straight is valuable in itself.
> MARTHA GELLHORN, *THE FACE OF WAR*, 1959.

Any authentic record seems valuable because from thousands of [. . .] stories we can construct a picture out of the jigsaw of formless details.
> BRYHER, *LIFE AND LETTERS TODAY*, OCTOBER 1941.

The Second World War inspired an outburst of women's writing, creating a rich and moving legacy for readers in the years to come. In books and magazines, letters and diaries, countless women – some of them writers by profession but many of them not – put down on paper their versions of the war. A selection of that material is reproduced here, telling us what the war felt and looked like to the women experiencing it. 'Fiction pales by comparison,' wrote Diana Trilling in 1944. Non-fiction was acknowledged as the best medium for keeping 'the record straight', as Martha Gellhorn put it. But the record of the war is not one record. An anthology with its 'jigsaw of details' can help to give a more complete picture, a fuller record than a single account. It can also try to do justice to the immense variety of experience that opened up to women at the time, as well as to the extraordinary literary talent that took this opportunity to flourish.

THE FUNCTION OF WRITING IN WARTIME

This is just a typical experience of hundreds of simple people who never thought they would have to face anything like it. So I record it.
> VERE HODGSON, 4 JANUARY 1942, *FEW EGGS AND NO ORANGES*

The memories being recorded and published in recent years add immeasurably to our understanding of the war. This anthology contains no oral accounts because it has a different emphasis. It shows how women wrote

1

the war at the time, what it looked like from their perspective as they tried to shape and make sense of their experiences. How did they want to present the war to themselves and others at the time? How were they constrained by that very war itself in how they might write it? Memory has its own controlling pressures, some of them nostalgic; the writing of a particular moment is born out of different needs.

For some women, writing itself became an imperative and symbolic act, keeping 'alive something that is vital to us', and now 'needed more than ever', as Rumer Godden wrote to her sister in April 1940.[1] Freedom of expression was frequently extolled as one of the principles the Allies were fighting for, and the pen was a weapon available to both sexes. At the beginning of the war Virginia Woolf used an uncharacteristically bellicose image about her writing when she described 'the little pitter patter of ideas' as 'my whiff of shot in the cause of freedom'. 'Thinking', she wrote in 1940, 'is my fighting.'[2] This desire also lies behind Elizabeth Bowen's suggestion that all wartime writing is 'in a sense [. . .] resistance writing'.[3]

Writing filled many needs. For some, 'keeping the record straight' became an obsession. 'I am hardly awake in the morning when I reach for this book to write in it,' noted Sarah Gertrude Millin in 1942.[4] She published a book for each year of the war, mixtures of news reporting and personal commentary, which were her way of imposing order on the war. Leonora Eyles, another professional writer, had a more specific obligation. *For My Enemy Daughter* was the letter that could not be sent to her daughter who had married an Italian and was living in Italy. Julia Tremayne was also cut off from her daughter, and her as yet unseen granddaughter. Living on the German-occupied Channel Island of Sark, she could not send letters to England, but wrote to her daughter frequently. The letters were then hidden carefully, 'and as shooting seems to be the penalty for most things I must make my cubby-hole very safe'.[5] Writing letters, even if they could not be sent, created a reassuring fantasy of communication.

Others used writing to keep in touch more directly, the war making letter-writers out of many who had not been accustomed to express themselves on paper. This was the last great age of letter-writing between families split up by evacuation, military service and war work. The collections of letters in the Imperial War Museum testify to the literary powers developed by many women who often wrote as the family's correspondent to absent members. Women's particular skills as letter-writers were recognized in the practice which spread among servicemen abroad of asking visiting female celebrities to write home for them. Elsie and Doris Waters ('Gert and Daisy'), Joyce Grenfell, Eleanor Roosevelt and Adele Astaire were all inundated with requests and complied good-naturedly. Joyce Grenfell tried 'hard to make each one different and try to imagine the homes the letters are going to. But it takes time. However, it seems, mysteriously, to give pleasure.'[6]

With personal letters written to strangers, the traditional categories of letters (written to others you know), books (written to others you do not know) and diaries (written for yourself) started to blur. The movement seemed to have been towards the public. The private form of the diary sometimes took on the function of a letter. Vere Hodgson started her diary in order to send it to her cousin in Rhodesia; Hilda Silberman duplicated her letters to friends in America 'as a general news-letter from England in wartime'. She must have been one of the pioneers of this new form of letter, and was 'gratified' when recipients forwarded them to the local press. 'Thus a wider circle gets direct news from Britain.'[7] Books, on the other hand, often seemed to want to forge a more personal note, to close the distance between author and reader into an intimate conversation between two people. In 1940 Naomi Jacob began *Me – In War-Time*: 'You must take it as a very ordinary woman, trying to discuss with you her everyday problems, which, it may be, are the same problems as you, yourself face.' Two years later Vera Brittain cast her controversial pacifist pamphlet, *Humiliation with Honour*, in the form of letters addressed to her fifteen-year-old son. Letters were a powerful wartime form. Vera Lynn's popular radio programme 'Sincerely Yours' was billed in the *Radio Times*, 'To the men of the Forces: A letter in words and music from Vera Lynn.'

Naomi Jacob 'trying to discuss with you', Vere Hodgson sending her diary abroad, Joyce Grenfell writing to the 'wives, mothers and a sweetheart of four of the very ill boys in the big orthopaedic ward' – whether they broaden or contract the traditional form, they all illustrate the same phenomenon: the function of women's wartime writing as friendship. It is not surprising that friendship should be particularly important in wartime, and writing could sustain and develop comforting relationships. Anne Frank's *Diary*, perhaps the most famous of all women's wartime writing, is addressed to Kitty, the diary with its own status as the best friend much needed during Anne's time in hiding from the Nazis. In June 1942, when Anne received the diary, she wrote on the flyleaf: 'I hope I shall be able to confide in you completely, as I have never been able to do in anyone before, and I hope that you will be a great support and comfort to me.' By September the *Diary* was addressed to other friends as well as Kitty, and Anne added to the flyleaf:

> I have had a lot of support from you so far, and also from our beloved club to whom I now write regularly, I think this way of keeping a diary is much nicer and now I can hardly wait for when I have time to write in you. *I am, Oh, so glad that I took you along.*

The diary remained vital. 'I will write my diary and keep sane' was Naomi Mitchison's resolution at the beginning of the war.[8] Like many others, she recognized how helpful writing could be in affording her a measure of control over her life. Joan Veazey strapped her diary to her wrist so that she could write as she worked through the Blitz in her husband's London parish,[9] an ingenious device but presumably a bit awkward. It shows how important keeping a diary must have been to her. Others faced more than awkwardness for the sake of their diaries. Bessy Myers was imprisoned by the Germans in France in 1940, and realized what an incriminating document hers was – 'I must be mad, mad, mad'.[10] Before the war was over women were rereading their diaries to remember themselves as they had been, and the selves they had written and created in the earlier years of the war.

There was another impulse for some of these wartime writers, as the sub-title of Vere Hodgson's *Few Eggs and No Oranges* suggests: 'A Diary Showing how Unimportant People in London and Birmingham Lived through the War Years 1939–1945'; Hilda Silberman's title, too, *Unimportant Letters of Important Years*. The word 'unimportant' appears again and again in women's descriptions of themselves. So does 'ordinary'. Why this insistence? In part, it seems to be a signal, a woman declaring her place in the ranks of the People's War. Partly too, it was a recognition of the significance of this particular moment in history, when ordinary existence was intersected by the extraordinary phenomenon of war. It was also a flag waving in celebration of ordinary life, those virtues of British life to be valued, defended, fought for, and carefully documented. The writer needed to make the ordinary visible and therefore valuable. Margaret Robson explained that she was publishing her late husband's letters 'because I thought that there was room for a war book which was not written around some exciting incident or escape, but showed war as it really was from the point of view of the ordinary front-line soldier'.[11]

Through writing, then, women could memorialize. They could also reach out, personalize, soften the sharp edge of war. ATS women who packed spares for tank repairs going overseas often included personal notes, a prac-tice frowned on by the army. Landgirls put messages in sacks of potatoes and Red Cross knitters tucked notes into the toes of socks going out to India. Children's clothes and shoes coming to Britain from America some-times held a letter and a prayer or a blessing for the recipient.

Writing could also help to keep the war at bay, which could be one reason why wartime writing is often more light-hearted and flippant than we might expect. Anita Leslie worked as an ambulance driver in France, a harrowing experience, yet her accounts came as a surprise to her family: 'We were rather shocked, dear, by your very frivolous letter.'[12] Writing could offer a useful turning away from war. Anne Lee-Michell commented later on her wartime diary: 'Many entries now seem to me facetious. I think we craved humour during our anxieties and that I recorded anything that made us laugh.'[13]

4

To write is also to have a voice for others. Some of the women in this collection have written on behalf of others who were unable to do so: those in concentration camps, those who died, those living in unbearable conditions, and especially those too young to write for themselves. They also wrote to protest against anti-semitism and racism.

WOMEN AND THE LITERATURE OF WAR

You would need to be half-dead not to feel observant and curious *now* about the general scene – and all our note-taking, the good with the bad, will be useful some day, to those whose job it will be to 'compose' this time, in terms of history or of art.

KATE O'BRIEN, *THE FORTNIGHTLY*, 1941.

As truthful as history but as readable as fiction.

VERA BRITTAIN, *TESTAMENT OF EXPERIENCE*, 1957.

Women have always had a role in war and the literature of war. From *The Iliad* onwards, when Hector tells his wife Andromache how she will grieve and 'ache again' after his death in battle, women have had their place as watchers and mourners, and as symbols of what men are fighting for. These are passive roles; until this century women were rarely involved in war and rarely wrote about it. It was with the First World War that they entered the arena of war, nursing and driving ambulances near the front lines, making munitions and filling men's jobs at home. These new experiences laid the foundations for the new genre of women's war writing, which rapidly established itself with a crop of poems, journals and novels.[14] With the Second World War the relation between women and war expanded and intensified dramatically. For the first time in this country the whole population was involved in the war, the women and children as well as the men. Bombs are no respecters of age or sex. And for the first time in the history of this country, women were conscripted into the forces or war-related jobs.

These new and stirring times for women had to be recorded, and in new ways. Choices were made on the first day of the war, as Virginia Woolf's diary for 3 September 1939 shows: 'M(abel) said train very empty. I believe little exact notes are more interesting than reflections.' They certainly were, and Woolf was not alone in her appreciation of the small facts rather than the large acts of war. It was the effects rather than the deeds of war which interested women writers. War was forcing new conjunctions between public and private in their own lives, and these conjunctions called for expression. New hybrids emerged as women writers blended previously discrete genres such as journalism, fiction and autobiography. Sometimes they anticipated later literary developments. Clare Boothe's description of her writing looks towards the New Journalism of the 1960s: 'I was interested far less in events themselves than in the effect they had on people's hearts and minds. Above all, I was interested in how *I* felt about how they felt, which is a highly emotional and egoistic approach that would disqualify anybody at once as an "objective journalist".'[15] She and other women used their brief to exploit the 'personal angle' in order to explore the effects of the war upon the individual.

Vera Brittain's success with her First World War *Testament of Youth* had shown how a 'new type of autobiography', as she called it, could do justice to women's experience of war. This autobiographical impulse combined with women's traditional propensity towards the novel, and with the documentary styles of the 1930s, to initiate some strikingly apt innovations. In 1941 Inez Holden published *Night Shift*, a highly acclaimed series of sketches of work in an aircraft factory. It is narrative by snapshot, setting up and wilfully shattering the expectations of fiction. At the end it abruptly shatters itself when the factory is suddenly blown to pieces. Kay Boyle's novel, *Primer For Combat* (1943), parallels a sympathetically observed report of the fall of France with a more bitterly described story of a marital break-up. Sarah Gertrude Millin's books put detailed journalism alongside disjointed accounts of her own experience and opinions, while Amy St Loe Strachey's *Borrowed Children* (1940) mixes diary and case-history, story and sociology. Strachey's hope seems to be that the intractable problems created by evacuation will be dissolved by the wish-fulfilling structures of romance. Edith Olivier and Storm Jameson provided themselves with fictional personae for their wartime diaries, and Gertrude Stein brandished her own wonderful mixture of history, geography, and stream of idiosyncrasy in *Wars I Have Seen* (1945). Elizabeth Bowen said that she wrote short stories instead of novels because 'during the war [. . .] it would have been impossible to have been writing only one book'.[16] Some of these books *do* seem to be more than one book, as they stretch and improvise in order to accommodate and express new experiences.

GRIEF AND WOMEN'S WRITING

Denny took the measurements (for the blackout) and began to add them up. Seeing the tea-table with [. . .] the children and the big boys still there I began to cry. I had to keep on going out during tea-time to cry on the stairs.

NAOMI MITCHISON, *YOU MAY WELL ASK, A MEMOIR 1920–1940*, 1979.

The girl in the green-grocer's shop was red-eyed this morning: her husband had been killed in Germany. I didn't sympathise: that would have seemed bathetic, somehow impertinent. Another assistant mentioned it. The girl said briefly: 'Worse has happened to others,' and walked off.

MARY SEATON, 'THOUGHTS FROM HOME', *LEAVES IN THE STORM*,
SCHIMANSKY AND TREECE (EDS), 1947.

I am very much aware that I am not describing the emotional aspect of all this but it is not easy.

MARGERY ALLINGHAM, *THE OAKEN HEART*, 1941.

In men's war writing women mourn, but grief seems to be strangely absent from women's war writing. In the public arena at least, women seem to have felt the pressure of male codes of behaviour, to the extent of being unable or unwilling to show grief openly. Even the customary forms of condolence were infected by this reticence, as Virginia Woolf noticed: '"Please, no letters" I read this twice in *The Times* Deaths column from parents of dead officers.'[17] Woolf saw this as part of 'the myth making stage of the war we're in', in which women seemed to be caught up in the myth of the British stiff upper lip. Public grief would have been unpatriotic, feminine, weak. Writing towards the end of the war, Mary Seaton commented on 'the lack of ostentation in today's grief. It isn't just that mourning arm bands and memorial services in the village church are out of fashion. People's feelings are becoming more proudly their own affair.'[18]

The low visibility of grief in their published writing shows how women's values and emotions can never wholly enmesh with those of a nation at war. Part of women's public war language must be silence. This was almost national policy, with restraint and suppression impressed upon wives writing to their husbands away on active service. Women's magazines advised their readers not to worry their menfolk with tales of hardship or confessions of infidelity. Suppression becomes a characteristic mode for women in wartime. Perhaps this accounts for some of the popularity of the 1945 film *Brief Encounter*, a celebration of heroic suppression.

With careful attention, however, the significant gaps and silences reveal themselves: those moments, for example, when Naomi Mitchison and others go off to cry on the stairs. Or there may be a brief, painful revelation, such as the parenthesis which punctures a breezy letter about a son's departure for training: '– the nightmare I have envisaged ever since he was born: that the youth of his generation should be ruined as was my own. –'[19] Books with titles like *No Time for Tears* and *No Time to Weep* remind us of the presence of tears and weeping, even while stoically brushing them aside.

WAR FROM THE WOMEN'S PERSPECTIVE

Didn't women have their war as well?'

VERA BRITTAIN, *TESTAMENT OF EXPERIENCE*, 1957.

The women's perspective of the Second World War seems to have three distinctive hallmarks. First, it is largely anti-war, although in a submerged way. In 1938 Virginia Woolf published *Three Guineas*, which starts from the question 'how are we to prevent war?' This would have been the desire of practically all the writers in this anthology, many of whom would also have agreed with her about the relationship between war and the construction of gender: 'No, I don't see what's (to) be done about war. It's manliness; and manliness breeds womanliness – both so hateful.'[20] War is, then, basically a male activity, to which women must always stand at an angle, however implicated they are.

Secondly, at the time, women recognized the transience of their wartime experiences. Hilary Wayne was speaking for many women when she said that 'in the ATS one felt one was suspended – disconnected from pre and post-war life'.[21] It was this very sense of disconnection, of difference whether for good or bad, which impelled women to record what they knew would be the most highly charged moments of their lives. They did not know when the war would end but they acknowledged its status in their lives as an exceptional parenthesis.

The third characteristic of the women's perspective is that it was largely outlawed by the literary world of the time. The proliferation of small magazines has often been noted, but there were surprisingly few contributions in them by women. The explanation for this was given by the leader of the pack, Cyril Connolly, editor of *Horizon*:

> We take the line that experiences connected with the blitz, the shopping queues, the home front, deserted wives, deceived husbands, broken homes, dull jobs, bad schools, group squabbles, are so much a picture of our ordinary lives that unless the workmanship is outstanding we are prejudiced against them.[22]

This list effectively bans most female experience. Luckily, the women themselves did not take the Connolly line, and reached for their pens.

In compiling this collection I have, with a few exceptions, included only published material, most of it now out of print. Given the demands of war work and the shortages of paper, the amount that was written and published during the war is astounding. But reading was of course a good way to get through some of the tedium of the war, and books and articles about the war were popular. There was, according to the official historians, 'a striking increase in the expenditure on books'.[23] 'New books appear daily,' Hilda Silberman noted in 1942, 'but in small editions and are quickly out of print.' This anthology is an attempt to rescue a fraction of the ephemeral literature of wartime books and magazines, letters and diaries.

I have chosen only what was originally published in English, and mainly from the standpoint of Britain. Boundaries had to be drawn somewhere. There are a few accounts from France, but the Far East is almost entirely missing. I have included some American women as the relationship between Britain and America was such an important part of the experience of the war in Britain.

The Imperial War Museum keeps a huge collection of unpublished writing available for public inspection. Between eight and nine hundred items on the Second World War, ranging from a single letter to multi-volume memoirs, are by women. Retrospective memoirs predominate, but there are some contemporary letters and diaries. The unpublished pieces in this anthology come from or via the Imperial War Museum: private voices of love or grief which are missing from the published accounts.

I have tried to choose what was written during the war or soon afterwards, but this has not always been possible; there are inevitably some exceptions, and also some gaps. Accounts of top secret work, for example, would have to be left till later. Sexual revelations would for the most part come later too, although the collections of personal letters in the Imperial War Museum show women writing about sex with admirable openness and frankness when they can be sure of a sympathetic reception. But on the whole there is little overt sex in this version of the war, and there is little from working class women either.

The American Martha Gellhorn listened to two WAAFs at work in a control tower and commented on 'the girls' voices that sound so remarkable to us (it is hard to decide why, perhaps because they seem so poised, so neat)'. So poised, so neat: these words could well describe much of the prose in this anthology. It is for the most part the prose of middle-class women. Many people hoped that the war would break down class barriers, and to some extent it did, with middle-class women going into factories, extending their limited circles of acquaintance and so on. But as can be seen from the paragraph in which Rose Macaulay welcomed the way the war would 'resolve class distinctions', and yet at the same time remarked how 'the less well instructed pronounced "*sireen*" for "siren",'[24] the barriers could not come down overnight. Nor would working-class women unused to writing suddenly rush to put down their experiences in print. Some of their accounts are coming out now, and a missing part of the picture is being completed.

This anthology's version of the war may, then, be an incomplete one; nevertheless it offers a wonderful body of literature to appreciate, and a way into women's wartime life as it seemed at the time. The value of this contemporary perspective is highlighted with particular neatness by the cover picture, the meaning of which has shifted considerably over the years. Abram Games's recruitment poster for the ATS is one of the war's most famous images of women. At the time it was highly controversial: there was too much lipstick, too much glamour. This was not how wartime women should be depicted. The uproar reached the House of Commons and the poster was withdrawn. Fifty years later the Blonde Bombshell, as she was known, returns to grace a collection of her contemporaries' writings. She seems now not so much provocative as confident and assured, just the image to represent the millions of women who responded to the war with 'hearts undefeated'.

Notes

1. Letter of April 1940, quoted in Rumer Godden, *A Time To Dance, No Time To Weep*, Macmillan, 1987.
2. Entries for 16 September 1939 and 15 May 1940, *The Diary of Virginia Woolf*, Vol. V 1936–1941, ed. A.O. Bell, The Hogarth Press, 1984.
3. Elizabeth Bowen, Preface to the American edition of *The Demon Lover*, 1945, reprinted in *Collected Impressions*, Longmans, 1950.
4. Sarah Gertrude Millin, *The Pit of the Abyss*, Faber and Faber, 1946.
5. Julia Tremayne, *War on Sark*, Webb & Bower, 1981.
6. Joyce Grenfell, Hyderabad, 18 December 1944, *The Time of My Life, Entertaining the Troops, Her Wartime Journals*, ed. J. Roose-Evans, Hodder & Stoughton, 1989.
7. Hilda Silberman, *Unimportant Letters of Important Years 1941–1951*, The Favil Press, 1951.
8. Naomi Mitchison, *You May Well Ask, A Memoir 1920–1940*, Gollancz, 1979.
9. See Michael Moynihan, *People At War 1939–1945*, David and Charles, 1974.
10. Bessy Myers, *Captured, My Experiences as an Ambulance Driver and as a Prisoner of the Nazis*, George Harrap, 1941.
11. Postscript to Walter Robson, *Letters from a Soldier*, Faber and Faber, 1960.
12. Anita Leslie, *Train to Nowhere*, Hutchinson, 1953.
13. Quoted in Moynihan, *People At War*.
14. See Claire Tylee, *The Great War and Women's Consciousness*, Macmillan, 1990.
15. Clare Boothe, *European Spring*, Hamish Hamilton, 1941.
16. Elizabeth Bowen, op. cit.
17. Virginia Woolf, entry for 3 June 1940, *The Diary of Virginia Woolf*, Vol. V.
18. Mary Seaton, 'Thoughts from Home', *Leaves in the Storm*, eds Schimansky and Treece, Lindsay Drummond, 1947.
19. Quoted in Naomi Royde Smith, *Outside Information, Being a Diary of Rumours*, Macmillan, 1941.
20. Letter to Shena, Lady Simon, 25 January 1941, *Leave The Letters Till We're Dead, The Letters of Virginia Woolf 1936–1941*, ed. Nigel Nicolson, The Hogarth Press, 1980.
21. Hilary Wayne, *Two Odd Soldiers*, George Allen & Unwin, 1946.
22. *Horizon*, January 1944.
23. E.L. Hargreaves and M.M. Gowing, *Civil Industry and Trade*, HMSO & Longmans, 1952.
24. Rose Macaulay, *Life Among The English*, Collins, 1942.

Chapter one

PRELUDE

Throughout the 1930s Germany was re-arming. Most people in Britain hoped to avoid a war, but felt it was inevitable after the 1938 Munich Crisis. Thirty-eight million gas masks were issued, and trenches dug for air-raid shelters. Many women writing at this time were sceptical of all politicians, and women's magazines often made the point that with more women in power, war could be averted. But although there were some famous pacifist exceptions, such as Vera Brittain and Sybil Thorndike, most came to agree with the view that Nazism must be resisted by force.

With the approach of war came the urge to write. Reporters such as Martha Gellhorn, Virginia Cowles and Clare Hollingworth were already covering the European scene; but the idea of reporting a war also appealed to women who were not journalists. Polly Peabody was a young American Red Cross worker who managed to get herself to Norway at the beginning of the war. From there she filed her first newspaper story: 'It was terribly exciting, and I felt as if I were a character in a Hollywood movie. The word "scoop" became a thrilling new addition to my vocabulary. Writing had always been a day-dream on which I had dwelt during solitary hours.' The war made Peabody's dream come true; she worked as a war reporter and published *Occupied Territory* in 1941.

Other women with no such ambitions for professional careers as writers also reached for their pens; many diaries were started in 1939. Some of these, including Nella Last's, were kept for Mass Observation, the social survey organization set up by Charles Madge and Tom Harrisson in 1937. Why did women bother to sit up late with their diaries, and add to the labour of their wartime days? A good reason is suggested by one diarist, Anne Lee-Michell: 'Perhaps I felt dimly that we were assisting, however remotely, in historic events.' And as the war went on those left feeling lonely and vulnerable found comfort in confiding in their diaries.

VIRGINIA COWLES
The 1938 Nuremberg Rally

I saw the spirit of Nazi Germany flowing through the ancient streets of Nuremberg like a river that had burst its dams. A million red, white and black swastikas fluttered from the window-ledges, and the town, swollen to three times its normal size, resounded to the ring of leather boots and blazed with a bewildering array of uniforms.

Although the vast regimentation of modern Germany was a phenomenon which only the machine age could produce, at night the medieval background became curiously real. The clock swung back to the Middle Ages. The long red pennants, fluttering from the turreted walls of Nuremberg Castle, shone in the moonlight like the standards of an old religious war; the tramp of marching feet and the chorus of voices chanting the militant Nazi hymns had all the passion of an ancient crusade. It was only when you heard the sudden whine of a silver-winged fighter, travelling at three hundred miles an hour, that you were jerked back to the grim reality of 1938.

That grim reality had cast a dread shadow over the Party Congress, for this was 'crisis week'. Never in history had a crisis been more cold-bloodedly manufactured. For days the world had known the exact form it would take, even the date of its culmination. It had watched the attack against Czechoslovakia growing in violence, and now, with the German Army mobilized, it waited for the crescendo to be sounded by Hitler's speech, dramatically planned for the last day of the Congress. [. . .]

The idea of the superman was encouraged by the vast displays in Nuremberg. Everything that was done was done on a gigantic scale. The power of the spectacles lay not so much in their ingeniousness but in their immensity. The keynote was always repetition and uniformity. Instead of a few gilt eagles there were hundreds; instead of hundreds of flags there were thousands; instead of thousands of performers there were hundreds of thousands.

At night the mystic quality of the ritual was exaggerated by huge burning urns at the top of the stadium, their orange flames leaping into the blackness, while the flood-lighting effect of hundreds of powerful searchlights played eerily against the sky. The music had an almost religious solemnity, timed by the steady beat of drums that sounded like the distant throb of tom-toms.

One night I went to the stadium with Jules Sauerwein to hear an address Hitler was making to Nazi political leaders gathered from all over Germany. The stadium was packed with nearly 200,000 spectators. As the

12

time for the Führer's arrival drew near, the crowd grew restless. The minutes passed and the wait seemed interminable. Suddenly the beat of the drums increased and three motor cycles with yellow standards fluttering from their windshields raced through the gates. A few minutes later a fleet of black cars rolled swiftly into the arena: in one of them, standing in the front seat, his hand outstretched in the Nazi salute, was Hitler.

The demonstration that followed was one of the most extraordinary I have ever witnessed. Hitler climbed to his box in the Grand Stand amid a deafening ovation, then gave a signal for the political leaders to enter. They came, a hundred thousand strong, through an opening in the far end of the arena. In the silver light they seemed to pour into the bowl like a flood of water. Each of them carried a Nazi flag and when they were assembled in mass formation, the bowl looked like a shimmering sea of swastikas.

Then Hitler began to speak. The crowd hushed into silence, but the drums continued their steady beat. Hitler's voice rasped into the night and every now and then the multitude broke into a roar of cheers. Some of the audience began swaying back and forth, chanting 'Sieg Heil' over and over again in a frenzy of delirium. I looked at the faces round me and saw tears streaming down people's cheeks. The drums had grown louder and I suddenly felt frightened. For a moment I wondered if it wasn't a dream; perhaps we were really in the heart of the African jungle. I had a sudden feeling of claustrophobia and whispered to Jules Sauerwein, asking if we couldn't leave. It was a silly question, for we were hemmed in on all sides, and there was nothing to do but sit there until the bitter end. [. . .]

The most fashionable gathering-place in Nuremberg was the Grand Hotel. [. . .] Outstanding in the English group were Lord and Lady Redesdale and their daughter, the Honourable Unity Valkyrie Mitford. [. . .] To Unity, National Socialism was a Left Wing revolution and Hitler the champion of the downtrodden masses. There was no doubt that the latter was flattered by her admiration and sincerely fond of her. He often telephoned her, gave her presents, and in public treated her with deference. Although the Nazi Party leaders fawned over her in public, in private they were jealous of the friendship. Tom Mitford told me that when Unity went to Germany they often refused to tell Hitler she had arrived. The only way she could get into communication with him was to wait in the street, sometimes for hours, hoping to catch his eye when he passed. [. . .]

Her rather naive observations on Hitler were at times strangely revealing. When I asked her what she talked with him about, she replied, 'Gossip'. He liked to hear the anecdotes his advisers were apt to overlook. For instance, when Madame de Fontanges, the French journalist, fired a revolver at Count de Chambrun, the French Ambassador in Rome, declaring that the latter had tried to thwart her romance with Mussolini,

Unity related the episode to Hitler. She said he thought it very funny and laughed delightedly, saying what a narrow squeak it might have been for 'poor old Mussolini'.

According to her, Hitler had a sense of humour and liked company. [. . .] The remark that struck me most was her comment on Hitler's talent as an imitator. She claimed that if he were not the Führer of Germany, he would make a hundred thousand dollars a year on the vaudeville stage. He often did imitations of his colleagues – Goering, Goebbels and Himmler – but, best of all, he liked to imitate Mussolini. This always provoked roars of laughter. 'And sometimes,' added Unity, 'he even imitates himself.'

BELLA FROMM

Flight from Germany

Paris, 6 September 1938:

The last two days were a nightmare: At the last minute I discovered that I needed a Belgian visa, because of the one hour's ride at night through that country. I could not get it without photographs. It took a great deal of scurrying around, but it was all finally arranged.

At nine o'clock the night express came thundering into the station. Farewells and tears. At the far end of the platform, in civilian clothes, was Rolf. We had agreed that he was not to run the risk of being seen with me at the train. Blurred by my tears, I could hardly see his face. The train had already started. Good-by, Rolf . . . God bless you . . .

Four and a half years ago my child, Gonny, had left on the same train, from the same station, in her adventure in search of freedom and a new life. And now, I too was going on the same quest.

The heavy luggage was booked, sealed, and stamped. My few suitcases were in the rack above me. The passport was in order. I traveled luxuriously in a Pullman sleeper. Perhaps for the last time. I had not spared money, because I had to leave the rest in Germany anyway. Exhausted, I went to bed.

About 2 A.M. I was badly frightened by the sudden apparition of two uniformed figures. Drugged by my first sound sleep in weeks, my senses momentarily reeled with terror.

'Frontier pass control,' one of them announced gruffly.

I asked them to let me put on some clothes, but they made me leave the door open while I dressed.

'Emigrant's passport!' announced one. 'Jewish bitch! Trying to smuggle out her valuables, I suppose.'

I kept my mouth shut. They turned everything inside out. They took the soles from my bedroom slippers. They squeezed the toothpaste from the tube.

'Have you anything that should not be taken out of the country?' demanded one.

'You've seen for yourself everything I have,' I said.

'You Jewish whore!' one shouted at me. 'Trying to smuggle out all that jewelry.' He pointed to the little heap that had been emptied out on the bed.

'I am not trying to smuggle anything out,' I said. 'All that has been the property of my family for generations. Here is the permit issued by the Foreign Exchange Office.'

'We'll have to check on that with Berlin,' said he. 'We reach the frontier in half an hour. You'll have to get off the train.'

My protests were futile. I said I should miss the boat.

'Then take the next one.'

They seemed to be deliberately unaware of how hard it was to obtain passage. Cancellation or even delay was impossible, with so many hundreds eagerly awaiting their turn. I had a vision of being sent back to Germany and having to go through the business of laboriously collecting my exit papers all over again. My heart almost stopped.

The two went outside for a whispered consultation. When they returned, they submitted a statement for me to sign:

'I am a Jewish thief and have tried to rob Germany by taking German wealth out of the country. I hereby confess that the jewels found on me do not belong to me and that in trying to take them out I was eager to inflict injury on Germany. Furthermore, I promise never to try to reenter Germany.'

I signed. I had to get out of this country. This was a country to get out of if you had to do it naked.

Half an hour later the train crossed the border. I was in safety. My heart was pounding and I began to cry. Tears of liberation. But I was still uneasy until the train stopped at the Gare du Nord.

The statement, together with my jewels, had gone into the pockets of my tormentors. I am sure they will go no farther up the line. If they reappear, it will be in the shop of a pawnbroker.

9 September 1938. S.S. Normandie:

Safe aboard this gorgeous boat! It is almost too much for me to believe. Then, when I do become acutely aware of my good fortune, I feel almost guilty, remembering the unfortunate ones who wait, trembling, desperately hoping for their chance to get out. There *must* be a way to help.

The magnificent ship glides through the waters to the new land. I cannot get myself to join in the gay cheerfulness on board. There is an atmosphere of luxury and freedom from care, but I am not yet in a mood to breathe this air. I find I cannot yet stand fun and laughter.

STEVIE SMITH
Where is Czechoslovakia?
1939

Friendship and the revolt from friendship is the stuff of life. I am so grateful to my darling friends, to all my darling friends, but for the moment adieu. When I get home my noble aunt is reading the papers. At the time I was writing this the number of people reading the papers was more than usual. To keep out or not to keep out of war, that was at that time the question. Now, perhaps we are already again at war, perhaps not. My aunt is a staunch Tory, and equally staunchly she is regarding Germany as the ultimate enemy. Unlike many of the people who live in my own high-class suburb, she is well read in the political game. To-night is the night of the announcement of the flight of the Premier. Flight into darkness, say some, echoing the beautiful title Schnitzler chose for his suicide novel. I am listening at the house of a friend, an old mamma, she is really the church friend of my aunt, or the church sweet enemy, since my aunt carries on her church work in a fury of disagreement with the other ladies. Mrs A., we will call her, has a radio, which my aunt and I have not. My aunt does not like 'the noise.' Mrs A.'s radio announces the flight. On this great day of stress Mrs A. has not seen a paper. She has been too busy. So I say: 'The news looks serious. Japan is coming in with Germany. That will be not so hot for Australia.'

Mrs A. pants rather; she is making a wool rug and the colours must be matched nicely. She pants: 'Oh, yes, Australia! Mr A. has bought a new car.' So now the great news comes through that the Premier is flying to Berchtesgaden. 'So that is the best news I have heard today.' 'What is?' says Mrs A. 'That the Premier is flying to Berchtesgaden.' 'Oh,' Mrs A. says. 'Oh.' Then she says: 'Mr Parker was just in. He said: "Why are we interfering in Czecho-Slovakia?" ' I am rather intrigued by this piece. Bottle Green, I guess, is calling all suburbs. Now, I hurry to say to you that I am

16

not high hatting the suburbs; suburbs are very OK in many ways. I use the term spiritually, not geographically. I am thinking of the people who say: 'Where the hell is Czecho-Slovakia?' These people often don't live in suburbs at all; suburbs (it is unfortunate for suburbs) is a term of abuse, and these people earn abuse. Their forefathers, I guess they said: 'Where the hell is Waterloo?' 'Where the hell is Trafalgar?' But they would have known what the hell all right if Napoleon had invaded England. So they will know what the hell all right if Germany goes on her *Drang nach Kolonien*, like hell they will, like hell. So Mrs A. has two sons just down from Oxford, just the right age. I said, *just the right age*. So Mrs A. says now something so sad to make the angels weep, and so ridiculous. Alas, that human beings have the special privilege to be so often at the same time ridiculous and sad. So what does Mrs A. say? 'Whatever happens my boys will not be involved – because we have all signed the Peace Pledge.' Oh, sad echoing of fiendish laughter! Oh, the hollow laughter that goes echoing round the halls of hell upon these words. 'We have signed the Peace Pledge.' And already upon my eyes there is darkness and a great wind blowing over dead battlefields, and the stench of death without honour, and the ridiculous sad cry: We never knew. 'Oh, now I must go!' I say. 'Yes, you have heard the news,' says Mrs A. with a meaning note. Oh, yes, I suppose I am very rude, to hear the news and go.

CICELY McCALL

The Women's Institutes' Annual General Meeting, Earl's Court

This was June 1939. England was still at peace.

In this year only a few months after Munich, only three months before the invasion of Poland, the Associated Countrywomen of the World, the international body which binds together Women's Institutes all over the world, had held a week of meetings in London. Twenty-three countries had been represented, and nine of these representatives came to Earl's Court. One by one they were called to the front of the platform. Some wore national dress. Some neither spoke nor understood English. But all of them understood the applause and the smiles which greeted each fresh announcement.

America, Sweden, India. One by one they came forward, made their bow, and sometimes said a few words.

Latvia, Norway . . . Germany!

She was a tall woman. Her shoulders were flung back, her face set as she stepped on to the platform. There was a second's tense silence, as though suddenly nine thousand pairs of lungs had contracted, and their hearts too. Then came deafening applause. It rang round the hall tumultuously. It fell, then grew again in increasing volume as though each perspiring delegate on that very hot June morning could not enough say:

'Welcome! We are all countrywomen here today. We are non-party, non-sectarian. We wish for peace, goodwill and co-operation among nations. You have had the courage to come here in spite of rumours of wars. We bid you welcome!'

The strained look had gone from the German delegate's face. Amazement had taken its place. Amazement and pleasure. As she stepped off the platform she hesitated, almost stumbled. Perhaps she could not see very well. We shall never know what message she carried back to her country when her eyes were dried. Now, in this fourth year of war, is she still alive? Does she remember?

Chapter two

THE OUTBREAK OF WAR

B ritain declared war on Germany on 3 September 1939. The most immediate effect on the women of Britain was the mass evacuation that then
followed: one and a half million mothers and children were removed from
supposed danger areas and sent into the country.

In this way the war forced itself dramatically into the homes of many,
whether they were evacuees or what were hopefully called 'hostesses'. The
'home front' would become one of the great phrases – one of the great
monuments even – of the war, but the home itself was one of the war's first
casualties. It was broken into and broken up by evacuation, and by
conscription too, as husbands and sons were called up to active service.
Further problems faced women at work. Figures for women's employment
went down at the beginning of the war, as the government adopted a policy
of limiting 'non-essential' production not related to the war effort to a few
firms. Industries such as textiles and pottery, which traditionally employed
a large number of women, were cut back, but the new jobs in munitions
were slow in coming. Professional women lost ground too. Elaine Burton,
an administrator dismissed from her job at the beginning of the war, wrote
her well-researched book *What of the Women?* (1941) to argue for the
more efficient use of women's labour.

The favoured tone for women's writing at the outbreak of war seems
to have been one of determined light-heartedness, combined with a desire
to show some practical spirit. Jan Struther's Mrs Miniver and E.M.
Delafield's Provinicial Lady both dash gallantly up to London to search for
worthy war work – 'Driving, for choice' according to Mrs Miniver. *The
Provincial Lady in Wartime* chronicles the doings of September and
October 1939: 'Spend large part of the day asking practically everybody I
can think of, by telephone or letter, if they can suggest a war job for me.
Most of them reply that they are engaged in similar quest on their own
account.'

MARGERY ALLINGHAM
Evacuation, Day One in the Country

I don't know what sort of invasion we all had in mind, but we were not unduly optimistic. We had certainly been warned. From the beginning the evacuation scheme had come in for criticism. To read the country letters in the newspapers just after the Munich crisis you would have thought that everybody in the towns was a vermin-infested T.B. carrier; and naturally in the face of such a howl of fury the newspapers did what they always do when confronted by the really unpopular and shut down on the whole story like a clam. This was particularly unfortunate, because the scheme could have done with an airing, especially that part of it which affected adults. [. . .]

We all agreed there was no need to worry anyone who didn't want evacuees. I was particularly vehement about this, I remember, because I felt with a passion left over from my own childhood that the important thing was to put the youngster where someone wanted him first and worry about his living space afterwards. 'Better a dinner of herbs . . .' in fact, every time. And there were in Auburn literally dozens of people who said yes yes, they thought they had room for another little old boy or a nice little girl.

Meanwhile the time went on and on. One by one we slipped home for lunch and raced back again, but still no one came. I was frankly fascinated by the evacuation scheme, and had been from the beginning because it seemed to me to be the most revolutionary of all the Government measures, not excluding conscription. After all, one's own fireside is the citadel of freedom, and it did seem extraordinarily dangerous if any local authority could legally invade it. However, since the art of being governed is to do the necessary voluntarily and in one's own way before anyone starts shoving, and since Britain has that art at her finger-tips, I did not anticipate any real trouble; but I did feel the whole scheme might have been better had it been given the usual thorough shaking out in the high winds of Parliament and Press before it became law.

At that time no one knew much about it, for it had never been published out of Hansard as far as I could find out. All we knew then, and that mainly from hearsay, was that when an adult was billeted on you you got five shillings a week from the Post Office, and she was expected to buy her own food and cook it on your stove if you let her. It was made pretty clear that you were expected to let her do that, but no other details appeared to have been considered at all. Nothing about washing up, nothing about bedding, nothing about fuel, nothing about cooking utensils. It sounded like a fine source of trouble and quarrels all round to us, 'worse than the war,' and we congratulated ourselves on the ninety children. Whatever a child does you can't very well quarrel with it, and in our experience in Auburn half the trouble in a lifetime comes from quarrels.

Meanwhile it was nearly three o'clock in the afternoon, very hot and very dusty. We began to worry they would not get down in time for them to have their tea and get safely installed before the black-out. Mrs Moore hoped they hadn't been travelling all day and wondered if they wouldn't be starving, and Doey said he'd been informed that they would all have rations.

Presently Mr Moore shouted from the playground, and we all popped out; but it was only a big coloured van arriving. It swung down through the elm avenue and pulled up outside the school. The driver and his mate turned out of their seats like automatons, opened the doors, and began to drag out wooden food cases. They did not smile or speak or look at us. They brought the stuff straight in, dumped it in a corner and went back for more, moving quickly and as if they were working in their sleep. It was the first time war strain had come to Auburn, and it was odd and impressive, like the first puff of ack-ack fire in a blue sky. They looked as though they had been at work for seventy-two hours, as they probably had. There were red rims round their eyes, and their faces were grey and dirty. When someone asked them about the evacuees they snapped at us, and one man took off his coat, rolled it in a ball and threw it in a corner. Then he put his head on it and went to sleep.

Thinking it over, we were curiously unexcited by all this when one considers how interested we usually are when anything a little bit different arrives. We expected excitement, I suppose, and were saving it for the children. At any rate we took no notice of the sleeping man or his lorry, as far as I remember, apart from regarding them both stolidly. We examined the stores. There were quantities of it; bully beef, two sorts of tinned milk, and a considerable number of tins of biscuits as well as several quires of brown paper shopping bags.

Doey said suspiciously, 'There's a lot there, isn't there?' But at that moment a message came over from the Lion to say that eight buses were on their way. This delighted us all, and Mrs Moore got the kettles boiling. We were fidgeting about making last-minute preparations, when Doey, who had been thinking over the message, suddenly said, '*Eight* buses?'

I said, 'Oh, they'll be those little old-fashioned charabanc things.' And he said, 'Very likely.'

I was wrong. Mrs Moore, who was by the big window which looks on to the road, saw them first. There they were, as foreign-looking as elephants. There were eight of them, big red double-decker London buses, the kind that carries thirty-two passengers on each floor, and as far as we could see they were crowded. They pulled up, a long line all down the road, with a London taxicab behind them. A small army of drivers and officials sprang out, shouting instructions to their passengers.

It was a difficult moment. We locals were all doing arithmetic. Twice thirty-two is sixty-four; eight times sixty-four is five hundred and twelve; and the entire population of Auburn is under six hundred and fifty. We hoped, we trusted, there had been some mistake.

It was at this point that Doey made the second discovery. *They weren't children.* They were strange London-dressed ladies, all very tired and irritable, with babies in their arms.

We attempted to explain to the drivers, but all the time we were doing it it was slowly dawning upon us that we should never succeed. The drivers and the officials expected us to be hostile. They had read the newspapers. They were very tired, and moreover they were so nervy and exhausted, more with the emotional effort than anything else, that they were raw and spoiling for trouble. Doey and I, on the other hand, were just plain terrified. Finally we persuaded them to wait for just ten minutes while we found out if there had been a mistake, and we all went into the Lion to telephone authority at Fishling.

Authority at Fishling sounded a bit rattled also, and we gathered that our difficulties were as nothing beside the troubles of others, and that we'd kindly get on with what God and the German Chancellor had seen fit to send us. So we said 'All right,' and went back. It was the beginning of the war for us in Auburn, the first real start of genuine trouble.

Fortunately there was plenty to do. As a reception committee we had hardly shone, and the immediate need seemed to be to remove any unfortunate first impressions.

To our intense relief the buses proved to be not quite full. There were just over three hundred souls altogether, many of them infants, but they looked like an army. They trooped into the school, spread over the rooms and the playground and sat down, all looking at us with tired, expectant eyes.

There appeared to be no one actually in charge of them now they had arrived. The bus drivers went away with the buses, and the two schoolmasters and one young school-mistress who had come down with them were due to rush back as soon as possible to rejoin their own schools evacuated somewhere else in the east country.

The utter forlornness of the newcomers was quite theatrical. To our startled country eyes their inexpensive but very fashionable city clothes were grand if unsuitable, and with the myriads of babies in arms and the weeping toddlers hanging to their skirts they looked like everybody's long-lost erring daughter turned up to the old homes together in one vast paralysing emotional surprise.

They did not talk much, except to catch one's arm and say, 'Get me off soon, please. I'm very done up,' which was piteous in the circumstances.

22

They had no luggage except brown paper carriers containing the babies' immediate necessities, which was fortunate, for they had had an air-raid warning or two on the way down and had been bundled into shelters and out again. Moreover, they were not the ordinary East End cockneys, with whom we have some kinship and whom we had expected. These girls came from the suburbs well our side of the city, and most of them were obviously better off in actual spending money than the majority of Auburn families. Somehow this made it more difficult.

What we did not understand at all at the time, and which would never have occurred to us if some of them hadn't told us about it afterwards, was that they were nearly all great cinema-goers and had been seeing newsreel pictures of refugees for months, so that when their turn came they dropped into the part more or less automatically. To us who did not know this, of course, their silent hopeless gloom, indicative of utter exhaustion, was terrifying and incomprehensible. After all, they had only come thirty-five miles, and that in a bus. In normal times they might easily have done the trip for pleasure. We wondered what in God's name was happening up there in London.

Meanwhile, of course, our position (Doey's and mine) was rather delicate. It's one thing to arrange with a valued neighbour and client to receive two small girls, and another to send her instead two weeping young women and eight children under seven between them.

Also another problem had arisen. It was Anne who produced it. This was the first time I ever saw Anne. She came up, forcing her way through the crush and roaring with laughter. Her gaily painted face was quite different in its happiness from almost everyone else's, and she was hatless. She touched my arm, and I saw that she was wearing a wildly patterned green and purple silk dress, which, like the lady's in the ballad, was 'narrow . . . that used to be sae wide.' Tony, nearly two, clung to her neck and screamed with delight.

She said, 'Here, I say, where's the clinic?'

The word rang a faint bell. As far as I could remember there was a welfare clinic at Flinthammock which was held every Thursday afternoon, or something like that. This did not sound as if it was going to be much use to Anne, however, for she said she was 'due' in ten days or so, and that there were about twenty others like her. They 'had ought' to have had pink tickets, she said, but what with the rush and one thing and another they'd come along without.

Since it seemed to be our business, I assured her it would be quite all right. I had come to the conclusion that this was probably the end of the world, and that Dante was evidently going to have a hand in it, as I had always feared he might. I also felt wildly indignant that it should be Englishwomen who were being herded about in this abominable way. I do not defend this insular and prideful reaction, which shocked me out of the corner of my eye, so to speak, at the time; but I feel bound to mention it because it was so strong.

Meanwhile we were getting a move on as best we could. I sent as many people as I dared over to Margaret and Christine, and Doey sent some home to Mrs Doe. Mrs Moore and Mrs Gager somehow got tea for everybody, and at the same time we sent out a general SOS. There was nothing formal or resounding about it, as far as I remember, but rather an agonized shout of 'Somebody come!'

Miraculously Auburn responded. It turned up like the Navy or the Fire Brigade or one's parents, and, having taken one horrified, outraged look at the scarifying sight in the big schoolroom, it took the situation in hand.

It was extraordinary. People who had no room, who loathed the idea of strangers, and who had declared in all honesty that while they were prepared if necessary to die for their country, they could not and would not stomach a child in their house for ten minutes, came up to the sunny playground with unwilling, conscience-driven steps, paused at the doorway of the big school aghast, and then went in and collected some weeping young mother and her infants and carried them home with tight lips and grim eyes.

The entire business became more and more unreal as it went on. We went back into a Bret Harte or Dickensian world in which stony hearts dissolved in acid tears and piteous rosy-faced babies smiled their way into private fortresses. It was a frightening experience, a sort of return to simplicity by way of an avalanche; or as though God, tiring at last of our blasted superiority, had taken us and banged our heads together. [. . .]

It occurred to me at this point that we were only one village out of hundreds, probably thousands, all suddenly confronted by this remarkable invasion, and that all over the country startled people must be opening their doors like this to tired and sometimes angry strange girls and their heavy-eyed children. Somehow that reflection did not make our immediate problem seem any more simple.

Meanwhile Jane had discovered the Ring Farmers. They were not called that yet, of course; that came later. At this time they were just one vast loving family who did not want to be separated even for a night. There were nineteen of them: a matriarch who had been married twice and her younger children, two families of her married duaghters, a daughter-in-law and at least one baby apiece. Most of the girls were remarkably pretty, Jessie Matthews types, and they were very smart if in a rather dressed-up way for Auburn. They all had soft voices and that delightful impudent direct intelligence which belongs to the city. Mama outshone them all, however. She was well over fifty, and looked like some fine Shakespearean actress playing the Queen of Denmark before the trouble started. Her expression was imperious and her carriage regal. She was wearing a black halo hat which suited her, and she drew me away from the others and said, 'How about letting us stay here till the morning? You know what the girls are. We ought to get the kids to sleep. We'll be all right by ourselves. We don't *want* billets, my dear, not to-night. Just find us a few necessities, and we'll manage.'

Well, of course they couldn't stay there because there was no black-out in the big room for one thing; but we did fit them up for the night in the schoolroom behind the chapel, and the big old-fashioned pew forms fitted together made cribs for the babies. Mr Spooner, who looks after the chapel, worked like a slave to make them comfortable. Bill got out his lorry, and Albert and Charlotte, and Alan their eldest, loaded it with camp beds dug out from the junk cupboard and mended at speed. Everybody lent something, blankets or crocks or food, for the night.

Mama received everything with the gracious ease of a Duchess at a bazaar. She was never hurried, never hesitant, and always charmingly smooth and polite. If she needed anything we had forgotten, she indicated it rather than mentioned it. Someone said she couldn't have taken in things better if she'd been a sausage machine.

When the flow ceased she dismissed us gently with thanks and a Mona Lisa smile. There was no need for us to think of them for quite a time, she said. They'd manage.

As I came back I saw Albert and Charlotte in the Queen's yard, and we eyed each other very thoughtfully for a minute before we all burst out laughing at the same thing. The old woman thought she was pretty smart. The joke was, of course, that we weren't being done; we were just being generous. I wondered if the old lady, with all her town intelligence, would ever get the exquisite subtlety of that one.

This slightly peculiar humour of ours, which is scarcely ever understood or even suspected by the townsfolk, may be a little hard to follow, because of course on the surface the townee always appears to come off best. On this occasion Mama had our crocks, our beds, our blankets and our food, and we had no means of knowing if we should ever see any of them again. However, the whole thing goes far deeper than that and is the outcome of a thousand years' experience of living next door to the same families. We had certainly risked a few odds-and-ends, but think of the position in which she had put herself. If she and her family were proposing to live amongst us for any length of time the definite information we should have in a few days' time about her innate honesty, her reliability as a borrower, her generosity and her cleanliness was practically beyond price.

STORM JAMESON
City Without Children
1939

The children were sent out of London over the weekend. [. . .] Over half a million children were hurried out of the city. Some further hundreds of thousands went independently, packed off to relatives and boarding schools in the country. On Wednesday, September 6, London looked as it would look if some fantastic death pinched off the heads under fifteen. [. . .]

In the centre of London, the City proper, there are squares that have changed little if at all since the eighteenth century. The houses have become the offices of sedate firms. Unless they shout, little marble-playing boys are not ordered off, and not many weeks since I watched children playing in one of these squares a game with flat stones that was probably old in Troy. The children have vanished. Two big paunchy business men, carrying rolled copies of *The Times*, self-conscious with gas masks in canvas boxes slung on their shoulders, stroll across in the sun. The steps going down into a small church are well sandbagged. It is as dark as a crypt in this sunken place, and nearly full of people praying, as people have prayed here for five centuries, for help in the day of trouble and lamentation. Without looking up, a woman said in a loud voice: 'My son! Oh, my son!' To what listener?

The streets are lively with typists and office girls, going home. Many of these girls are only two years older than a sister who has been evacuated. On one side of an age line you are still a child who must be protected. A step, and you have become a young woman with handbag, toeless sandals, and gas mask, who must go to the office as long as the office is there. It seems a pity. But one cannot save everybody. So these older children walk jauntily on their long thin legs, carrying their masks with a touch of coquetry.

F. TENNYSON JESSE
A Letter to *The Times*
1939

'Sir,

'While from all my friends in the country comes praise of many town-children evacuees – and, without exception, praise of all the secondary-school children – complaints are pouring in about the half-savage, verminous and wholly illiterate children from some slums who have been billeted on clean homes. Stories with which one cannot but sympathise are told of mattresses and carpets polluted, of wilful despolation and dirt that one would associate only with untrained animals. The authorities, with plenty of time to prepare, seem to have failed both in the physical and psychological examination of the evacuees, although the mechanics of the great trek have been so well ordered.

'Now one hears that both women and children of the roughest and uncleanest types are going back to their own "homes". At the present time, when Britain is fighting for liberty, no Briton would suggest dictatorship methods, but surely something short of these can be evolved to prevent these unfortunate children from being allowed to return to the appalling conditions whence they have been rescued? It is not fair that they should disrupt small houses, but is it not possible to cause (to coin a phrase) "grass-orphanages" under the care of skilled and sympathetic teachers, to come into being? Let the mothers go back if they will. It does not matter so much what happens to adults, but surely children should not be allowed to go back to conditions which shame a nation fighting for civilization.

'In the course of my work I have, in the last few years, attended many trials at the Central Criminal Court, and am nearly always horrified by the low physical and mental standards of the accused persons. Stunted, mis-shapen creatures, only capable of understanding the very simplest language and quite incapable of thought, moved by impulses at the best sentimental, at the worst brutal. During a trial when accused and witnesses are of this sub-human sort, it is as though a flat stone in the garden had been raised and pale wriggling things that had never seen the light, were exposed. No one who knows anything of Criminal Courts will contradict me.

'These children, of whom the country residents so reasonably complain, are bound to grow up into just such sub-human savages, unless we seize this opportunity of saving them. I do not, of course, say that all crime is due to the appalling conditions in which most men and women who find

27

their way to our courts live when young – there have been several trials in the last two years which have shown that men, who have had every advantage in youth, can be brutal, treacherous and base. But I do say that no child who has not been shown the rudiments of decency and in whom imagination has not been encouraged, stands a chance of being a good and happy citizen.

'War has lifted the flat stone – these disgraces to our educational system have been forced out into the light. Do not let us, even though a certain amount of arbitrary arrangements may be needed, let them creep back beneath their stone. This is, and I repeat it with every emphasis of passion at my command, an opportunity which, if we miss it, we do not deserve to have given to us again.'

I could have written more forcibly, but after all one has to be careful of the words one uses to Auntie *Times*.

NELLA LAST
A Son's Last Day At Home

Thursday, 14 September 1939

The last day of having a 'little boy' – for so my Cliff has seemed, in spite of being twenty-one at Christmas. He has been so thoughtful and quiet these last few days, and so gentle. I watched his long sensitive fingers as he played with the dog's ears, and saw the look on his face when someone mentioned 'bayonet charging'. He has never hurt a thing in his life: even as a little boy, at the age when most children are unthinkingly cruel, he brought sick or hurt animals home for me to doctor, and a dog living next door always came for a pill when it felt ill – although as Cliff used to complain, it never noticed him at other times! It's dreadful to think of him having to kill boys like himself – to hurt and be hurt. It breaks my heart to think of all the senseless, formless cruelty. I looked at his room to-day: he and his brother, though deeply attached, liked their separate rooms and, although it meant more work, I like privacy myself too much to have denied them it. I thought of the crowd he would have to live in, and of how, unless for an occasional dance etc., he prefers a tramp over the hills with a pal – or even just Aunt Sarah's old dog. He likes to sit before the fire with his legs stretched out, munching an apple and reading, sitting for hours on end, designing and making his Christmas or birthday cards and little witty tags for Christmas presents.

He always likes a few flowers in an old tankard on his bedside table, a clean serviette, the cat on the window sill at his elbow and the dog by his feet while having meals – such little unimportant things to ask, and yet to be denied for only God knows how long. We who remember the long drawn-out agony of the last war feel ourselves crumble somewhere inside at the thoughts of what lies ahead.

Tonight I looked a bit washed out, so after tea I changed into my gayest frock and made up rather heavily. When Cliff came in with his friend, he said 'Oho!' and raised my face with his finger: 'Hm! Quite good but just a *wee* bit tartish!' – and he wiped my lips and cheeks, kissed me on the tip of my nose and turned me round to see if Jack approved. Jack and he insisted on making toast and scrambling eggs – I think they are proud of this little accomplishment! No one could eat it though, and I felt myself going cold – a funny little sign that I'm best to be in bed.

JAN STRUTHER

Mrs Miniver's 'Peace-In-War'

London, 5 October 1939

Dearest Susan,

I have come back here to find a job, as Starlings now seems to be running perfectly all right, nursery, evacuees, and all. I don't know yet what kind of job I can get, if any. Driving, for choice. What I hanker for, of course, is to be put at the beck and call of some very important hush-hush sort of man who needs to be driven very fast in a long-nosed powerful car to mysterious destinations. From time to time my passenger would glance down at his watch, then backwards over his shoulder, and say briefly, 'Step on it, Mrs M.' And I should see in the driving-mirror a supercharged straight eight, disguised as a grocer's van, rapidly gaining on us . . . Yes, definitely, that would be just my cup of tea. But either this type of man is dying out – which I should deplore – or else, which is more likely, he does his own driving.

In the meanwhile I am helping at whatever odd jobs I can find – addressing envelopes, rolling bandages, &c. – and enjoying, more than I can say, being back in London, which is unbelievably impressive.

The funny thing is that although the floodlighting experiments used to reveal a whole lot of architectural beauties which one didn't know, the black-out reveals even more. One loses the details of buildings, but sees their outlines properly for the first time. That is, when there's any vestige of a moon. And even when there isn't, one still discovers new things by hearing, touch, and smell. For instance, I had never noticed before that the area railings in this Square were of such a pleasing design. Now I know them intimately, by touch. And I can tell when I'm getting near to the Air Raid Shelter at the corner by the damp jutey smell of the sandbags. In fact, the whole of London now smells most pleasantly of jute – even indoors, because of the stuff one uses for undercurtains. It is one of the best scents in the world: partly, I suppose, because it reminds one of those rickety tents one made out of sacking as a child.

As for the balloons – you've probably read a lot about them in the papers already, but I can't help that, I have *got* to talk about them. They are the most delightful and comforting companions in the world. You see, I hadn't been in London at all since war broke out, and when I travelled up five days ago, by the late train, I don't mind admitting I was feeling rather jittery. There was a serene gold sunset, with oast-houses sticking up against it like black cats, and all the way up in the train that wretched lovely line from *Antony and Cleopatra* kept running in my head: –

Finish, good lady; the bright day is done,
And we are for the dark.

I went to bed very sore about the shins from falling over a station barrow, and hating the house with neither Clem nor the children in it, and with Mrs A. looking more than ever like John Knox; and altogether everything was rather grim. But when I looked out of my window early next morning and saw all those fat little silver watch-fish floating overhead in a clear sky, I felt completely reassured. They really are quite beautiful, although – like puppies – they manage to combine this with being intrinsically comic. From time to time they are taken down: ostensibly to refill them with gas, but really, I suspect, to scrape off the barnacles. I only wish, once they've got them down, they'd paint faces on them like Chinese dragons. I'm sure it would add to their deterrent effect. The best thing of all, which nobody had prepared me for, is that on windy nights they *sing*. It's like going to sleep on a ship at anchor, with the sound of wind in the rigging. Only, thank goodness, London doesn't rock – yet.

There, I have finished letting off steam about the balloons. *Liberavi animam meam*, as Uncle John always used to say when he had just been particularly offensive to poor Aunt Sarah. Like many well-read but ill-tempered people, he thought a Latin tag excused everything. But Aunt Sarah didn't know any Latin. Bad Luck.

As for other things, all I can say is that Hitler, poor misguided man, has made the biggest mistake of his life in giving us a month of this kind of peace-in-war in which to become calm, collected, and what's more, *chic*. Of course, the people who are natural born dowds still manage to make their gas masks look dowdy, but those who are normally well-turned-out somehow contrive to make them into a positive decoration. It isn't only a question of having one of the many expensive and pansified cases which are on the market, though I admit they help: it's more that most people have now learned to carry the things with an air – with *panache*. You might think, walking about London, that everybody was going off to a picnic with a box of special food.

Another thing: you know how in normal times, when they come back to London in the autumn, English women make no attempt to keep on wearing light, bright colours. They just mutter 'Fogs' in a defeatist manner, put away their summer handbags, gloves, scarves, and so forth, and then throw up their arms and drown in a sea of black, navy, dark brown, bottle, and maroon, as the fashion catalogues would say. This year, wearing white 'accessories' has become literally a matter of life and death – or at any rate, of wholeness and injury; and you've no idea how much more cheerful the place looks. But it's odd, isn't it, that the aim of 'protective colouring' should now be to detach us from our background, not to melt us into it? This war will have to introduce a new word for that process, just as the last one introduced 'camouflage'.

Talking of stockings, I remember Teresa saying last year that one of the most awful minor catastrophes in the world was when one's suspender gave way at a party: how one felt quite discomfited, and lop-sided, and alto-gether at a loss until it was done up again. Well, I think that's the main difference between September, 1938, and now. Then, we felt only too distinctly the uncomfortable *ping*! of the elastic. But now we've had time to do it up again; and we feel more than equal to coping with the party, however long and strenuous it may be.

How silly it was of him to allow us to become not only angry but bored. This nation is never really dangerous until it's bored.

Yours ever, with much love,

CAROLINE.

ROSAMOND LEHMANN

A Review of *Mrs Miniver*
1939

Here are the sayings and doings of Mrs Miniver, familiar to some of us in more ephemeral form in *The Times*, now collected all together in one pretty pink and blue volume, so that her countless admirers may derive a more permanent pleasure from her charm, her wit and wisdom. 'Boxed, and in a gay binding,' this work seems destined for the drawing-room table, or for the best spare room, where the perusal of one or two of her little adventures should help the week-end guest to drop off at night soothed, smiling and serene.

Mrs Miniver is, we know, secure in the heart of the majority of her public; and I must be taken as speaking only for a minority, upon which she exercises an oppression of spirits which, since it is caused by such a charming person, appears at first sight due to mere jealousy and spite. Yet surely it is odd that anyone so tactful, kind, tolerant, popular, humorous and contented, should arouse such low feelings, even in the ever-dissatisfied minority? And then, if one happens to dislike the spectacle of so much success, why not simply ignore it, and turn away? Why read, as one must, with exasperation, the column she has with such modest triumph made her own? Why does one look out for her next appearance with such feelings as the deserving poor must entertain for the local Lady Bountiful, or the inmates of a Borstal Institute for a certain kind of official visitor?

One trouble is, one can't ignore the successful; and to enable one to forgive them there is needed some quality alien to Mrs Miniver. It is not so much that we are irritated by her being pleased with herself: blissfully married, mother of three, well off, well read, she has a right to be pleased: is it perhaps the way she has of masking her colossal self-satisfaction with tender self-depreciation? 'See what a silly I am!' It is in her humility that we suspect her most. [. . .]

Now the war is upon Mrs Miniver, as it is upon all of us. But whoever is defeated, she'll come through. Having plenty of courage and common sense, she will cope successfully with evacuees and increased taxation, even if necessary with bombs. The airy balloon that hovers so lightly above our heads may shrivel a little, but it won't collapse. Inheriting (despite her tendentious name) no long traditions, or rather inheriting only mixed bits and pieces of outworn and debased ones, she will be adaptable, and come up shaken but intact, whatever new society emerges. For whether Right wing or Left wing, the right are always right, and always with us.

COMPETITION AND CORRESPONDENCE IN THE *NEW STATESMAN*

16 December 1939
Professor Harold Laski has written a book entitled *The Danger of Being A Gentleman*. The usual prizes for not more than 200 words from a book of that title.

SECOND PRIZE

Curious, thought Mrs Miniver, pensively nibbling a *langue-de-chat*, how difficult life was becoming for people who happened to have come out of the top drawer.

She poked the fire, tilting the tarred logs until a stream of molten lava poured down. Yes – that was symbolic . . . The black stream (or would it, perhaps, be a Red one?) would soon pour ruthlessly down over the Clems and the Carolines, the Tobys, Judys and Vins; over their luncheon-parties and shooting-parties, and all the civilized fun which they had so long and so lightheartedly enjoyed.

Unless – unless what? Wasn't there something they could do about it, some means of preserving all that was gay and lovely in their tradition, while purging it of all that was dangerous and bad? She felt a faint stirring in the back of her mind, as of some small wood animal waking from its winter sleep. . . .

But just then the telephone rang. The trouble was, thought Mrs Miniver as she reached out to answer it, that one never quite had time to get to the bottom of one's deeper thoughts. That, perhaps, was the Danger of being a Gentleman. . . .

K. Watkins

23 December 1939

CORRESPONDENCE

SIR, – I am afraid I must plead guilty to a slight deception.

When I saw the announcement of your competition No. 512, I felt pretty sure that I could write a far crueller satire on 'Mrs Miniver' than could any of my detractors. I therefore tried my hand at it, and sent in the result over beyond my wildest hopes, and as my close connection with Mrs Miniver precludes me from accepting the prize, I have no choice but to reveal myself.

Would you be so good as to send the prize to the competitor who was next in order of merit – or, if you prefer it, to the Association for the Relief of Distressed Gentlewomen?

17 Halsey Street, S.W.3   Jan Struther

F. TENNYSON JESSE
It is a Very Queer War

11 September 1939

It is a very queer war. Our little social life, such as it was – quiet but pleasant – has come to a complete end. Noel Streatfeild, complete with gas mask and tin helmet, dashed in for lunch, full of stories about the firemen and ambulance drivers at the station where she is an A.R.P. warden. She was going down in the pitch black the other night, dressed in her slacks and dark blue sweater, when a voice with a French accent murmured to her: 'Would you not like to come home with me, pretty boy?' It was one of the French Bond Street tarts. 'Shut up, you fool!' said Noel.

'*Mon dieu!*' said the tart.

4 November 1939

The A.R.P. authorities informed us that it is very important during an aerial bombardment to sit with a cork in your mouth, as the blast from a shell (even a long way off) may snap your jaws to and then, not only may your tongue be cut off, but your ear-drums are blown in. So we ordered our old man to produce us three corks for us to take upstairs, and when he served the coffee after dinner the solemnly presented Tottie with three corks on a little tray in the most correct manner imaginable, remarking: 'Your corks, sir!'

VERILY ANDERSON

A FANY is Court-Martialled

My plans for concealing my fears under a dashing adventurous life came to nothing. For one thing, now that war had been declared, there was nothing for the moment to fear. Eagerly I volunteered to be sent abroad; but when the time came to be posted from London I found myself instead back in Sussex in a house I knew well, with about thirty other FANYs, including Elizabeth with her unstuffed palliasse.

We were commanded by a bubbly-haired old actress who, as the niece of a senior army officer, took her position very seriously. In her talk she mingled a certain amount of army jargon, picked up at her uncle's breakfast table, with the normal chatter we understood of hats and actors and horses. Sometimes, judging by her modes of addressing us, she saw us as Mayfair Debutantes and sometimes as Men Going Over The Top.

The idea behind our camping in this big and beautiful house was that we should be able to drive ambulances for the army. At first we had no ambulances, and hung about wistfully wishing we had. Then we were allotted an assortment of commandeered furniture-vans, fish-carts, and carriers.

Within a week of our collecting them, I had the misfortune to be the first FANY to crash one into a gatepost.

The C.O. came running out to look at the damage. Several army expressions must have floated up from her subconscious, but for the moment all she could say was a reproving,

'Really, Bruce, it's too tiresome!'

She went back to her office, which she called The Orderly Room, and must have sat down to think hard of something with more of a military tang.

A few minutes later, while I was getting ready for lunch, two FANYs of the quiet, useful, obedient type came into the bedroom which I shared with four others (including one whose claim to fame was that her husband had been fallen on by Queen Mary in her recent motor accident). The two FANYs stood in a waiting attitude, one each side of me.

'Want to borrow a comb?' I asked affably.

'You're under arrest,' said one.

'I'm what?' I asked.

'Under arrest. We've had orders to close in on you and march you to the orderly room without your cap or belt.'

I giggled. This was just the sort of joke Elizabeth and I had with each other, but it was funnier coming from these two.

35

'Oh,' said one to the other, 'she can't. The C.O. never thought of that. Our belts are stitched on to our tunics.'

'Then, without your cap, fall in!' said the other.

'I say, are you serious?' I asked with some surprise, now remembering the episode of the fallen gate-post.

'C.O.'s orders. Quick march.'

I put on my tunic and, still buttoning it, trotted merrily along between them, hoping to meet Elizabeth on the way downstairs. But Elizabeth was not about. To my amazement, everybody we passed turned away as though in shame. I had knocked a good many gate-posts down in my time, but nobody had ever before felt so deeply about it as this.

In the orderly room I had an idea which I felt might interest our dramatic C.O. I saluted her.

'You can't salute without a cap on,' she remembered, and then gave various conflicting orders to my escorts.

'The Prisoner To Be Confined In A Cell,' she ended up and I was marched away to the green dressing-room which I had known as such since I was a child. I sat down on the bed waiting to see what would happen next. I could hear my escorts moving about outside as they guarded me.

Soon one of them brought my lunch on a tray. Her eyes were downcast and the tray shook a little. After all that ceremonial, I expected dry bread and water, which is what we were given as children when we were sent to bed in disgrace. I was quite surprised to be allowed ordinary sausages and mash, which was followed by apple tart brought by the other escort.

To my intense delight, secreted in the apple tart was a slip of paper on which dear Elizabeth had written, '*Keep a stiff upper lip for the honour of the Third*.' I was glad her eyes were not downcast.

A few minutes later I heard weeping outside, followed by muffled foot-steps.

The gardener's wife came in to take my tray away. She handed me a box of chocolates.

'I dunno, I'm sure,' she said. 'One of the young ladies give me this to give you. The one outside was crying her eyes out and saying she couldn't go on. And half of them downstairs wouldn't touch their lunch. You'd think there'd been a murder. Three left the table sudden-like, and that pretty young Lady Victoria burst into tears and ran upstairs in a dreadful state.'

'But what's it all about?' I asked. 'What's happened?'

'Haven't they told you?'

'No.'

'You're going to be court-martialled.'

'Oh, dear!' I said, 'Then I'd better clean my buttons.'

My next visitor was the M.T. sergeant, a tough-looking lady who was rarely seen out of oily overalls.

'Please tell me,' I asked her anxiously, 'did I kill somebody?'

'Who? You? Not that I know of.'

'Then what's this all about?'

'You've done something serious, my gal,' she said, taking her cigarette out of the corner of her mouth. 'You've damaged government property.'

'But this place belongs to my father's churchwarden.'

'As far as we're concerned, it's government property. What I want to know is, would you prefer to be tried by men or women?'

'Men,' I said, 'every time.'

'I think the C.O. would prefer to keep this to ourselves. So I'll tell her you'd rather have women. I shall be on your side, of course.'

This was something new. So far the sergeant had never found herself able to be on my side.

'I'm the prisoner's friend,' she said, smoothing down her Eton crop and wiping her hand on the seat of her overalls.

'Oh,' I said. 'Who'll be my enemy?'

'The president of the court. That's the C.O. Rather fun, eh?' She rollocked out of the room.

As my guard had mutinied, it was the M.T. sergeant who escorted me down to what used to be, before the arrival of the FANYs, the small drawing-room. The C.O. had herself chosen a jury and three witnesses, who had been nowhere near the gate-post at the time of the impact.

I though of Elizabeth's message and tried to see how funny it all was. But the jury and the witnesses were all so painfully embarrassed that I began to feel as though I was having my appendix out in a public waiting-room. The only person who appeared to be enjoying herself was the prisoner's friend. She seized the opportunity of making hay with her senior officer, whom I found myself feeling quite sorry for. After all, the C.O. had obviously set out to do what she felt was her duty to the country.

Two greyhounds wandered in and, rather as though they had come into church, were hustled discreetly out.

My mind wandered off on to other things while the president and the prisoner's friend became more and more irrelevant, only occasionally attracting the unwilling attention of the jury.

I was surprised out of my reverie by the pronouncement,

'Not guilty.'

'But surely –' I started to object, then thought better of it. If the gate-post had been proved still intact, let it rest at that. I was dismissed.

The tension was broken. I was surrounded by FANYs, jury and otherwise, shaking my hand and congratulating me as though I had shot the winning goal in a school match. One of the dormitories instantly gave a feast for me, delving under their beds to produce drinks and cakes and fruit. The C.O., delving back again into her subconscious for an appropriate term, brought out a beauty.

'If you'd been found guilty, there would of course have been The Question of Mitigation Of Sentence.'

NELLA LAST
Whistling up the Spirits

Wednesday, 1 November 1939

I know by Cliff's letters it's the little simple things of home and his former life before he was a soldier that are dearest. I often wonder what his thoughts have been when he was writing my letters.

He said he liked the snap of him and me together. It was like his 'own picture' of me – always gay and kind and 'firm'. He felt I was one of the things to 'hold on to' and know I would never change. Wonder what had gone 'agley' – he does not often show his feelings. Odd he should think I am always gay. Come to think of it, down at the W.V.S. Centre they think I'm a 'mental tonic', as old Mrs Waite put it.

I must be a very good actress, for I don't feel gay often. Perhaps, though, I'm like the kid who whistled as he went past the churchyard to keep his spirits up, for down in my heart there is a sadness which never lifts and, if I did not work and work till I was too tired to do anything but sleep when I went to bed, would master me. Like the little Holland boy who put his hand in the hole in the dyke and kept back the trickle of water that would have quickly grown to a flood, I *must* keep my dykes strong enough – or else at times I'd go under.

I got a dozen chintz bags made tonight – such pathetic, brave little bags with a square of tracing paper stitched on. They are 'hospital supplies', to use to put a soldier's little treasures in, out of his pocket, if he is wounded and taken to hospital. There are huge stacks of them to make, and when I thought of all the W.V.S. Centres all over England making the same numbers, I could have wept. It's little things like that which seem to bring home to me the dreadful inevitableness of things, with everything prepared for a three years' war. The chintzes I sewed would have made such gay cushions or curtains – or romping children's overalls.

Wednesday, 29 November 1939

I wish sometimes I was a religious woman and could find comfort and faith in bombarding God with requests and demands. I think people must be born like that, though. I try sometimes to pray that Cliff will not have to go to France – will come out of the Army – but feel in some queer way presumptuous, and just ask for comfort and help on his journey. My next-door neighbour has every religious service on at all hours, and finds comfort in it. I wish I could do so – I would only find irritation at the loud noise. She says she prays God to strike Hitler dead. Cannot help thinking if God wanted to do that he would not have waited till Mrs Helm asked him to do so.

VITA SACKVILLE-WEST
Country Notes

September [1939]

With the prospect of devastation hanging over us, the impression of fecundity produced by the countryside the past fortnight strikes one as painfully ironical. All crops seemed to come to fruition at once: the corn, the apples and the hops. These things happen every year, but this year one noticed them more poignantly than usual. For one thing, a number of the ordinary farm workers had been called away to grimmer jobs, and their place was taken by amateur improvised labour. Skinny little boys from London raked the chaff and cavings from under the threshing machine; handsome, elegant young men waiting to be put into uniform heaved trusses of straw from stack to cart; schoolboys climbed into apple trees and picked, for once legitimately, the huge green cookers into bushel baskets. Everything hummed with liveliness; the thresher hummed literally, so did the drying-fans in the oasthouse; there was a constant burr from stackyard and oasts; the air smelt of hops; dust-motes flew about; large horses stood waiting patiently between the shafts of large waggons; peaches and nectarines on the wall ripened so rapidly that the blush came over them as over the cheeks of a girl; figs turned as brown as Syrian sailors. A sudden hurry woke the somnolent farm to life; everyone took a hand, grateful for the physical activity which puts a stop to thought; everything bore its own particular fruit. This teeming effect has been increased by the quantities of extra children straying all over the place, as though country families were inordinately prolific. Swinging on gates, smeared with blackberry juice in the lanes, they have turned the country into a warren. Some of them, I understand, are not too popular with their hosts and hostesses. There is one story of two little boys, left behind to play while the farmer and his household went out to work; on his return he found a cloud of feathers and a squawking barnyard full of completely naked chickens. Decidedly, being in the country is great fun.

Then there are the land girls, an unfamiliar sight in the orchards and among the cows; picturesque in their brown dungarees, tossing their short curls back and laughing. I came across two of them picking plums; very young they were, and standing under the tree loaded with the blood-red drops, their arms lifted, the half-filled baskets on the ground beside them, they could scarcely have looked prettier in their lives than on that sunlit morning.

Black-out

In contrast to the sunlit days came the starlit nights. I could imagine nothing more desirable and mysterious than these black secret nights, were it not for the sinister intention behind them. I suppose that one should not allow the intention to impair one's appreciation of this new beauty of the starry night. The moon has gone, and nothing but stars and three planets remain within our autumn sky. Every evening I go my rounds like some night-watchman to see that the black-out is complete. It is. Not a chink reveals the life going on beneath those roofs, behind those blinded windows; love, lust, death, birth, anxiety, even gaiety. All is dark; concealed. Alone I wander, no one knowing that I prowl. It makes me feel like an animal, nocturnal, stealthy. I might be a badger or a fox. All voices are stilled as though by a hand laid over noisy mouths. The experience is a strange one, making me feel more like myself and more unlike myself, more closely united to those who share my roof yet more divorced from them, than ever I felt before. I think of all the farms and cottages spread over England, sharing this curious protective secrecy where not even a night-light may show in the room of a dying man or a woman in labour.

The black-out is inconvenient to the man drying the hops from dusk to dawn. I stroll round to the oasts, and find one door left open beneath the shadow of the staging. They have hung a green silk scarf over the central lamp, so that the glaucous light of under-seas tinges the lime-washed walls to the very colour of the hops themselves. War brings an unforeseen strangeness to these small interiors of illumination.

I continue on my rounds. The Londoners' children in the village are asleep by now in their improvised beds. The landgirls, tired out, are asleep

40

also, their brown dungarees exchanged for striped pyjamas. The four young men whom I watched at supper, four boys at the beginning of lives probably to be lost, the boys who slung the sheaves in early morning, are asleep also. All these people gathered under various roofs are asleep.

The place I love; the country I love; the boys I love. I wander round, and towards midnight discover that the only black-out I notice is the black-out of my soul. So deep a grief and sorrow that they are not expressible in words.

Chapter three

HORIZONS DARKEN

In April and May 1940 Germany invaded Denmark, Norway, Holland, Belgium and Luxembourg. At the end of May the British Expeditionary Force was evacuated from Dunkirk; a month later France surrendered.

Because Britain was never invaded, it remained to some extent on the edge of the terrible sufferings and devastation in mainland Europe. People could not see fully the horror of what was going on in Europe: the persecution and oppression, the life under an invading power, the many millions put to death or forced to become refugees. But there were glimpses, indications, echoes.

Eye-witness accounts by English and American women in France during the summer of 1940 reverberate with shock. With their eye on the effects of war rather than its acts, they show the characteristics of women's war reporting at its best. Their standpoint is the margins of war, explicitly and democratically among ordinary people; their focus is highly angled, picking out significant detail. Even Tom Harrisson, who found little to praise in his article on 'War Books' for *Horizon* in December 1941, paused to admire Cecily Mackworth's *I Came Out Of France* for its 'epic quality and sympathy'.

Those women who did manage to leave France or other parts of Europe sometimes had exciting adventures – the usual stuff of war stories – and books such as Bessy Myers' *Captured, My Experiences as an Ambulance Driver and as a Prisoner of the Nazis* (1941) began to appear. An interesting feature of women's writing about scrapes and escapes is the way the authors often insist on their ordinariness in other circumstances. Etta Shiber, for example, was imprisoned for helping English servicemen who had been left behind after the evacuation from Dunkirk to return to England. What she did showed courage and initiative, yet she continually describes herself as a timid middle-class lady, 'an ordinary woman with no particular taste for adventure'.

Escape to England was not always the end of the story. With the threat of invasion spreading, the popular press worked up public opinion against Austrians and Germans in England, most of them victims of Nazi oppression. In the summer of 1940 nearly four thousand women were interned in segregated quarters on the Isle of Man. These were dark days, and it is heartening to find women joining in the tireless work on behalf of the refugees: among them were the MP Eleanor Rathbone, Secretary of the Parliamentary Committee on Refugees, and the Austrian Eva Kolmer, who collaborated with François Lafitte on his powerful 1940 Penguin Special, *The Internment of Aliens*.

CECILY MACKWORTH
The Power of Propaganda

It was gradually becoming apparent to what extent the German Fifth Column had been organized throughout France. The sick refugees who passed through my dispensary told me stories which, separately, meant nothing, but became significant when viewed as a whole. At every station there had been benevolent men and women waiting to give false information; nurses who had separated children from their parents and then, when inquiries were made, turned out to be unknown to any of the Red Cross organizations. Notices appeared mysteriously on the walls of town halls and churches, warning the population to leave immediately, signed with the seemingly authentic signature of the mayor. False rumours had been put about with such consistency that it became clear that they were not rumours at all, but perfectly timed propaganda. Refugees from remote corners of the south assured me with absolute conviction that the Germans had been close behind them as they left their homes. At this time it really seemed as though the world had gone mad. The feeling that it was impossible to trust anyone was extraordinarily oppressive.

KAY BOYLE
The Fall of France

26th June. Yesterday was a day of downpour, and of quiet and moving grief among the people here. There was a ceremony of mourning on the square in the rain, and the soldiers passing through lounged about as the wreath was placed on the monument of the last war's dead. Two of them turned their backs and did not salute when the French flag was raised. Afterwards the women returned quietly and sat down, raw-eyed, behind the counters of their shops. None of them have any news of their men – none; and Germany is claiming a million and a half prisoners for the duration of the war.

1st July. One feels the need badly now of seeing people, watching things, hearing things said. Every café table seems to have become a sort of refuge, and people who have never before set eyes on one another find themselves sitting down and looking into each other's faces for the answer, not understanding yet how it has happened or why it has happened, but only that we share a disastrous fate in common, and that is the fate of sudden and incredible defeat. They tell you the story of their own experiences, or the experiences of friends, or merely of people they have heard about somewhere, as if in saying these things over and over they must somehow find the explanation in the end.

POLLY PEABODY

In France, August 1940

I went to the American Red Cross to find out if anything more had been heard of my unit, which was still sitting up in Sweden, and also to offer my services in whatever capacity they might be required.

The personnel of the American Scandinavian Field Hospital I was told, were at that very moment on their way back to America.

After exchanging a few Red Cross smiles, which are enough to make milk curdle, I was given the job of ambulance driver at the American Hospital in Neuilly, and the work consisted of transporting food and clothing to the various prison camps, to relieve in some degree the hell to which the prisoners of war were subjected.

Most of the men slept on the damp ground, were underfed and lightly clothed. They all suffered from dysentery, of which many died. Thousands of parcels were packed for prisoners, but the tragedy was that they seldom got delivered.

One day, while I was working at the hospital, a little man, all bent with age, and whose small eyes had faded with the years, appeared with a parcel for his prisoner son. He held the bundle wrapped in newspaper under his arm, and spoke with a sort of excitement:

'You know, I have come a long way to bring it – I also had to wait for hours in line before I could get it, and at my age it is not so easy, but I know it'll make him happy – poor boy.'

I asked him what was in the package. 'A steak,' he said triumphantly. I refrained from telling him that the steak would be rotten by the time it reached his son, but I informed him that all packages had been momentarily stopped: I thought he was going to cry. 'Ah! Mamzelle, he must be so hungry.' For a few minutes he stood gazing at the rumpled newspaper which the fresh meat had already stained: then without another word he turned and hobbled away.

Meanwhile, the Germans told the prisoners that at home no one was thinking of them, or cared, as they were too busy messing around with dirty politics. These conditions altered with time, and the lot of the prisoners improved: but in those August days they were shocking.

Lists of prisoners and casualties were on sale outside subway stations and on the news-stands. This was the only way in which the people of Occupied France learnt what became of their men.

I remember a woman who had apparently just bought one of these lists. She was standing on the side-walk, glancing through the long line of names, when suddenly she raised a clenched fist to her mouth to stifle a scream. For a moment she swayed: then, with the crumpled paper over her eyes, she sobbed and sobbed. The newspaper woman tried to console her, while passers-by lingered a moment and looked at her with sympathy, and went on their way shaking their heads. There was hardly a woman in France who didn't have a brother, husband or son or other relation they couldn't account for. At first, they said, 'He is surely a prisoner.' They all clung to that hope until sometimes the bitter truth was known.

Many people stopped me to ask questions or advice, on account of the uniform I wore. I was in a store once, when a woman approached me. She had a dazed, angry expression.

'Look,' she said, 'this is what I received this morning,' and held out a dirty piece of paper, the corner torn off a full sheet. The paper bore the stamp of a Red Cross, and on it was scribbled in pencil the name of a man, his regiment, number and the two words, 'gravely wounded.' That was all. The man was her son.

The case of the prisoners of war was close to everyone's heart, and it is still the hatchet which Hitler holds over the heads of the people. 'If you don't play along with us,' they say to the French, 'you will never see your men again.'

SYLVIA LEITH-ROSS

Leaving France

There were also hours and hours spent outside the Portuguese Consulate in Toulouse. I had been into a bookseller's shop to buy a map. When no other customers were near, the bookseller leant over the counter: 'I see you are English. I, I like the English. They gave Shakespeare to the world. You must get out of France at all costs! And Mademoiselle who is with you, she is so young. You must not stay another day. Get a Portuguese visa, then perhaps the Spanish will give you a transit visa, even though the frontier is closed.'

And so the greatness of Shakespeare led us to the Portuguese Consulate where, hemmed in by the crowd, we found a Canadian doctor and his French wife, marooned as we were, and without a car.

Together, we worked our way into the house, and step by step, up the stairs. In the Consul's office, intending travellers were putting in the visas on their own passports, writing on the corner of the mantelpiece, on the windowledge, and on each other's backs. The Consul stamped them cheerfully by the hundred. We were the only British subjects. At last we got through, though what we intended doing with our visas, we had no idea.

There was just room in the Austin for Dr W. and his wife. As we drove out of Toulouse, we passed bands of young men on bicycles, lads just under military age. Each had a bundle tied to his bicycle, and each rode swiftly, head down. Where to? They probably did not know.

We had long stretches of road to ourselves. There were moments when it was difficult to remember the war, so quiet was it. Then we would come on a level-crossing and have to wait while a train went by, very slowly, full of soldiers crowded into goods vans. They also did not look as if they knew where they were going to, with their white, unshaven faces. Once we passed the remnant of a Senegalese regiment. They marched heavily, wearily, their big feet in heavy boots, covered with dust. Their faces had gone a deep leaden grey, frightening when one sees it in an African.

We drove till late, and stopped at a small inn in a wayside village. The innkeeper and his wife had little food left, but would do their best, they assured us. There was a room vacant in another house where we could sleep. They had no news to give us; refugees had passed by in great numbers, but were now lessening. Of the Spanish frontier, they knew nothing reliable, nor of what was happening on the coast. We were eating fried ham when someone mentioned Bordeaux. It was good ham, but Mrs W. said she preferred ham cured *à la façon de Bordeaux*. Madame could not agree, and defended her local method. They spoke with fervour and animation, like two artists discussing some rare method of mixing paints or varnish.

It was eleven o'clock at night; all of us were worn with mental and physical fatigue; the future was a black chasm; the present heavy with difficulty and danger. Yet these two Frenchwomen had the courage and the vigour and the integrity, to sit down and discuss, at length, the merits of two ways of curing ham. . . . For a moment, it seemed to me ridiculous, then a kind of awe came over me. In the midst of unimaginable disaster, they were being true to themselves, they were being French. Nothing could stop them from thinking that cooking was an art of importance. In the face of ruin and desolation undreamt of, they threw out the challenge. It was not cured ham they were defending, but the right of France to be herself, *envers et contre tous.* [. . .]

We turned due south to St Jean de Luz. The town was full of people milling to and fro, of abandoned cars, and mounds of luggage. The British Counsul sat in a room above a café, and dealt with a throng of nationalities, which had somehow acquired British passports. He was kind and competent. There was a British ship in harbour. We were to embark at five o'clock.

Down on the quay, there was a confusion of soldiers and sailors and civilians, of lorries and ambulances, arms and stores. Every now and then, a French officer would stop one of us, and whisper: 'You are English. Can I get to England? I must go on fighting.'

ETTA SHIBER
The Indifference of the Comfortable

My only desire now was to forget all that had happened to me; but as the days went by, and the first joy of release passed, I was overcome with a new anguish – one which was associated with the period which I had hoped to put behind me. It was, oddly enough, the result of the width of the gap between my new life and the events through which I had just passed. For, all about me, I saw people leading their normal calm existences, unaware, apparently, of the importance of the enemy threat. I had been a part of the war, although a small part, and I could not regard it with detachment myself, or remain unmoved when I saw others doing so.

Sometimes I would look about me in the streets, at the carefree crowds and say to myself: 'And yet we are at war!'

For me that fact had changed a whole existence. For millions of others it had also changed – or cancelled – existence; and while those about me seemed so unhurried, I knew that other thousands were striving and dying, and that every minute lost to help them would mean for them, not sixty seconds more of discomfort, but the end of life itself.

I couldn't forget the faces of those I had left behind me – Kitty, Father Christian, Tissier, Chancel, all the others, with whom I had lived an existence so different from that I know at present. With them, almost against my own will, I had been able to save some few lives – but how many more who could be saved still remain in peril! How many in France and in other countries under the heel of the oppressor suffer, struggle, and die!

The indifference I meet everywhere frightens me. I believe in human solidarity – but so many live unconcerned with the pains of their millions of brothers under the yoke! I believe in divine justice – even in our materialistic world – but I know it works through the instrumentality of human beings sufficiently in tune with it to strive for its execution. And as I see how many there are who put their own comfort above the efforts necessary to save millions of helpless beings, I feel guilty myself – guilty for being here now, in a place of safety, busied with matters of no importance, while this clash of the forces of good and evil is shaking the world.

Yes, I am troubled by a sense of guilt. Some who are alive today may be shot tomorrow; and how can anyone rest knowing that he might be able to contribute to saving precious human lives if he is not doing so?

CYNTHIA SAUNDERS
Tribunal Day
1939

The KC* laid his black hat and coat on a red leather chair underneath the trellised window overlooking the High Street, rubbed his hands and said, 'A cold morning, Sergeant.' 'Yes, Sir, very cold,' the policeman answered. It was ten o'clock. The door opened and the interpreter came in, shook

* King's Counsel

hands with the KC and the Sergeant, and said cheerfully, 'Let's turn them all down this morning and get to lunch early.'

'I'm sorry you're feeling so bloodthirsty, Miss Simmons,' the Sergeant said, 'make them think we're in Germany, eh?'

At 10.15 enter the first alien. It was quite a way from the door to the two chairs placed at a discreet distance from the little table behind which the Judge sat. On his left was the Sergeant, acting as secretary, taking down everything that was said; on his right the interpreter.

'Are you Grete Schmidt?'

'Yes,' a large, homely woman replied.

'When were you born?'

'Eighteen, six, ninety-three,' came the answer in Teuton fashion, meaning June 18th, 1893.

'And when did you come to England?'

'One, five, thirty-five.'

'Are you Jewish?'

'No.'

'What is your religion?'

The buxom cook spread herself. She had wanted to say so much, but the questions came a little too fast.

'Me? I believe in the Lord, and He made the world a very big place and I don't understand why people should always be being told they must go home.'

The interpreter smiled, the Sergeant smiled and the Judge passed his hand over his mouth.

'Nevertheless, Miss Schmidt, why are you in England now?'

'Because I like England. I don't like Austria with Hitler there.'

'Have you any money over here?'

'O yes, Sir, I save.'

'In a bank, Miss Schmidt?'

'No, Sir – one's pocket is one's best friend,' and she drew out a little leather satchel with pound notes.

Miss Schmidt had excellent references and 'her lady' was outside. Exempted from internment until further notice.

Next, an elderly Jewish couple. The man limped badly, walking with a stick. He sat down with some difficulty. 'Excuse me, I am lame – the Nazis,' he said. 'I am sixty-five today, my birthday.' The Sergeant leant across and shook hands with him. 'Congratulations.' Then the old Jew broke down for a few seconds. So did his wife. Miss Simmons looked away to the window and the Judge waited patiently.

The questions began. When it came to his former profession he had a rare one. He had made the printed silk ribbons often used on wreaths. 'Hitler took my business, my grandfather founded it, you see in the concentration camp they broke my leg . . . and in the High Street my wife knows . . . but you see I have come here . . .' He was dithering helplessly. Shades of former cross-examinations.

Miss Simmons translated, adding that it would be kinder to serve, and de-restrict.

The Judge thought so, too, and asked her to translate how he hoped they would both have a peaceful time in England. They tottered out, their registration books endorsed: 'Victims of Nazi Oppression, exempt from Internment and from all restrictions applicable to enemy aliens.' A little shred of happiness for past miseries. The Tribunal had been sitting for three weeks, but it took a few seconds to recover from this.

'Next, please.'

The door opened and a very beautiful youngish German woman tripped across the floor up to the two chairs, of which she took one and lifted it firmly to the table, sitting down immediately opposite the Judge (a thing he could not bear). Miss Simmons caught the Sergeant's eye and the Judge's, but not the beautiful woman's, who was out by every means in her power to win or die. She wheeled and charmed the KC in vain. It only got her case postponed for Home Office and other files to be sent down from London.

'Only she is too like a copy-book spy to be real,' the Judge observed to Miss Simmons at luncheon.

'Next, please.'

This was an Austrian boy of 19, parlourman in the house of a Staff Captain. Yes, he waited at table (and overheard everything), no, he wasn't a refugee (and so had deliberately become Stateless), but Austria under Hitler, &c. Rather a tall story. Anyway unsuitable for employment in Staff Captain's house. Tribunal had no power to make him leave or be dismissed; only power to intern or exempt from internment with or without travelling restrictions. Interned.

Then four refugees, then luncheon, and another half-dozen, all straight-forward cases.

Finally, about 4.15, the last for the day.

She spoke very little English, and answered every question in monosyl-lables. She was not a refugee. She had had two sisters over here in service, like herself, who had gone back to Germany shortly before the war started. Why had she stayed? No answer. Had she deliberately stayed? Yes. Would she like to go back now? No. Was she a member of the *Arbeitsfront*? No. Had she voted when the German ship came? No? Why not? No answer. It was getting late and the Tribunal was getting no further. A shame that the last case should be so tedious. It was no use starting all over again. Suddenly Miss Simmons had an idea. Had the young woman any special friend in England? Yes. Who?

'My employer –'
'Are you engaged?'
'He's the father of my child.'
That, too, may be the price of refuge.

DIANA MOSLEY

Internment in Holloway
1940

The beautiful hot summer weather went on and on; the garden at Denham was full of flowers. On Saturday afternoon I fed the baby and put him in his pram. I took my book into the garden. A maid appeared.

'There are some people at the door who want to speak to you,' she said.

'What sort of people?'

'Three men and a woman.'

I knew at once they must be police. Journalists sometimes hunt in couples, and one or two had come since M.'s* arrest asking rude and irrelevant questions, but three men and a woman sounded more like police. I went to the door, and a warrant for my arrest was produced. The woman came with me while I put a few things in a small box; 'enough for a week-end,' she said. I was thinking about the baby and the bombing of London which, since France had fallen, was expected hourly.

He was eleven weeks old that day. I asked where I was to be imprisoned; I had heard of a women's prison at Aylesbury; but it was to be Holloway, therefore I decided, much as I longed to take him, that I must leave him with Nanny, who would take both babies to Rignell where they would be as safe as it was possible to be. Since, however, the policewoman had said 'a week-end', I thought I should do my best to be able to continue nursing the baby when it was over, and then wean him in the usual way. It was supposed to be bad for a baby to have a complete change of diet. I hugged the babies, and Nanny who was in tears, and was driven away.

The police motored me to London along empty roads; we were there in no time. Hoping to be able to nurse the baby again I asked my escort to stop at Bell and Croyden in Wigmore Street, the policewoman came with

* Oswald Mosley, Leader of the British Union of Fascists and Diana's husband.

me and I bought a contraption called a breast pump. I should have been wiser to have got the salts and bandages which women use who do not intend to nurse their babies; I should have had far less pain. At Holloway prison the great gate opened and the car deposited me the other side of a yard.

Then came the strange procedure called in prison language 'reception'. I was locked into a wooden box like a broom cupboard. It had a seat fixed opposite the door; if you sat on it your knees touched the door. There was no window but light came in from the wire netting roof of the box. Here I remained for four hours. This was in the nature of a practical joke on the part of the prison authorities, for there was no reason why I should not have been taken straight to my cell after the usual formalities. There was nobody else arrested under Regulation 18B that day.

I collected my thoughts. My ideas about prison came from American films, and I envisaged cells of which one side would be made of iron bars, all giving on to a landing, like a zoo. The walls of my cupboard, painted a dirty cream colour, had been scribbled on by former denizens; there were a few swear words and cryptic sentences. 'Fraser is a cow,' was one. I tried to read the book I had brought with me, a pocket edition of Lytton Strachey's *Elizabeth and Essex*. It was not an ideal choice but I had snatched it up as I left my room.

After a couple of hours the door was unlocked for a moment and I was given a chipped enamel plate with a vast sandwich upon it, also an immense mug of thick china made in the shape of a bobbin with a waist but no handle, containing a hot brown liquid which I guessed was supposed to be tea though it looked more like soup. I was thirsty but dared not drink. I missed the baby in an almost unbearable way. I left the sandwich untouched. After a while I heard other prisoners arrive and being locked into the adjacent boxes, and for the first time I heard the odd noise made by women prisoners, particularly prostitutes. They shout to one another in a sort of wail that is more like song than speech. It was to become a familiar sound over the years; also the accompanying shouts of the wardresses: 'Be quiet, you women.'

After about four and a half hours in my box I was taken out to see the doctor, an unprepossessing female with dyed hair and long finger nails, varnished dark red. I told her that I had been nursing my baby but that I could look after myself, and when a bath was mentioned I said I had had one that morning which seemed to satisfy her. Then a wardress took me to F Wing.

She made me go first, an act of apparent courtesy which, like so much in prison, is not quite what it seems. Wardresses must always have their prisoners in front of them; if they were following there's no knowing what they might take it into their heads to do: run away, for example.

As she unlocked the door and we stood in the entrance to F Wing a babel of voices suddenly fell silent and a sort of gasp went up. Dozens of women, many of them in dressing gowns, were standing about in groups, most had mugs in their hands. I did not know it, but it was ten minutes before they were due to be locked in their cells for the night and for this reason they were all on the landings. They crowded round me with kind expressions of sympathy; they knew I had left a little baby and were furious on my behalf. I knew very few of them, though they were members of B.U. [. . .]

Before I arrived the 18Bs had decided to eat together at trestle tables set up in the space between the cells on the ground floor. They took it in turns to fetch the food in huge metal containers from the prison kitchen, and to wash up. Washing up was a nasty affair, the plates were battered enamel, the forks bent and old, there was no soap and very little hot water. As soon as I decently could I abandoned this communal style of living. I got a china plate of my own and avoided the dreadful enamel. In any case I could not eat the prison food, except for the delicious bully beef; I made my ration of this last several days, otherwise I lived on prison bread and Stilton cheese sent me by M.

LIVIA LAURENT

Internment on the Isle of Man
1940

We arrived at the camp on the Isle of Man. Compartment by compartment we were unlocked, let out and received by a smiling, gushing lady. 'This way dear.' She had helpers who were told where to take us. 'Three for the Hydro, six to the Towers, eight to Seaview, four to the Strand Café. You have lost your friend dear? Never mind, you will find her again. No one gets lost here.' We were pushed, counted, torn apart. Else and Lotte just vanished, only by hanging on to Matilda's rucksack did I manage not to get lost myself.

We found ourselves tramping down a lane. 'This is where you are going to live,' a cheerful girl told us. She knocked at the door of a boarding house. 'Two internees for you, Mrs Drinkwater.' Mrs Drinkwater was outraged. 'I have no room. What will they think of next,' and slammed the door in our faces. So that was that. Back to the station, which was already deserted. The smiling lady was just on her way home. 'Mrs Drinkwater had no room for these two,' our guide told her. 'Mrs Drinkwater? Who is Mrs Drinkwater? Who are you?' she wanted to know. I just looked the other way. This was a farce. Matilda would burst in a minute, I could see it coming. 'But they've just arrived'; the girl got flustered too. 'Ah yes, so they have, take them to the Bay View, plenty of room there. Goodnight, you'll be happy there.' She was gone.

The streets were quite empty already. This was the Bay View. 'Just knock at the door, all the best, goodnight,' and before we could thank her, the girl had disappeared. We knocked. Nothing happened. We knocked again. A face showed in a window: 'Who are you?' 'We are new, suposed to live here!' 'The landlord is out.' 'Can't you let us in?' 'Impossible, the door is locked. You can't get in, we can't come out. Wait!' She was back in a second. 'Catch,' she threw us bananas, oranges, apples.

I settled down on the steps and wondered if we were going to spend the night there. Matilda's mood suddenly changed and she became hilarious. There were people hanging out of all the windows now; trying to be helpful, laughing, feeling sorry for us. 'You'll be put in jail for overstepping the curfew!' 'That's O.K. with me, we've just come from there. Give me Holloway anytime. At least there is a bed for everyone.' 'You've been at Holloway?' The little brunette who had thrown us the oranges looked scared. It suddenly dawned on me that most of the people here hadn't been in prison at all, they had been sent here straight away.

'There is Mr Harrison, he'll help you!' A young curly-headed clergyman was coming towards us. After much wandering about we eventually landed in a small private house with one small bed for two people. [. . .]

We were not all alike, and our lives differed considerably. What was, for me, the better part of a year a time of comparative contentment and inner freedom, was, for others, the most frightful strain and unhappiness. Those who lived in the big hotels and suffered from the gossip and constant malicious attacks of others, those who stayed in small houses and were used by unscrupulous landladies as maids of all work, those who were torn away from husbands and children, those who knew their families to be in the front lines of London, in the trenches of Swiss Cottage, Bloomsbury and Maida Vale, those who had not yet learned to think of themselves as removed from their own background; and all of those who were not quite consciously determined to make the best of it, at whatever cost.

There were others who liked the absence of responsibility, the fact that no decision was required of them, for some it was their first real 'holiday' as they called it, others enjoyed the easy companionship, the chance of meeting people they wouldn't have met in the ordinary course of their lives; and Mrs Becker who had kept the little haberdashery shop in a back street of Manchester was happy and proud to dry dishes, graciously handed to her by Mlle Adele, the great singer and opera star. [. . .]

When I left my companions that afternoon, though arranging to meet again, I knew that that companionship was over. It had been over the moment we left Holloway. It happened to everybody. I met Leni. 'How is Gretel?' They had been inseparable, always walking arm in arm. 'We quarrelled,' and a long story of Gretel's misdeeds followed. Hildegarde walked around by herself. 'Where's Rita?' 'Don't mention that name to me, I never want to see her again,' she flared up. On the small territory allotted to 4,000 people, many lonely walks were taken, many tales of horror told about the friends of yesterday. Why was this necessary? Did people's natures come out in this so-called freedom? Had they only been subdued in Holloway? The story went that a sedative had been mixed in our food there, that's why we had been so peaceful and placid in prison. Quite possible, it would make as good an explanation as any. [. . .]

Dame Joanna Cruickshank (the Camp Commandant) was deeply grieved to find that some of us had not been quite straight with the authorities. It was hard for her to say, but say it she must, there were some internees who had actually reverted to dishonesty in order to obtain some of their own money. Not without reluctance she found herself compelled to employ this method* which, as she fully realized, punished innocent and guilty alike. She sincerely hoped it would not have to be for long. It was as painful to her as it must have been to us. As soon as we would show ourselves worthy of her renewed trust, she would reconsider the issue. And there was something else she had meant to say to us for a long long time. Happiness was of own making; place, conditions and circumstances were of no importance. All that mattered was to be happy!

While she went on talking at great length, imploring us to be happy at all costs, I watched the people as they were listening. There was old Mrs Kaiser, a grandmother, who had brought up a large number of sons and daughters, who had been a good wife and mother, and was nearing the conclusion of a full and varied life. Being poor, she couldn't have been one of those so rightly punished for embezzling their own money, but she looked crestfallen and apologetic just the same. There was little Miss Schwarz, a Bible student, who would rather have died than infringe the slightest regulation, however ridiculous, looking sad and guilty. There were countless others, teachers, successful business women, women who had done their jobs in life as well as anybody, and who had every right to be proud, independent, and confident, looking like children in a charity school, cowed and utterly crushed. There were little murmurs of regret, someone went so far as to say 'I'll never do it again,' although I am convinced she hadn't done anything at all, and the general atmosphere was unbearable.

* Of stopping the billing system with local shops.

The only failing of these women was the fact that they had the wrong kind of passport; very few of them had enemies, still less would they have indulged in any act of malice. But the fact alone was sufficient to over-shadow any other consideration for their personal value, their own integrity. And they accepted it. The terrible thing was their own acceptance of it, making it possible for a technical matter to influence their character, their courage, touch their very souls. [. . .]

The Service Exchange – the name explains itself – presented a highly intricate system for providing and exchanging work. Those who worked full-time had the chance of making 2/7 a week, for the remainder they were given vouchers. So a teacher who worked at the school, or gave private lessons, could have a jumper knitted in return, or have her hair done, or her clothes repaired. There was a laundry working full time, a hairdressing saloon, dressmakers, toymakers, weavers, spinners, fortune tellers, people who would type for you, or write a competent English letter, others who would take your children for walks or clean your mackintosh by a special method, guaranteed Viennese; even legal advice was to be had. Gardening came under the scheme too, and everywhere you saw people working in small allotments, later on in the fields, getting ready for the spring. And a good job they made of it.

FLAVIA KINGSCOTE
Internment in Italy
1941

Soon the cold spell relaxed and early summer came to Tuscany. In the hotel garden where we were allowed to walk at will, supervised by a pleasant carabiniere, lilac and irises bloomed in profusion, and all through the night and during much of the day the song of nightingales filled the air. It would have been difficult to have chosen a better suited spot in which to recuperate from the various strains and stresses of the last month, and personally, I was glad our stay here looked like being a long one. We were all very relieved, and many of us extremely surprised, to learn our whole party was to be released when the protracted negotiations regarding our line of departure were completed. Even today I cannot understand why the Italians let us all go unquestioningly, including young men of military age, but it was enough then to know we would eventually be leaving, and for the present I sat back and enjoyed the peace and beauty of my surroundings.

We were allowed out for two hours in the morning and another two in the afternoon, during which time we were given complete freedom within the bounds of the 'campo', a disused horse-show ground resembling a football field, about fifty yards distant from our three hotels. Apart from this we were also allowed to go for walks every afternoon in groups from each hotel accompanied by detectives. These walks grew longer and less formal as the weeks passed, our escorts at first lacking enthusiasm, but gradually the novelty of going for country walks took hold of them, and instead of trudging gloomily behind us along a mile or two of tarred road they would vie with each other, each trying to take his own particular group the longest and most cross-country hike, bringing us back long after the allotted time laden with wild flowers and other trophies.

The inhabitants of Chianciano accepted us without undue excitement or curiosity. Once the novelty of our presence wore off they settled down again, and soon realized what a piece of good business we represented. It was estimated that during our four or five weeks' stay we consumed more wine and beer than is normally drunk in two years, Chianciano being, after all, a spa for heart and liver troubles. The shops did a roaring trade not only in clothes but in sweets and cigarettes which were still to be had in unlimited quantities. The people, while remaining reserved, showed a distinct friendliness towards us, and it was from their lips we learnt of the loss of the *Bismarck* long before it was officially reported in Italy. They can only have heard of the sinking from the BBC, and their manner in conveying it to us with downward-pointing thumbs and sardonic grins, left little doubt as to their satisfaction.

A POLISH REFUGEE

How it Feels to be a Refugee
1943

We brought away nothing valuable from Warsaw – but there was one thing that we did bring, or rather it brought us. That was our car. We ought not to have had it. It was only my idiotic sentimentality. When we came to the French port we had no more money to buy new tyres and we ought to have left it there. I looked at it standing abandoned on an open platform. It had grown a little dirty and worn. I remembered how we had driven it out of our own garage and I thought of the times we had been together since, over what dreadful roads we had driven, and through how many countries. I remembered how we had slept in it when we had no money to pay for a hotel. And I thought to myself, there is my good friend which not a single time has let me down, and I couldn't bear to lose it. So it came with us. It stands now in a garage, and I am still paying five shillings a week, and from time to time I have terrible rows with my husband about it. But so far I have won, and we still keep it. Sometimes I go for a little and sit in it. It is like home.

It isn't easy to be a refugee. And yet, when you have lost so much, it seems as if you are given something in exchange. We have lost our houses and our possessions. But many of us have found a stronger faith in ideas. [. . .] Often I have heard people say, 'You refugees are a queer lot – you seem to have lost touch with reality. You have the most impossible ideas.' Then I think not only of Chopin who wrote his music in exile, I think also of Pilsudski, who planned the new Poland in a German prison, and of Masaryk who planned in exile the new Czechoslovakia. And perhaps the greatest work of the spirit written by man in exile is the Book of Revelation, which St John wrote on the Isle of Patmos. For myself I have always believed in ideas, but never so much as now.

Chapter four

PREPARING FOR THE WORST

The evacuation of the British Expeditionary Force from Dunkirk was followed by the Battle of Britain – the daylight dogfights between German and British planes over British soil. In the summer of 1940 Britain prepared to be invaded. Barricades, tank traps and miniature forts appeared; signposts, village and street names disappeared. An appeal to the public for weapons netted twenty thousand shotguns and pistols; these went to the Local Defence Volunteers, later known as the Home Guard.

Women sometimes felt marginalised in these fevered preparations, as they were not allowed to join the Home Guard until 1943, and then only as auxiliaries. But they were keen to do their bit: Home Guard wives proved themselves proficient at mixing Molotov cocktails – bottles filled with resin, petrol and tar to lob at invading Nazi tanks – and the MP Edith Summerskill founded the Women's Home Defence Organization to teach women how to use firearms. The novelist and playwright Margaret Kennedy made her own five-point invasion list of 'things we ought to do', which included having a large sum of money 'ready to be sewed into my stays' and a knapsack of iron rations. She prepared for mobility; the official advice was to '*stay put*'. Meanwhile the shortage of jobs for women was still acute, and a magazine article by the MP Eleanor Rathbone entitled 'The Waste of Woman-Power' was one of many protests that appeared in the press.

Invasion fears bred rumour and gossip. The government response was heavy-handed, aiming much of its propaganda at women. Two housewives gossip on a bus while Hitler and Goering sit smugly behind them in the famous 'Careless Talk Costs Lives' poster. Concern for public morale prompted Duff Cooper, head of the newly formed Ministry of Information, to invite the nation to 'join the ranks of the Silent Column', to 'fight against gloom' and 'be silent rather than say anything depressing'. His initiative was met with dismay and derision, his team surveying public morale denounced as Cooper's Snoopers. Dorothy L. Sayers helped to lead the movement against the Ministry of Information campaign, which was seen as both patronising and intrusive; by August the Ministry agreed that 'the word "morale" must not be used again'. The Queen never gave the speech written for her by A.A. Milne, in which she was to entreat her country-women 'to remember, when you are tempted to spread these rumours, or these ugly thoughts of hatred, just to say to yourself, "The Queen asked me herself not to. She asked *me*." '

Judging by what women published at the time, the government's fears of invasion hysteria among women were exaggerated. Or perhaps the women who made the effort to write – or who were accepted – for publication were themselves aware of the need to allay fear. Rebecca West faced the issue with characteristic directness in her article 'If The Worst Comes To The Worst'. Other writers, such as Naomi Royde Smith, were less direct, and took the sting out of rumour and gossip by playing with them.

The mood of the writing at this time seems to be one of realistic determination; this entailed closing down the emotional temperature. *England's Hour*, Vera Brittain's collection of essays on wartime London (written in 1940 and published in 1941), was much admired in America, where it was described approvingly as 'a completely unsentimental book'. In England, however, it was condemned by E.M. Delafield and others for its 'sentimental approach'. More in tune with the prevailing mood were the 'Rebuilding Britain' articles with titles like 'Hopes For The Future', urging readers to 'work to prepare for peace'. The heroine of the moment was Mary Cornish, a children's escort on the torpedoed ship *City of Benares*, who looked after six boys in an open lifeboat for over a week, and was celebrated by Elspeth Huxley in *Atlantic Ordeal*.

61

NESCA ROBB
The Struggle for Employment

When I first went to the [Women's Employment] Federation, early in 1940, the Emergency Register contained over nine thousand names. It did not, except in a few special cases, deal with teachers, who were held to be in a reserved occupation, or with certain categories, such as doctors and dentists, who had their town emergency schemes. Apart from these we had records of women capable of infinite varieties of work; qualified in social and domestic science, in secretarial and business experience, in the arts and sciences, as lawyers, linguists, architects, statisticians. Yet of the eager volunteers who had come forward in the preceding summer, overflowing the Marsham Street offices and leaving the interviewers breathless before their onslaught, only a tiny fraction had been absorbed into any form of national service. What indeed could they have done, during those months of torpor? This did not, however, mean that all those who, in September, had been safely in employment, were still employed in the spring. The country had been disorganized for peace without as yet being organized for war. Many businesses, from caution or necessity, had reduced their staffs. The evacuation of all kinds of concerns – business houses, schools, institutions and private families – had raised new problem for workers. Some, with special family ties, could not follow their employers; others, especially women with business or professional connexions of their own, found that their clients were dispersed and that, in the harder conditions of the day, there was little hope of finding new ones. The luxury trades and the arts were the first and hardest hit, but there was probably no single profession unaffected. Meanwhile, slowly, but to the unemployed woman very perceptibly, the cost of living began its inevitable rise.

The younger women were on the whole the lucky ones. They could join the Women's Services or the Land Army. As the younger men were the first to be called up, it was natural that their feminine contemporaries should take their places in junior posts. Most of the temporary civil servants, including practically the whole secretarial and clerical staffs of Government offices, were recruited also from the lower age groups. Even these advantages were not stable. There were long periods in which the Services stopped recruiting, in which there was no further extension of office staffs and no demand even for voluntary workers.

For the older women the position was much worse. For months on end it seemed that the country had no place for them and was completely indifferent to their problems, if indeed it realized that they had any. How some of them existed, or were expected to exist, during that time was hard to imagine. Some were entitled to unemployment benefit, but many were not; and as a rule they had heavier responsibilities than their juniors. Their age debarred them from the few forms of service that showed any wish for recruits, but there were no civilian posts for them to fill.

The class perhaps most seriously affected were the older office workers of all kinds. Hundreds of them were out of work and often in acute difficulties. Yet they could well have undertaken most of the routine Government jobs which many of them had held in the last war, and so released younger women for active work or training. The whole problem of woman power was indeed horribly bungled. It was doubtless impossible to reabsorb the new host of unemployed women into industry without some delay; but no explanation of this state of affairs, no guidance or encouragement of any kind was given by those in high places. There was no large-scale provision of training for the services that would clearly be needed later on. Every now and then the press would break out into headlines proclaiming that so many women were wanted, or that a training scheme for this or that was on the point of opening. When this happened we were invariably besieged by inquirers. Unhappily it generally proved that the women were not wanted after all; that the training scheme's opening was indefinitely postponed, or that it provided only for an infinitesimal number. Investigation seemed always to reveal some new nightmare's nest of muddle.

It was disheartening for all; for some it was excruciating. I shall not readily forget those days of the late spring and summer when things seemed to have reached complete stagnancy and one sat at one's desk feeling like the oracle of hope deferred. If one placed a candidate at that time, one felt as if one had saved a life – but how rarely could it be achieved! As a rule one could only take down the applicant's qualifications, explain, encourage and sympathize as best one could and refer her to all other possible agencies on the forlorn chance of something turning up. There were those who came back to us repeatedly after fruitless searches, each time a little more unhealthily transparent, a little bluer under the eyes and more pinched about the lips. They were marvellously uncomplaining, but the signs were clear. Fortitude is an inspiring sight, but there are few spectacles more painful than that of a fortitude that is being slowly disintegrated.

One acquired, too, an uncomfortable insight into the way in which much of women's work is underpaid. The principle of equal pay for equal work is still very far from being put in practice. That it is not generally adopted may be partly due to a belief, still widely held, that women work only for themselves and are never burdened with family responsibilities. Very few of the hundreds who came to us were without some such burden. There were widows with families to educate, wives whose husbands were invalided or out of work, single women who were supporting younger brothers and sisters, or, most often, some aged or infirm relative. It was sometimes unbelievable how many people our clients had been called upon to help out of salaries that made by no means lavish provision for one. Again, the older generation was the most affected, but the country has lost many volunteers for the Services and other war organizations because no provision is made for dependants and one cannot save much out of two-thirds of a soldier's pay. It is charming to be told, as Mr Chesterton was fond of telling us, that we are all queens and beings hallowed and apart; but the values lately set on female lives and limbs reveal a different attitude. Between the extremes of pretty speeches and flagrant unfairness there must be some mean of common sense and plain justice where women are concerned. Perhaps that is one of the things that will be discovered in the new Britain.

Another problem that was continually brought before us was that of women who for the first time in their lives wanted work and had never been trained to do anything. These were mostly middle-aged women, often mothers of families, who had hitherto been comfortably off or even rich. The war, with its tale of falling investments and ruined businesses, had thrown them suddenly into the struggle for employment. They were often charming people, intelligent and cultivated, who had probably run their homes admirably; but the fact remained that it was almost impossible to place them. The only posts for which they were positively qualified were those of house-keepers in private houses; and here again, owing to war conditions, the demand was limited. Some of them had married young and never given a thought to possible vicissitudes in the future. A great many had, however, the same story to tell. 'My parents did not think it worth while to spend money on educating the girls.' 'My father (it generally *was* father) wouldn't hear of his daughters doing anything.' These sentiments are unfortunately not yet out of date. Sometimes I wondered if parents who have deliberately stopped their daughters from training for a profession, are compelled to watch from another world the havoc they have wrought in this. It would often be a pretty Purgatory. Neither marriage nor private means give any guarantee that a woman will never have to work for her living. The instability of human fortunes is more marked than it has ever been in our lifetimes; and the scales are weighted more heavily against the unqualified. Some form of sound training and some experience of work are very necessary investments for a daughter's future. The lack of them can be a deadly handicap in time of need.

NAOMI ROYDE SMITH
Rumours

After the withdrawal from Norway, Quisling rumours ran like wildfire. My early tea was brought up one Sunday morning with the announcement that the Town Clerk had been arrested as a spy. Sleepy though I was I refused to believe this news. It was entirely untrue. There is, however, a circumstantial tale of a local clergyman's daughter who was able to denounce as a spy a British officer quartered on the vicarage. She heard him going late at night to the lavatory: but he never pulled the plug! This un-English behaviour excited her suspicion, she reported it, and her guest was discovered to be signalling with a flash-light from the window of the retreat.

Our best rumour, however, was a real sensation. One morning I noticed a distant smell of hot onions. As I was repainting chairs at the time I thought this might be due to some war economy in the composition of the enamel I was using – or that onions had been added to the cheese and cocoa which the daily woman requires with her elevenses. An hour later I went off to have my hair shampooed and learnt that there had been a gas alarm from Southampton. Air Raid Wardens, in gas-masks, had paraded the town, school children had been put into *their* gas-masks; the hair-dresser had been told to close all the windows and warn his clients to keep their heads well into the basins. The agitation was at its height when a message came through to say that the pollution of the atmosphere was not of Enemy Origin. A local pickle factory had had a fire and onions and vinegar frying and boiling together had produced a miasma blown by the wind in our direction.

DIANA COOPER
Preparing for Invasion

After Dunkirk we talked exclusively of parachutists, of how they would come and deceive us by being dressed as nurses, monks or nuns with collapsible bicycles concealed beneath their habits. An English uniform would have been a better disguise for the expected invaders. Orders and suggestions overwhelmed us. We must stay put (how does one do it?). We must not spread alarm or dismay (I must therefore hold my tongue). We must fill our ginger-beer empties with an explosive prescription, label it 'Molotov Cocktail' and hurl it at the invading tanks. We were advised to feed the enemy's cars with sugar to neutralise their petrol. Place-names were obliterated on roads and stations. Barricades of wagons and tree-trunks were successfully obstructing our own movements. We must 'Be like Dad and keep Mum' (very funny, we thought), and the children must not have kites or fireworks. We had killed our black-widow spiders when war came, and now the Zoo's Home Guard were trained riflemen. To have been hugged to death by a bombed-out bear would have been an anticlimax. One zebra only got a run for his money and streaked round Regent's Park pursued by the Zoo's secretary, keepers and the public. We had all given our weapons, binoculars and dainty opera-glasses to the Home Guard. In June the ringing of church-bells was stopped, so that they might ring again for invasion. It sounded a topsy-turvy order. Their silence, and the dark-ened houses that betrayed no cheer or welcome and were no longer symbols of shelter, affected me acutely.

A difficult suggestion that had a foolish appeal for me was to equip one's car with an all-covering armour of small pebbles between sheets of tin. This naturally never materialized and I was disappointed.

MARGARET KENNEDY
Bright Little Jokes

We are all keeping a check on our emotions. We are a little guarded in what we say for fear of inadvertently annoying people, or straining nerves already taut, or deepening the general depression. We avoid controversy or provocative sallies; what would normally be stimulating arguments might easily sharpen into quarrels just now. One tries to short-circuit emotion rather than to share it. The 'genial current of the soul' is dammed up, and we fall back on bromides and bright little jokes.

FRANCES PARTRIDGE
German Parachutists

May 13 1940
Everyone makes jokes about the likelihood of German parachutists landing in our Wiltshire fields dressed as nuns or clergymen – a good farcical subject on which to let off steam. This afternoon I was alone in the kitchen when the doorbell rang, and there on the step stood three tall bearded men who addressed me in strong German accents, and wore something between clergyman's and military dress! Aha! I thought, the parachutists already. But when they asked for Mrs Nichols I realized that it was some of the Brüderhof, a community of Christian Pacifists of all nations who live the simple life near Swindon. Curiosity was too much for me, so I asked them to have some tea. Two were very unattractive redheads with scarlet mouths above their beards. It was the maddest of mad hatter tea parties, consisting of me and these three Jesus Christs, all looking at me sweetly and speaking in gentle voices. I told them we were pacifists. 'Are you persecuted much?' they asked, rather taking the wind out of my sails. I felt as if Jesus Christ had mistaken me for John the Baptist.

NAOMI ROYDE SMITH
Rumours of Invasion
September 1940

A protean rumour which has shown itself in various forms during this month has reached here in what may be its final and true shape.

It began with a reported tocsin in Cornwall, spreading to Hampshire, heard by many and given a headline in the morning papers about three weeks ago: the Germans had landed somewhere in Dorset; in Kent; in Lincolnshire. This was officially denied. Then a whisper started that the corpses of German soldiers, in full battle dress, had been washed up all round the coast. Presently the horrid detail that each corpse had its hands tied behind its back was added. I felt that this was a sheer Quisling intended to foment indignation against the Royal Navy. Who else could have had this notion or the opportunity of doing such a thing? Then the tale grew into patent absurdity. The whole of the Channel from Weymouth to Devonport was *covered* with the corpses of stricken armies. The retailer of this piece of nonsense had pointed out to those who brought it to him that, if this were true, the entire population of the Reich must have perished, also that no corpses drowned in the North Sea would get far beyond the Straits of Dover as the tide there would wash them to and fro. After that the rumour died down, but today it has come back in a more plausible form. The Invasion had a dress rehearsal last week. The RAF attended it. The embarked *Wehr* did not like the prospect. A suspicion that this was no mere rehearsal produced a stampede. The hospitals of Northern France are now filled with German soldiers, all shot in the back by the bullets of their commanding officers.

AN ENGLISHWOMAN
An Invasion Alarm

From an Englishwoman to a friend in America, 8 September 1940

We had an invasion alarm last night. (Please, Censor, don't cut all this out; it is quite harmless and will be useless information to the enemy by the time it arrives.) Phil and I were at the flicks when just in the middle of the most exciting part of *The Thin Man* a message was flashed on the screen requiring all troops to return to their barracks at once.

We found that the invasion password had been given by telephone just before we got back. Phil seized his rifle and kit and dashed off to report at HQ.

I was just starting to wash my hair before the midnight news when the bell went and I went down to admit a very young, very solemn soldier. He announced that he had come to phone a message and stand by our phone throughout the night for further orders for his unit who were stationed in defensive positions around. I suggested that he leave his kit in the outer hall – 'No, I'll not do that.' He obviously considered that the safety of Britain hung on his every act.

So he piled his rifle, tin helmet, gas mask, etc., beside the telephone. Then he gazed dubiously at the instrument, scratched his head: 'I've never done this afore.' I said: 'What, do you mean to say you've never used a telephone?' 'Never.' I showed him which way to hold the receiver and how to dial and explained about the number being engaged. Then I went off to hear the midnight news. When I came down about 12.30 meaning to get him some food, I found him still clutching the telephone with sweat pouring from his head and not a thing happening! I got him connected up with his HQ then and stood by telling him what to say.

VERA BRITTAIN
And So – Farewell!

Towards the end of June 1940, many conscientious parents throughout England find themselves confronted with a heartbreaking dilemma.

Simultaneously with the collapse of France, the Government announces an official scheme to send thousands of British children to the Dominions. Canada, South Africa, Australia and New Zealand broadcast enthusiastic offers of hospitality. In the United States, a Committee is formed under the Chairmanship of Marshall Field of Chicago to rescue Europe's children; it is even possible, we learn, that the adamant immigration laws may be modified in order to admit a hundred thousand boys and girls of British stock to America.

We feel certain that the Government would not sponsor so large a scheme unless it was convinced that horror and dislocation would come to this country with the downfall of Europe. The announcement of the plan seems to thousands of anxious parents a warning of 'things to come'. Earlier evacuation schemes have made no special appeal to them, for moving children from the town to the country was merely a method of redistributing the population; it assured neither safety, freedom from chaos, nor that sense of security which is the birthright of childhood. Emigration to the Dominions or America, where real freedom from war will be a gift from new territories unhampered by the evil nationalistic traditions of the quarrelsome Old World, is a proposition more hopeful and far more imaginative. The most resourceful and energetic parents decide to register their children immediately.

From the moment that the Children's Overseas Reception Board – to be known familiarly as 'Corb' – is established in the Berkeley Street offices of Messrs. Thomas Cook and Son under the Chairmanship of Geoffrey

69

Shakespeare, Under-Secretary of State for the Dominions, a queue of parents and children begins to stretch from the office door into Piccadilly. The opportunity of safeguarding the children's future appeals equally to the small households of Mayfair and the large dockyard families from Bermondsey and Chatham.

'If we must die,' say these fathers and mothers, 'at least we intend to save the next generation.'

Sick at heart, conscious that our obligations as parents may demand a sacrifice of a kind we had never contemplated, Martin and I debate the question for a weary week-end. Richard is at school in a so-called 'safe area', but Hilary, at Swanage, has already been summoned to the air-raid shelter, and her headmaster has finally concluded that no place nearer than Canada can now offer a stable life and an uninterrupted education. We ourselves have lived in the United States for long periods during fifteen years; we have friends tested by a decade of loyal affection. Shall we not be sadly remiss as parents if we fail to take advantage of circumstances so favourable?

'It's a terrible thing to do,' I protest, unable, after twelve years of careful rearing, to face giving up the children just when their personalities are developing and their fascination is growing every day.

'You're only thinking of yourself,' Martin replies inexorably. 'It's the children's interests that matter, not your feelings.'

I agree with him miserably. 'I know that. I'm only trying to decide whether it's better for them to have danger with me or security without me. As you feel so certain, you're probably right.'

After one more night of agonised indecision, I accompany Martin to the offices of the Children's Overseas Reception Board. Two humble units in a long line of troubled questioning parents, we make our inquiries. The woman Member of Parliament who answers them happens to be a personal friend.

'Don't hesitate,' she advises us. '*Get them out!*'

She hands us several alternative application forms; one is a request for permission to make private arrangements without waiting for the government scheme to come into operation.

'Look here,' she adds, 'you could afford to pay for their passage, couldn't you?'

We admit that we could. 'The children have been to the United States before,' we continue. 'They both hold re-entry permits.'

'Well, then, there's nothing to wait for. They're in quite an exceptionally favourable position. Fix up their passages yourselves, and you'll be making room under the government scheme for two more children whose parents can't afford to send them on their own.'

We decide to take her advice and book provisional berths for Richard and Hilary, never dreaming that in three weeks' time, when the operation of the government scheme has been impeded by the loss of the French fleet and the resulting shortage of convoys, we and other middle-class parents who have acted with similar promptitude will have our distress increased by accusations that we have abused our 'class privileges' at the expense of children from state-aided schools whose interests under the scheme we believed ourselves to be serving.

When we visit the Passport Office to obtain passports for Richard and Hilary, there is certainly no evidence that the queue of parents which stretches to the end of Dartmouth Street is composed of 'wealthy escapists'. For over an hour we stand waiting in the company of an ex-army corporal, who is using his savings to send his family to a Canadian sergeant whom he knew in World War No. 1.

'Yes,' he explains, 'I'm sending the wife and kid. She don't want to go, but I tells her: "You mark my words, it'll be the only life, after this war. The boy won't 'ave 'arf a chance here, compared with over there. When it's all over," I says to her, "I'll come out and join you." ' [. . .]

The morning so long dreaded has come. Last night I delayed as long as I could over drying Hilary's slim fairy-like body and brushing Richard's thick nut-brown hair. Sleepless, I looked at their sleeping faces – Richard's long dark eyelashes motionless on his cheeks, Hilary's fair serene face as unperturbed as an angel's. Modern children, endowed as though by some law of compensation with a calm emotional detachment which they cannot have inherited from their war-ridden parents of the Lost Generation, they neither fear nor even speculate about the adventure before them.

We join the waiting boat train at Euston, our luggage-laden taxicab hemmed in a long cavalcade of vehicles which threads its way laboriously through the newly barricaded entrance to the station. Just in time we board the train and discover that it is crowded with children – children of both sexes and all ages, babies whose fortunate mothers are justified in leaving an invasion-threatened country and going with them, older children who vary from five or six years old to the school ages of fourteen and fifteen. Most of them are being accompanied to the boat by their parents – miserable mothers and fathers of whom some are even now torn cruelly with indecision. On the way back to London we are to meet an unhappy father whose departing wife, right up to the moment of embarkation, announced her intention of returning to London with her boy and girl.

Like the rest of the children in the train, Richard and Hilary remain philosophical, even with regard to the dangers that they may encounter on the way to Montreal.

'Wonder if we'll meet any submarines?' speculates Richard, voicing with no inhibition of fear the secret dread that tears at our hearts, challenging our resolution, making us perpetually uncertain whether we have acted for the best. It is the parents, not the children, who are suffering; at least we can thank God for that. As the crowded train rolls inexorably onwards, the hackneyed verse of a familiar hymn seems to beat into my brain with the roar of the wheels.

'If Thou should'st ask me to resign
What most I prize, it ne'er was mine.
I only yield Thee what is Thine.
    Thy Will be done!'

At the docks we are ushered into a large covered shed, to wait for what seem indefinite hours till the immigration officials arrive. Tired out already by the long train journey, the dozens of babies lift their voices one by one in loud wails of protest, and soon the dock resembles the parrot-house at the Zoo. Looking up and down the huge enclosure at two or three hundred weary older children sitting with mute resignation beside their suitcases, we conclude that the immigration officials cannot be fathers. At last a number of stewardesses take pity on the waiting families; they bring cartons of milk and packets of biscuits, which they offer to children and parents. Martin and I feel that the biscuits would choke us, but Richard and Hilary, seizing their supply with eager grubby hands, each zestfully consume eight biscuits and two cartons of milk.

A Canadian Pacific official approaches us.

'Are these the children who hold re-entry permits to the United States?'

Richard and Hilary move forward in proud assent. Now that the moment has come, my legs suddenly feel as though they will no longer sustain me. Oh, my darling children, is there time to call you back from salvation, even now?

With imperturbable dignity, Richard and Hilary march off beside the CPR official into the hut where the immigration officers are sitting. As we watch them from a distance, we notice a long file of girls from a Yorkshire convent school move towards the gangway, accompanied by their gentle nuns. Are these the wealthy, taking advantage of their privileges? They exist, perhaps on other liners; not many of them seem to be boarding this one.

Apparently without a qualm, the children exhibit their papers and their money. After answering several questions, they reappear with their escort.

'The only thing that worried me,' Richard confesses, 'was whether they'd let me keep the five shillings Granny gave me, as well as my ten pounds.'

'And did they, darling?'

'Yes,' chimes in Hilary. 'They didn't mind a bit. Richard said: "Have I got to give you my five shillings, because I'm only supposed to take ten pounds?" and the man said: "Never mind, sonny; we won't worry about that." '

A cold rainy wind blows suddenly over the docks. Beyond the enclosure we see now the grey-painted hulk of the anonymous liner, waiting to carry away from us the dearest possessions that are ours on earth. No – not our possessions. We never possessed them; they have always possessed themselves.

The CPR official approaches again. His manner is discreetly sympathetic.

'I'm afraid you'll have to say good-bye to the children now.'

'Very well,' we reply with outward equanimity. I remember then that I have brought no farewell gifts for either; that I was packing throughout the two hours that the children went shopping with their father. Oh, dearest Richard and Hilary – will you think of me as the careless mother who never gave you a parting present, when you bought her such a lovely bunch of scarlet carnations?

'Good-bye, Mummie! Good-bye, Daddy!'

'Good-bye, my own darlings. You'll look after Hilary, won't you, Richard? And you, sweetheart – you *will* do what Richard tells you on the boat?'

'We'll be quite all right, Mummie. Don't worry about us. We promise we'll look after ourselves till you come across too.'

'Good-bye, then, my loves!' ('*If Thou should'st ask me to resign What most I prize . . .*')

With the gallant pathetic courage of children, Richard and Hilary kiss us and leave us as calmly as though they are departing for a weekend visit to a familiar relative. Their eyes are bright; their faces do not change as they go with their guide to meet the unknown adventure.

At the entrance to the gangway, they turn and wave cheerfully. Then the tarpaulin flaps behind them, and they are gone.

ELSPETH HUXLEY

from *Atlantic Ordeal*

Mary Cornish started games. They played 'Animal, vegetable or mineral', and when that palled, 'I Spy'. But there were not so many things to be spied from a small boat in mid-Atlantic. Their companions, the boat's essentials – sail, mast, tiller, handles, a barrico of water and tins of bully; at sea the waves, spray, clouds and a few sea-birds. So many games needed paper and pencils to play. They needed concentration too, and this became harder and harder to achieve.

When games ran out, Mary Cornish started to tell stories. Dim recollections of *The Thirty-nine Steps* and *Bulldog Drummond* lingered in her mind. Now she tried to drag from her memory tattered shreds of these stories and others and to hang them on a new framework. It was a desperate task, for she was not by nature a story-teller, although fortunately a nephew had provided her with some experience of small boys' tastes. Captain Drummond was the hero: square-jawed, strong, lean, tough and fearless. In the first instalment he became deeply embroiled with a gang of Nazi spies. Aeroplanes, submarines, parachutists, secret wireless installations, master minds and cyphers were soon involved. The story reached a point where she could think of no way out for Captain Drummond, and the first instalment ended.

'Go on, Auntie – *please* go on!' they implored. They were promised more next day. Thereafter, there was no escape. The first instalment of the day, eagerly awaited, was given after the midday meal. A second instalment followed after supper – a few swigs of condensed milk sucked out of a hole punched in the tin – before settling down for the night.

To invent new episodes for Captain Drummond, twice a day, became almost a nightmare. Only the most thrilling adventures, the most hair-raising escapes, the most breathless fights, would satisfy her audience. Once, moved by a fit of nostalgia for the sight of green and growing things, Mary Cornish spoke of a garden she knew well in Devon. She described to the boys its blazing June flowers, its shady trees, the cool lawns and the smell of mown grass and moist earth; but this was not a success. The boys – although they were town dwellers who had never seen a Devon garden – became homesick, and the older ones grew restless; they wanted Captain Drummond dangling from the edge of a precipice, hidden in a Nazi bomber or chasing an enemy agent across the moors at night. Only in tales of action could they altogether forget their thirst and hunger, their cramp and cold, and the sea. [. . .]

All day long, eyes had raked the sea in vain; ears, strained to catch the drone of aircraft engines, had heard only the pounding of waves on the boat's timbers, and the cry of gulls. Now another night had fallen and long, weary hours of cold discomfort lay ahead. It was at such moments only that the boys' spirits fell. Sometimes a half-stifled whimper would come from under the blankets, and Mary Cornish would say brusquely: 'Don't you realize that you're the heroes of a *real* adventure story? There isn't a boy in England who wouldn't give his eyes to be in your shoes! Did you ever hear of a hero who *snivelled*?'

This spartan treatment worked every time. The boys' minds were turned from self-pity to the ever-distracting subject of their home-coming, to the delight of Mum and Dad, and the awed admiration of their school-fellows. Auntie was right; heroes don't snivel.

REBECCA WEST
If the Worst Comes to the Worst
8 June 1940

If the worst comes to the worst, and the Germans invade England, many of us will be hurt and some of us will be killed. We will see other people, possibly those whom we love, being hurt and being killed. Our homes may be destroyed, and towns which are dear to us, and woods and fields which are the fond background of our lives, may be horribly annulled. We may know fire as a pursuing enemy and hunger and thirst as our companions, so well that sudden death becomes a friend. Well, it might be far worse.

It would be much worse, to take one possibility, if we behaved badly. We all of us are bound to feel fear during the next few weeks. Anybody who did not would be defective, as defective as the politicians who did not become alarmed by the aggression of Nazi Germany. It is a wholesome reaction. When the bowel finds that it is harbouring an irritant, it uses every muscle in its wall to expel it, and the result is colic. When the mind becomes aware that it is faced with a dangerous experience, it floods the consciousness with a disagreeable sensation, designed to warn it that it will perish if it does not organize all its resources in self-defence. Do not be ashamed of your fear. Cherish it, obey it to the point of thinking quickly and acting vigorously in the interests of your safety. But conceal it.

Conceal your fear. Act on it, get the fire-hose and the sand-buckets ready, clear the attic. But do not express it in the disagreeable form in which it came to you. Should you do so, you may be condemning yourself and all whom you love to the pangs of a perdition far worse than the malaise of fear.

For fear and pain have one important characteristic in common. Their outward and visible signs give onlookers an exaggerated impression of what the person who is ill or is afraid is suffering. Anyone who has undergone pain so severe that it has to show itself in cries and movements knows that these often overstate the degree of discomfort that is actually felt. The body is calling for help, so it makes the appeal as strongly as possible. Amateur and inexperienced nurses are constantly deceived by this overstatement into believing that their patients are being subjected to a strain greater than they can bear, and anticipating their death or mental collapse. The experienced nurse, however, knows that there is a tough core in the human being which makes it keep hold of its life and its wits till it meets the germ or suffers the mechanical injury that simply will not be denied, and she knows that in ninety-nine cases out of a hundred the patient who says 'Give me prussic acid, I want to die', lives to want nothing so much as the longest possible enjoyment of life.

Fear, like pain, looks and sounds worse than it feels. When one is afraid of being killed in an air-raid or by a parachutist, there are all sorts of considerations which our mind checks up on the other side. There is the sporting chance we all enjoy of not being hit, the hope that somehow we may be able to perform some act of disservice to the enemy, the knowledge that the military operations of which these raids will be a part should end in a victory for England and freedom from Hitler. But fear, like pain, is an appeal, made for an urgent purpose. It, too, is always an overstatement.

Therefore you should not speak the words it puts into your mouth, or let it decide the expression of your face. For there will be no experienced nurses about you to know that you are not in such a bad case as you seem. We are facing an entirely new set of events, and there are no kind seniors to look after us, who have been through it all before. We have got to find out the code of conduct proper to the moment and apply it without help. We are all novices in this situation, even our governors. Therefore we might, if our code did not include the most rigid stoicism, contrive for ourselves a ruin which is worse than any pain we might suffer in warfare. If we say, 'We cannot bear the torture of waiting day after day for the bombs to drop on us', or 'We cannot bear having bombs dropped on us day after day because we are afraid of being killed', and if we say it again and again with the bogus poignancy of fear, it is possible that the Government might hear us and believe us. They might form the mistaken view that it was impossible to go on waging war when the civil population was in such a demoralized condition. They might then feel obliged to make terms with the Germans.

This would not mean peace. It would, indeed, mean that we should never know peace again, and that our children and our children's children should not see its return. Our young men would be taken from us to fight Germany's imbecile wars of aggression against Russia, America, Africa, and Asia, and when they came back to us they would have been trained in such delicate arts as machine-gunning civilian refugees. The rest of us would be forced to give our labour and every penny more than was needed for our bare subsistence to pay for these imbecile wars. As the background of our lives would be the fear of the concentration camp; and we would never again warm our hands at the fires of kindness and tolerance. Those of us who know Nazi Germany know that it is darkness; but we would dwell in the outer darkness which is the lot of the Czechs and the Poles today. Let us, therefore, bridle our fear and give the Government full opportunity to win the war.

And let us see to it that if the worst comes to the worst it finds us not only in command of our fear, but also beyond the power of surprise. Each of us should today examine his or her circumstances in an attempt to fore-tell what predicaments the war may bring us, and whether they could conceivably lead us to be a trouble to the authorities, thus conniving at our own enslavement. We should all of us go to our doors and say to ourselves, 'If the village was set on fire I should be naturally inclined to run away from it along that road. I must remember that I must not do that if there are German troops on that road, for then our troops and aircraft might be afraid to bombard it. I must find some other way; and even if there is no other way, I must not go on that road.' The problem will differ in every locality; but we must always find a like solution. Otherwise, however well we mean, we will be as dangerous as cowards and traitors.

If these most pardonable errors of startled flesh, fear and stupefaction, can in these present extraordinary circumstances compel us to guilt, there is consolation in the ease with which we can now achieve unparalleled distinction. That is a miracle: a miracle of a sort that was called to my mind the other day by a letter in *The Times* contributed by Lady Baldwin. She wrote suggesting that the flag of our patron saint, St George of Cappadocia, should be hung from every church tower in England. Excellent wife that she is, she probably wrote with the intention of forestalling those who would like to use Lord Baldwin for that purpose on their particular church tower. But her letter turned my thoughts to some inquiries I had made into the identity of our patron saint, two years ago, after I had spent a spring night wandering about the Macedonian foothills, from church to mosque and from mosque to pagan altar on the rocks, watching Christians and Moslems ask St George for children from barren wives and crops from barren lands.

He was not, as Gibbon falsely told us, 'a villainous army contractor'. Gibbon was a great man but the world is not even faintly like what he supposed. He was confusing George of Cappadocia with George of Laodicea, a thorough bad egg of a bishop who lived quite a couple of centuries later. Very little is definitely known about the true St George, who was martyred somewhere near Constantinople in the third century. The Pope Gelasius, looking into his case, could find out nothing about him and was driven to remarking tactfully that he was one of 'those saints who are justly revered by the people but whose actions are known only to God'. Yet the best scholars believed that he really existed; and there survives in the Near East a tradition which makes it probable that there did once live an heroic and virtuous person called George of Cappadocia, who had an extraordinary adventure with a wild beast amounting to a powerful intervention on the side of life against death.

Many are the miracles that are ascribed to him. Always he is putting in his spoke in favour of this precious though often highly disagreeable entity that we call life. He was for it, he wanted more of it, he would not have it downed. Once he saw some planks by the roadside, planks that were dead wood, cut and planed; he turned them back into trees. The sap ran up their veins, branches stirred in them, they put forth green leaves. This he did because they had been lying by the roadside to be built into a house, which was not at the moment needed. The urgent requirement was a wood which good men could use as an ambush against brigands.

When we were young it seemed as if the modern world had made planks of us. We had been drained of much of our natural vitality and forbidden to grow according to our instinctive bent, we were deprived of our individuality and planed down to uniform shape so that we should fit into a standardized and mechanized world. That world has fallen to pieces. Now we are living trees again. We must rely on our own individuality, for in a time of crisis there will be nobody to tell us how to behave. Our habit of natural growth, whether we are stunted or noble, whether we are sickly or sturdy, is what counts today. If we grizzle and chatter and prefer short term safety from the bombs instead of long term safety from slavery, then we are rubbish: dead wood by the roadside, timber for a house that will never be built. But if we are a quiet shelter to all those who come within our shadow, then we shall have the dignity of the living forest, and the worst will be far from the worst. Indeed, it will be better than the best that we could have hoped for in the days before this test.

Chapter five

THE BLITZ

Britain was not invaded at the end of the summer of 1940, but was heavily bombed. Between 1940 and 1941 about 43,000 civilians in Britain were killed in air raids, and about 17,000 during the rest of the war. A further 86,000 were seriously injured, and by May 1941 nearly one and a half million people had been made homeless in London alone – a far higher figure than the government had anticipated.

At the centre of the blitz women were working as Air Raid Wardens, fire-women and nurses, as drivers of ambulances and mobile canteens, and as members of voluntary organisations. These organisations could respond more flexibly to events than government agencies could, and the WVS in particular shouldered a huge amount of physical and emotional hard work. The Housewives' Section ran neighbourhood support groups, keeping records, giving food and shelter, sweeping and salvaging. At Incident Inquiry Points the WVS helped to identify casualties, to inform and comfort the bereaved.

The blitz spawned new forms of writing. In three weeks Clemence Dane put together *The Shelter Book*, 'A gathering of tales, poems, essays, notes and notions for use in shelters, tubes, basements and cellars in wartime.' It was published by the end of 1940, and the others followed suit, with reviewers recommending books for their 'shelterworthiness'.

Women writers were outspoken from the start. They described the terrible conditions in the East End of London, the shortcomings of a cumbersome bureaucracy, the looting and the nightly trekking out of city centres into the countryside to find respite from the bombing. They sympathised with the irritation people felt at the 'we can take it' attitude attributed to them by the media. But they also recognized what Barbara Nixon calls the 'dogged equanimity, which was an unspectacular form of genuine courage'.

Compared with the wartime casualty toll worldwide, the British air-raid figures were mercifully low. Women's accounts of the blitz are characterised not so much by a litany of suffering as by restless shifts of perspective and swings of mood. A heightened awareness of reality, a sense of the absurd and the theatrical – 'life is being lived temporarily on a public stage' wrote Elizabeth Bowen – these all come from the nervous tension of the time, and express it perfectly.

VIRGINIA WOOLF
Thoughts on Peace in an Air Raid
1940

The Germans were over this house last night and the night before that. Here they are again. It is a queer experience, lying in the dark and listening to the zoom of a hornet which may at any moment sting you to death. It is a sound that interrupts cool and consecutive thinking about peace. Yet it is a sound – far more than prayers and anthems – that should compel one to think about peace. Unless we can think peace into existence we – not this one body in this one bed but millions of bodies yet to be born – will lie in the same darkness and hear the same death rattle overhead. Let us think what we can do to create the only efficient air-raid shelter while the guns on the hill go pop pop pop and the search-lights finger the clouds and now and then, sometimes close at hand, sometimes far away, a bomb drops.

Up there in the sky young Englishmen and young German men are fighting each other. The defenders are men, the attackers are men. Arms are not given to Englishwomen either to fight the enemy or to defend herself. She must lie weaponless to-night. Yet if she believes that the fight going on up in the sky is a fight by the English to protect freedom, by the Germans to destroy freedom, she must fight, so far as she can, on the side of the English. How far can she fight for freedom without firearms? By making arms, or clothes or food. But there is another way of fighting for freedom without arms; we can fight with the mind. We can make ideas that will help the young Englishman who is fighting up in the sky to defeat the enemy.

But to make ideas effective, we must be able to fire them off. We must put them into action. And the hornet in the sky rouses another hornet in the mind. There was one zooming in *The Times* this morning – a woman's voice saying, 'Women have not a word to say in politics.' There is no woman in the Cabinet; nor in any responsible post. All the idea makers who are in a position to make ideas effective are men. That is a thought that damps thinking, and encourages irresponsibility. Why not bury the head in the pillow, plug the ears, and cease this futile activity of idea-making? Because there are other tables besides officer tables and conference tables. Are we not leaving the young Englishman without a weapon that might be of value to him if we give up private thinking, tea-table thinking, because it seems useless? Are we not stressing our disability because our ability exposes us perhaps to abuse, perhaps to contempt? 'I will not cease from mental fight,' Blake wrote. Mental fight means thinking against the current, not with it.

That current flows fast and furious. It issues in a spate of words from the loudspeakers and the politicians. Every day they tell us that we are a free people, fighting to defend freedom. That is the current that has whirled the young airman up into the sky and keeps him circling there among the clouds. Down here, with a roof to cover us and a gas mask handy, it is our business to puncture gas bags and discover seeds of truth. It is not true that we are free. We are both prisoners to-night – he boxed up in his machine with a gun handy; we lying in the dark with a gas mask handy. If we were free we should be out in the open, dancing, at the play, or sitting at the window talking together. What is it that prevents us? 'Hitler!' the loud-speakers cry with one voice. Who is Hitler? What is he? Aggressiveness, tyranny, the insane love of power made manifest, they reply. Destroy that, and you will be free.

The drone of the planes is now like the sawing of a branch overhead. Round and round it goes, sawing and sawing at a branch directly above the house. Another sound begins sawing its way in the brain. 'Women of ability' – it was Lady Astor speaking in *The Times* this morning – 'are held down because of a subconscious Hitlerism in the hearts of men.' Certainly we are held down. We are equally prisoners to-night – the Englishmen in their planes, the Englishwomen in their beds. But if he stops to think he may be killed; and we too. So let us think for him. Let us try to drag up into consciousness the subconscious Hitlerism that holds us down. It is the desire for aggression; the desire to dominate and enslave. Even in the dark-ness we can see that made visible. We can see shop windows blazing; and women gazing; painted women; dressed-up women; women with crimson lips and crimson fingernails. They are slaves who are trying to enslave. If we could free ourselves from slavery we should free men from tyranny. Hitlers are bred by slaves.

A bomb drops. All the windows rattle. The anti-aircraft guns are getting active. Up there on the hill under a net tagged with strips of green and brown stuff to imitate the hues of autumn leaves guns are concealed. Now they all fire at once. On the nine o'clock radio we shall be told 'Forty-four enemy planes were shot down during the night, ten of them by anti-aircraft fire.' And one of the terms of peace, the loudspeakers say, is to be disarmament. There are to be no more guns, no army, no navy, no air force in the future. No more young men will be trained to fight with arms. That rouses another mind-hornet in the chambers of the brain – another quotation. 'To fight against a real enemy, to earn undying honour and glory by shooting total strangers, and to come home with my breast covered with medals and decorations, that was the summit of my hope. . . . It was for this that my whole life so far had been dedicated, my education, training, everything. . . .'

Those were the words of a young Englishman who fought in the last war. In the face of them, do the current thinkers honestly believe that by writing

'Disarmament' on a sheet of paper at a conference table they will have done all that is needful? Othello's occupation will be gone; but he will remain Othello. The young airman up in the sky is driven not only by the voices of loudspeakers; he is driven by voices in himself – ancient instincts, instincts fostered and cherished by education and tradition. Is he to be blamed for those instincts? Could we switch off the maternal instinct at the command of a table full of politicians? Suppose that imperative among the peace terms was: 'Child-bearing is to be restricted to a very small class of specially selected women,' would we submit? Should we not say, 'The maternal instinct is a woman's glory. It was for this that my whole life has been dedicated, my education, training, everything. . . .' But if it were necessary, for the sake of humanity, for the peace of the world, that child-bearing should be restricted, the maternal instinct subdued, women would attempt it. Men would help them. They would honour them for their refusal to bear children. They would give them other openings for their creative power. That too must make part of our fight for freedom. We must help the young Englishmen to root out from themselves the love of medals and decorations. We must create more honourable activities for those who try to conquer in themselves their fighting instinct, their subconscious Hitlerism. We must compensate the man for the loss of his gun.

The sound of sawing overhead has increased. All the search-lights are erect. They point at a spot exactly above this roof. At any moment a bomb may fall on this very room. One, two, three, four, five, six . . . the seconds pass. The bomb did not fall. But during those seconds of suspense all thinking stopped. All feeling, save one dull dread, ceased. A nail fixed the whole being to one hard board. The emotion of fear and of hate is therefore sterile, unfertile. Directly that fear passes, the mind reaches out and instinctively revives itself by trying to create. Since the room is dark it can create only from memory. It reaches out to the memory of other Augusts – in Bayreuth, listening to Wagner; in Rome, walking over the Campagna; in London. Friends' voices come back. Scraps of poetry return. Each of those thoughts, even in memory, was far more positive, reviving, healing and creative than the dull dread made of fear and hate. Therefore if we are to compensate the young man for the loss of his glory and of his gun, we must give him access to the creative feelings. We must make happiness. We must free him from the machine. We must bring him out of his prison into the open air. But what is the use of freeing the young Englishman if the young German and the young Italian remain slaves?

The searchlights, wavering across the flat, have picked up the plane now. From this window one can see a little silver insect turning and twisting in the light. The guns go pop pop pop. Then they cease. Probably the raider was brought down behind the hill. One of the pilots landed safe in a field near here the other day. He said to his captors, speaking fairly good

English, 'How glad I am that the fight is over!' Then an Englishman gave him a cigarette, and an Englishwoman made him a cup of tea. That would seem to show that if you can free the man from the machine, the seed does not fall upon altogether stony ground. The seed may be fertile.

At last all the guns have stopped firing. All the searchlights have been extinguished. The natural darkness of a summer's night returns. The innocent sounds of the country are heard again. An apple thuds to the ground. An owl hoots, winging its way from tree to tree. And some half-forgotten words of an old English writer come to mind: 'The huntsmen are up in America. . . .' Let us send these fragmentary notes to the huntsmen who are up in America, to the men and women whose sleep has not yet been broken by machine-gun fire, in the belief that they will rethink them generously and charitably, perhaps shape them into something serviceable. And now, in the shadowed half of the world, to sleep.

BARBARA NIXON
from *Raiders Overhead: The Record of a London Warden*

That day [7 September 1940] London had changed. It was not only the damage, the shattered houses and the glass in the streets, often inches deep. And it was not a melodramatic change; it was more like a drunk man suddenly sobering up when he receives tragic news. At last people realised that there was a serious war on – a war that meant visible death and destruction, not only newspaper articles and recruiting posters and war memorials. And they did not like the realisation.

For troops who have been training and waiting for months, the long-expected attack can often give a sense of relief as well as alarm. But the British public had not had any training, physical or moral, to help it to withstand the nervous strain of being bombed. The ordinary man had not cared deeply about the betrayal of Czechoslovakia at Munich, although he knew that it was shameful, but he had cared less about the Poles. If he troubled to justify the declaration of war at all, it was on technical grounds that if we continued to give way to Hitler there would soon be no allies and no battlegrounds left. The first year of the war with its 'patrol activity' in front of the Maginot Line was commonly accepted as mystifying and ridiculous, and then dismissed as other people's business. Ten days before France collapsed, when I had expressed anxiety in the local pub as to what might happen if that country gave in, my remarks were received with indignation and scorn. When the collapse came, the French and the Belgians were just 'dirty traitors.' It was as simple as that. Only one person in twenty genuinely thought that the war was anything to do with him. Indeed, enthusiastic support could hardly be expected when so many people had friends or relations in factories, who were being told to go to the lavatory for an hour, or otherwise waste their time, because there was insufficient work to do.

The newspapers told the country that London could take it. But locally there were sour comments on what journalists knew about it. If London at that stage had been bombed as heavily and continuously as Cologne and Stalingrad, one hesitates to think what might have happened. In the last war there had been the pious cliché that the strain was nearly as great for those safely in the rear as for 'the loved ones at the front.' This time it was true, and the most common saying by men, as well as women, was that this wasn't war, it was murder, they wouldn't stand for it, and so on. The loudest cry, however, was: where were the guns? Where were these defences that had been praised as impassable?

All through Sunday and Monday the East Enders drifted miserably west-wards, looking for shelters; most of them had no baggage; they had lost everything; some carried pathetic and clumsy bundles of their remaining belongings; some pushed battered perambulators stacked with salvaged, broken treasures. They had nowhere to rest, nowhere to wash. In the West End attempts were made even to exclude them from some shelters. On a 38 bus in Piccadilly a wretched-looking woman with two children got in and sat down next to me; they still had blast dust in their hair and their tattered clothing; they were utterly miserable, and the lady opposite moved her seat and said, loudly, that people like that should not be allowed on buses. Fortunately, the conductor announced with promptitude that some ladies could take taxis. [. . .]

It is, perhaps, understandable that sleeping accommodation was not provided. It had, apparently, not occurred to the Government that raiding might be continuous throughout the night. One can say that it should have done so, as it certainly occurred to many ordinary citizens, at least by the time of Denmark's invasion. But the fact remains that it did not. The millions of bunks needed could hardly have been provided more quickly than they were, once the need for them was belatedly realised.

Again, the Government's argument that it was impossible to provide safety from direct, or very close, hits for the whole population was also tenable, if unpopular; and this is not the place to go into the relative strengths of the various types of shelter.

But lavatories – lighting – ventilation! For the lack of these there can be no excuse. Even if a raid is only going to last an hour, it is still frightening, and a lavatory is essential. There cannot be any argument about it. I have seen shelters which were built over the gutter, and this was left unscreened to run across the middle of the floor. In our area we were well off. There were chemical closets usually partially screened by a canvas curtain. But even so, the supervision of the cleaning of these was not adequate. Sometimes they would be left untended for days on end, and would over-flow on to the floor. On one of these occasions, with difficulty, we moved the offending article outside. We had already reported it the night before. In the morning the police said that it could not stand outside in the public gaze; we said that still less could it stand inside under the public's nose. Even a regu-lation-minded police-sergeant could see the force of this argument, and a report went from the Station to the Town Hall and had the desired effect.

Then the question of lights. I have been told by wardens that, for the first two months, shelters in some boroughs had no light at all. We had one hurricane lamp for about fifty people. How often in the small hours, if the raid had started early, there would be a wail of 'Warden! Warden! The light's gone out!' and children would wake up and howl, women grow nervous, and the men would swear. It is expecting altogether too much of people's nerves to ask them to sit through a raid in the dark. That one paraffin lamp also provided the only heating that there was in those days. It was bitterly cold that winter, and naturally, therefore, the door was kept shut. Some of the bigger shelters had ventilation pipes, but the smaller ones that held fifty people had only the door. In some, the atmosphere of dank concrete, of stagnant air, the inevitable smell of bodies, the stench of the chemical closets was indescribable. More than once I had to stop a conversation abruptly and go outside to avoid being sick. It is begging the question to say that they must have been dirty people. Cleanliness is almost entirely dependent on the provision of material facilities. Few of us would be as clean as we are if water were not laid on. Big stores and hotels in the West End provided some grand shelters, complete with amenities; but apart from these, ours were, in the early days, among the best in London.

Why did people tolerate such conditions? Since improvements have been made, newspaper columnists have often speculated on this question. Was it stupidity, or was it courageous endurance? Probably there was a little of each, but the main reason was fear. If you live in an old and rickety house that trembles at a passing bus, or at the top of a block of flats; if you have children, or are old and slow in moving; or if you were simply brought up to be nervous and uncontrolled – you are justified in being afraid. [. . .]

At night it was a dead city. The few small shops were barred and shut-tered, and the blocks of flats were deserted. If there was no gunfire or drone of planes it was quieter than the countryside. Even in an open field, the soughing of a tree in the breeze, the rustle of a rat in a hedge, or the wheeze of a cow, can still be heard. But here the silence was almost tangible – a literally dead silence, in which there was no life. It was difficult to believe that this was London, whose daily uproar never sank below a steady rumble, even in the small hours. After 10.30 p.m., when the public houses turned out the few hardy regulars, the silence was complete, only broken occasionally by the echoing footsteps of a warden, or policeman, on patrol. All the population was underground. When the silence grew overpowering, we went down into a shelter to reassure ourselves that there was still some life in this deserted city. [. . .]

Locally, after the first few nights, people began to select the company they preferred, and very quickly each of our shelters developed a distinct character of its own, which was dependent to a large extent on the shelter marshal. Mrs Barker, in charge of No. 2, brought down her gramophone, and her shelter was noisy and gay. With a lusty voice she led the singing, and kept it up till three or four in the morning if it was a noisy night. When a bomb burst within earshot she roared into 'Roll out the barrel' with admirable gusto. The next shelter was in the charge of a retired post office worker with silver white hair, and they were all very nervous and quiet: they even complained about Mrs Barker's gramophone, saying that the German pilots overhead would hear the noise and drop a bomb on them all! The younger people congregated in the next one, and it became known as the courting shelter. Those in the main road had a more casual population, and that necessarily meant a percentage of drunks and fights. In the large shelter near the railway station there were frequent raucous brawls; twice, women were delivered of children; and drunken adolescents gambled, and upset the chemical closets, and indulged in every form of anti-social behaviour. [. . .]

I had been fairly confident that I could behave reasonably well under gunfire and bombing, and the first seven nights had, more or less, justified my confidence. But what I was unsure of was what my reactions to casualties would be. I had never seen a dead body, I was even squeamish about handling dead animals, and I was terrified that I might be sick when I saw my first entrails, just as some people cannot stop themselves fainting at the sight of blood. At later incidents one forgot oneself entirely in the job on hand. But on this occasion, because I was unsure of myself, I was acutely selfconscious, and, as a protection, adopted as detached an attitude as I could. I had to watch myself, as well as the objective situation.

I was not let down lightly. In the middle of the street lay the remains of a baby. It had been been blown clean through the window, and had burst on striking the roadway. To my intense relief, pitiful and horrible as it was, I was not nauseated, and found a torn piece of curtain in which to wrap it.

The funerals of our fellow-wardens were a greater strain than the blitz itself. At first, the Town Hall made no official preparations for the burial of five of their service members – four wardens and one stretcher-party man – killed on duty. We made eight visits to various officials before they agreed to give municipal support to the arrangements the different families had already made. It was not that we ourselves wanted a 'fuss,' but for most relatives anything that can even make a pretence that their irreparable loss was worthwhile, or that it meant something to others as well as themselves, was at least a slight softening of their bitterness. And there was bitterness. There was still no real war; it seemed we would never be fighting back, and no war could ever be won by sitting down and 'taking it' as the press still encouragingly called it.

Moreover, there had been more in the air than mere high explosive on that last Saturday raid. The same night Hess had landed in Scotland, and was being fed on chicken and grapes, the papers said, because he had broken his ankle. A legion of theories and rumours spread about: some people were optimistic and thought it meant that Germany was cracking up, most were distrustful of the 'high-ups' in this country, a very few hazarded the opinion that the Germans were going to turn against Russia and wanted us out of it. But the upshot was always the same – a gloomy shrug, and 'If we're going to be sold out by Quislings in the end, why put up with all the bombing now?'

At the last moment the Town Hall authorised an official Civil Defence parade for the funerals, and lent us clean overalls for the two days. Members of all our services turned out and lined the streets, and did a slow march to the different churches five times in two days. I am sentimental, bordering on maudlin, by nature, and despite terrific efforts to think of something else, sniffed abominably. I was well jeered at for it by my old tough friends of '13,' who were evidently surprised.

But even the funerals would not go 'according to plan.' With poor Mackin's nothing would go right. He was a Communist, and at first there was delay because official stomachs could not digest the red cotton hearse cloth which his family provided, and justifiably insisted on. At the very last second, as we all about-faced, three young friends of his, who had obviously taken half an hour from work and run most of the way, arrived with a pathetic little bunch of red tulips. Despite the coachman's disapproval, they were fixed in position, and nodded and flopped proudly and jauntily in front of the grand official wreath.

When we halted at Mrs Trew's house to pick up Johnny (the one who had had the railings blown into him) the hearses became blocked in a cul-de-sac caused by débris, and took over an hour to be extricated. Then, to make up time, Mackin's hearse dashed off through North London to the crematorium at sixty miles an hour, and six of us in a stretcher-car, who were to be bearers, lost it and arrived too late. His requiem – the Internationale – as played by the organist, was unrecognisable, since the latter had never heard the tune before and had a limited mastery of his instrument. It was all dreadful. The only alleviation of one's misery was the thought that Mackin himself would have had a first-class laugh, saying that he had been a thorn in the flesh of the authorities all his life, and could still make them uncomfortable, even with his feet gone and a hole in his head.

ELIZABETH BOWEN
London, 1940

Early September morning in Oxford Street. The smell of charred dust hangs on what should be crystal pure air. Sun, just up, floods the once more innocent sky, strikes silver balloons and the intact building-tops. The whole length of Oxford Street, west to east, is empty, looks polished like a ballroom, glitters with smashed glass. Down the distances, natural mists of morning are brown with the last of smoke. Fumes still come from the shell of a shop. At this corner where the burst gas main flaming floors high made a scene like a hell in the night, you still feel heat. The silence is now the enormous thing – it appears to amaze the street. Sections and blocks have been roped off; there is no traffic; the men in the helmets say not a person may pass (but some sneak through). Besides the high explosives that did the work, this quarter has been seeded with time-bombs – so we are herded, waiting for those to go off. This is the top of Oxford Street, near where it joins the corner of Hyde Park at Marble Arch.

We people have come up out of the ground, or out from the bottom floors of the damaged houses: we now see what we heard happen throughout the night. Roped away from the rest of London we seem to be on an island – when shall we be taken off? Standing, as might the risen dead in the doors of tombs, in the mouths of shelters, we have nothing to do but yawn at each other or down the void of streets, meanwhile rubbing the smoke-smart deeper into our eyes with our dirty fists. . . . It has been a dirty night. The side has been ripped off one near block – the open gash is nothing but dusty, colourless. (As bodies shed blood, buildings shed mousey dust.) Up there the sun strikes a mirror over a mantelpiece; shreds of a carpet sag out over the void. An A.R.P. man, like a chamois, already runs up the debris; we stare. The charred taint thickens everyone's lips and tongues – what we want is bacon and eggs, coffee. We attempt little sorties – 'Keep BACK, please! Keep OFF the street!' The hungry try to slake down with smoking. 'PLEASE – that cigarette *out*! Main gone – gas all over the place – d'*you* want to blow up London?' Cigarette trodden guiltily into the trodden glass. We loaf on and on in our cave-mouths; the sun goes on and on up. Some of us are dressed, some of us are not: pyjama-legs show below overcoats. There are some Poles, who having lost everything all over again sit down whenever and wherever they can. They are our seniors in this experience: we cannot but watch them. There are two or three unmistakable pairs of disturbed lovers – making one think 'Oh yes, how odd – love.' There are squads of ageless 'residents' from aquarium-like private hotels just round the corner. There are the nomads of two or three nights ago who, having been bombed out of where they were, pitched on this part, to be bombed out again. There is the very old gentleman wrapped up in the blanket, who had been heard to say, humbly, between the blasts in the night, 'The truth is, I have outlived my generation . . .' We are none of us – except perhaps the Poles? – the very very poor: our predicament is not a great predicament. The lady in the fur coat has hair in two stiff little bedroomy grey plaits. She appeals for hair-pins: most of us have short hair – pins for her are extracted from one of the Poles' heads. Girls stepping further into the light look into pocket mirrors. 'Gosh,' they say remotely. Two or three people have, somehow, begun walking when one time-bomb goes off at Marble Arch. The street puffs itself empty; more glass splinters. Everyone laughs.

It is a fine morning and we are still alive.

This is the buoyant view of it – the theatrical sense of safety, the steady breath drawn. We shall be due, at to-night's siren, to feel our hearts once more tighten and sink. Soon after black-out we keep that date with fear. The howling ramping over the darkness, the lurch of the barrage opening, the obscure throb in the air. We *can* go underground – but for this to be any good you have to go very deep, and a number of us, fearful of being buried, prefer not to. Our own 'things' – tables, chairs, lamps – give one kind of confidence to us who stay in our own paper rooms. But when tonight the throb gathers over the roof we must not remember what we looked at this morning – these fuming utter glissades of ruin. No, these nights in September nowhere is pleasant. Where you stay is your own choice, how you feel is your fight.

However many people have crowded together, each has, while air whistles and solids rock, his or her accesses of solitude. We can do much for each other, but not all. Between bomb and bomb we are all together again: we all guess, more or less, what has been happening to all the others. Chatter bubbles up; or there is a cosy slumping sideways, to doze. Fear is not cumulative: each night it starts from scratch. On the other hand, resistance becomes a habit. And, better, it builds up a general fund.

Autumn seems a funny time to be bombed. By nature it is the hopeful start of the home year. The colours burning in the trees and weed-fires burning in the gardens ought to be enough. Autumn used to be a slow sentimental fête, with an edge of melancholy – the children going back to school, the evenings drawing in. Windows lit up earlier. Lanes in the country, squares in the city crisp with leaves. (This year, leaves are swept up with glass in them.) In autumn, where you live touches the heart – it is the worst time not to be living anywhere. This is the season in which to honour safety.

London feels all this this year most. To save something, she contracts round her wounds. Transport stoppages, roped-off districts, cut-off communications and 'dirty' nights now make her a city of villages – almost of village communes. Marylebone is my village. Friends who live outside it I think about but seldom see: *they* are sunk in the life of their own villages. We all have new friends: our neighbours. In Marylebone, shopping just before the black-out or making for home before the bombers begin to fill up the sky, we say, 'Well, good luck!' to each other. And every morning after the storm we go out to talk. News comes filtering through from the other villages. They say St John's Wood had it worse than we did. Camden Town, on the other hand, got off light. Chelsea, it seems, was hot again. They say they brought 'one' down on Paddington Green. Has anybody been over to Piccadilly? A man from Hampstead was here a minute ago; he said . . . Mrs X is a Pimlico woman; she's quite upset. Anybody know how it was in Kilburn? Somebody had a letter from Finsbury Park.

For one bad week, we were all turned out on account of time-bombs: exiled. We camped about London in other villages. (That was how I happened to be in Oxford Street, only to be once more dislodged from there.) When we were let home again we were full of stories, spent another morning picking up all the threads. The fishmonger said he had caught sight of me buying milk in Paddington. 'What, you were there too?' I asked. 'No,' he replied, 'I've got Finchley people; I was only over in Paddington looking after a friend.' We had all detested our week away: for instance, I had been worrying about my typewriter left uncovered in the dust blowing through our suddenly-emptied house; the fishmonger had been worrying about all that fish of his in the frig. with the power off. It had been necessary for several of us to slip through the barricades from time to time in order to feed cats.

Regent's Park where I live is still, at the time of writing, closed: officially, that is to say, we are not here. Just inside the gates an unexploded bomb makes a boil in the tarmac road. Around three sides of the Park, the Regency terraces look like scenery in an empty theatre: in the silence under the shut façades a week's drift of leaves flitters up and down. At nights, at my end of my terrace, I feel as though I were sleeping in one corner of a deserted palace. I had always placed this Park among the most civilized scenes on earth; the Nash pillars look as brittle as sugar – actually, which is wonderful, they have not cracked; though several of the terraces are gutted – blown-in shutters swing loose, ceilings lie on floors and a premature decay-smell comes from the rooms. A pediment has fallen on to a lawn. Illicitly, leading the existence of ghosts, we overlook the locked park.

Through the railings I watch dahlias blaze out their colour. Leaves fill the empty deck-chairs; in the sunshine water-fowl, used to so much attention, mope round the unpeopled rim of the lake. One morning a boy on a bicycle somehow got inside and bicycled round and round the silence, whistling 'It's a Happy, Happy Day.' The tune was taken up by six soldiers digging out a bomb. Now and then everything rips across; a detonation rattles remaining windows. The R.E. 'suicide squad' detonate, somewhere in the hinterland of this park, bombs dug up elsewhere.

We have no feeling to spare.

VIRGINIA WOOLF
Autumn 1940

Friday 13 September

A strong feeling of invasion in the air. Roads crowded with army wagons: soldiers. Just back from half day in London. Raid, unheard by us, started outside Wimbledon. A sudden stagnation. People vanished. Yet some cars went on. We decided to visit lavatory on the hill; shut. So L. made use of tree. Pouring. Guns in the distance. Saw a pink brick shelter. That was the only interest of our journey – our talk with the man woman & child who were living there. They had been bombed at Clapham. Their house unsafe. So they hiked to Wimbledon. Preferred this unfinished gun emplacement to a refugee over crowded house. They had a roadmans lamp; a saucepan & cd boil tea.

He laid rather a thin rug on the step for me to sit on. An officer looked in. 'Making ready for the invasion' said the man, as if it were going off in about ten minutes.

The nightwatchman wdn't accept their tea; had his own. Someone gave them a bath. In one of the Wimbledon houses there was only a caretaker. Of course they cdn't house us. But she was very nice – gave them a sit down. We all talked. Middle class smartish lady on her way to Epsom regretted she cdnt house the child. But we wdn't part with her, they said – the man a voluble emotional Kelt, the woman placid Saxon. As long as she's all right we dont mind. They sleep on some shavings. Bombs had dropped on the Common. He a house painter. Very friendly & hospitable. They liked having people in to talk. What will they do? The man thought Hitler wd soon be over. The lady in the cocks hat said Never. Twice we left. More guns. Came back. At last started, keeping an eye on shelters & peoples behaviour. Reached Russell Hotel. [. . .]

2 October

Oh I try to imagine how one's killed by a bomb. I've got it fairly vivid – the sensation: but cant see anything but suffocating nonentity following after. I shall think – oh I wanted another 10 years – not this – & shant, for once, be able to describe it. It – I mean death; no, the scrunching & scrambling, the crushing of my bone shade in on my very active eye & brain: the process of putting out the light, – painful? Yes. Terrifying. I suppose so – Then a swoon; a drum; two or three gulps attempting conciousness – & then, dot dot dot

---

ROSE MACAULAY

A Sample Corner of Total War
October 1940

Where an hour back two houses stood in this small street, there is a jumbled mountain of fallen masonry, rubble, the shattered débris of two crashed homes; beneath it lie jammed those who lived there; some of them call out, crying for rescue, others are dumb. Through the pits and craters in the rubbled mass the smell of gas seeps. Water floods the splintered street; a main has burst; dust liquefies into slimy mud. The demolition squad stumble in darkness about the ruins, sawing, hacking, drilling, heaving; stretcher bearers and ambulance drivers stand and watch. Jerry zooms and drones about the sky, still pitching them down with long whistling whooshes and thundering crashes, while the guns bark like great dogs at his heels. The moonless sky, lanced with long, sliding, crossing shafts, is a-flare with golden oranges that pitch and burst and are lost among the stars. Deep within its home a baby whimpers, and its mother faintly moans '*My baby. Oh, my poor baby. Oh, my baby. Get us out.*' The rescue squad call back. 'All right, my dear. We'll be with you in ten minutes now.' They say it at intervals for ten hours. Water and milk are passed down to those who can be reached. The rescuers work on. They are kind, skilful, patient, brave, thirsty men; they wish that a mobile canteen would turn up with hot tea or cocoa. They are friendly and polite; one of them mutters obscene oaths at Jerry as he zooms overhead, whooshes through the air, and crashes somewhere near at hand; another nudges him, indicating that a tin hat near him covers a female ambulance driver; he apologizes unnecessarily. 'Sorry, mate, didn't see you there.'

Someone is dug out; she is seventy-four, gay and loquacious; she does not cease talking as she is carried to an ambulance and driven to hospital, she is so pleased to be out. Half an hour later her married daughter is extracted; she has a grey, smeared, bruised face: she cries and is sick. 'Oh my back, my legs, my head. Oh, dear God, my children.' She is carried to an ambulance, driven away. 'The children are safe,' she is told. 'They will be out quite soon. You'll see them soon.' But she will not, for they are all dead, two boys of eleven and twelve, two babies of three and one. 'If only,' she moans, 'they didn't suffer much . . .'

Dawn is near. It grows colder. Still Jerry zooms and crashes, still the rescuers dig, saw, heave and console. 'All right, my dear, you'll be out in a jiffy.' There are only two voices to answer now; one exhausted woman's, and a baby's wail. Not much hope now for the others. At dawn the demolition squad, the ambulance drivers and the stretcher bearers are relieved by others; only inside the ruins the personnel remains the same.

'It's this every night now,' says a demolition worker, drinking a mug of cocoa on the pavement before he goes. 'This and fires.'

'There were a few casualties,' says a bland voice next day. 'But little material damage appears to have been done.'

A sample corner of total war. Elsewhere, men are being burnt alive, blinded, shot, drowned, smashed to bits when their planes crash. Civilian war deaths are no worse than those of the young men in the fighting forces; all alike are sentient human beings, dying suddenly or in agony. 'Eighteen of our planes were lost, but eight of the pilots are safe.' And ten not. Do not let us cant about 'women-and-children.' However it may be about children – and I admit that here our feelings outrun reason – it is no worse that women should be killed than men. It is all part of the blind, maniac, primitive, stupid bestiality of war, into which human beings periodically leap, spitting in civilization's face and putting her to confused rout. The alternative, here and now? No one can see any, except surrendering to the still more blind, maniac, primitive, stupid bestiality of Nazi rule over Europe, which would be to spit at and rout civilization even more earnestly.

KATE O'BRIEN
Cheffie

Yesterday someone told me that Cheffie has been killed by Hitler.

She kept a cheap restaurant on the unsuccessful side of Bloomsbury. I do not know when this restaurant began, but I have heard that Cheffie was there during the other war. She was from Derbyshire, she said, and I think she sometimes 'stunted' Derbyshire cooking. But that was never the point. The food she served was cheap and fancy, and sloppily served on fancy tables. But it was hot and you could have it at any hour of day or night, and you could have it if you didn't pay for it.

Sometimes in the evenings Cheffie wore a Spanish shawl; sometimes she wore black lace. She wore jade and coral and amber. Her hair was very black and her skin was soft, slackened leather. She was graceful, a bit too tall.

I don't know if she was wife, widow or maid, or what other name she had besides Cheffie. She seemed all right alone. She seemed complete.

Her fingers were long and strong; she was always gashing them with knives as she cut her superb, big sandwiches. You could ring up for sand-wiches at any small hour, if your party was waning. She cut them and sent them round with her love. No matter if it was three a.m., and you hadn't set foot in her restaurant for a years or more. No matter if you were too grand nowadays for her shady bohemianism and her paper napkins. You were always given the impression that Cheffie didn't see through you.

She had a startling, husky voice. If she was tired it boomed below human compass – if she had had a few drinks and the young chaps, geniuses and that, who had the run of her place, were baiting her out of patience.

Sometimes she was too conversational, too friendly, what you called a bore. She had a flat upstairs, and sometimes, if people were crying or quarrelling, she took them up there, or sent them up there, to settle their trouble some way or other. Anybody could sell her any old poster or mural design or wise-crack or publicity stunt. Anyone could talk her into anything. All that was necessary was to seem unhappy or put upon. 'Dear', she said in in her cracked, booming voice. 'Dear' and 'child'. I can see her going into the shelters with her jugs of coffee. I can hear her slow and not too obvious jokes. I bet she was welcome.

She was superstitious. I have been told that a few nights before she was killed a bomb fell, and everything shook in her rooms and nothing was broken. But a little Madonna on her mantelpiece that someone had given her because it looked like her fell over on its face. She did not like that. She said it was a bad omen.

95

A few of the unsuccessful and dreamy will remember her uneasily. A few – writers, sculptors and such – who were young lately and had hoped against hope that the world might be saved to give their slipping youth its last chance, will examine their consciences, lest they were ever superior or unkind to Cheffie – in any way she might have noticed. No doubt they were, and she noticed. But I think that it is no more than her due to guess that her bounty was as boundless as the sea. She censured no one. She fed and smiled at the liar, the cheat and the idler. She was a romantic and she died romantically.

STORM JAMESON
The Death of a Sister

24 February. It is not true that, two weeks ago, an air-raid killed my young sister; it is not true that she alone, of the five or six persons in the kitchen of the communal restaurant, was killed when a bomb demolished the place. She was a volunteer worker – a part of her war work – and when the bomb fell, since there were no other sounds, no gun-fire, she must have heard it come. It is not true that you don't hear the bomb which is going to fall near you. One of those daylight raids of single planes. Flying at a great height, they loose their bombs on some small unguarded town and make off. What are they? Young men making a practice flight? [. . .]

When old people die, surely with nothing left to want, unless it were another sunny afternoon to slip in among all those they have been gathering since childhood, one's anguish is without disbelief – even without despair. But there was so much she wanted. To see her children again; to work, to use her quick rather short fingers, young restless hands; to make plans. She planned as she moved, with the pure energy of delight. From everything of hers we touched, afterwards, it was the future sprang out. Even expecting that in a long war there would soon be no such frivolities, she had bought the cards for three more birthdays – for a boy of seven, eight, nine, and a girl five and six and seven. [. . .]

Why, God, take one so filled with the future? You could have taken me and that column of the past I am becoming. Why, why? [. . .]

I have to remind myself of what has happened. There is not a nerve in my body which consents to it. And now I know that what we say of the young dead, *They shall not grow old*, says only that the agony of their solitary going away remains, unchanged by time. The future does not spring from it, as it sprang from the laid table, and from the places where, under a handerchief or among books, she had hidden it. Nothing wears it down. And think that so many young are being hurried out of life before they have grown used to it, and this pain, this glacier, is covering Europe with its cold – where we have to live.

LORNA LEWIS
Food on Wheels
November 1940

4 a.m. . . . Not perhaps one's favourite hour for rising, especially when the All Clear hasn't gone. But here we are scrambling out of impromptu beds, loading up the mobile canteens with tea urns, milk jugs, cakes, sausage rolls, etc. Cramming stores into the vans, tea and snacks into ourselves, tin hats on to our heads. Pushing and blundering about sleepily with heavily-shaded torches, hoping to goodness that bombs and barrage won't break over us and the vans.

Then we're off for the East End shelters which the Ministry of Health has asked us to serve. Groping our way in the blackness we pause for each unfamiliar red light on the road. Maybe it's a road diversion due to a newly fallen unexploded bomb; or rubble and glass on the road from bombed houses; or a fresh crater. Anyhow, better treat all red lamps with respect.

My particular goal is down in one of dockland's poorest and most battered quarters. This shelter holds anything from 1000 to 1200 people and is under a big warehouse. Outside its entrance we open the side of the van, let down the counter, get out mugs from the drawers, by the light of a very small electric lamp. Then out of the darkness appear pale faces, the faces of men, women and children looking up at us. The sound of distant gunfire is drowned by coughing and a clamour of voices: 'Tea, miss. . . . Three teas, mate, and three nice cakes . . . Tea, ma . . . Five cups of you-an'-me, please. . . . Two very speshul teas for this lady, dear, and a sponge cake and bar of milk chocolate and a large woodbine.'

In this neighbourhood there's been no gas now for weeks. It is on the emergency efforts of our and other units that many thousands of London citizens go off to their work and the dangers of the day. From our van alone my colleague and I serve in under three hours about four hundred cups of tea. Soon the counter and the cash box are a mass of crumbs and stickiness, the floor is a flood of tea drips. Washing up is done in a small bucket and is on primitive lines; we can only hope that what the customer's eye doesn't see the heart doesn't grieve over.

DIANA COOPER
Shelter in the Dorchester

9 September 1940

It's not really the place to sleep, the eighth floor of the Dorchester. I never close an eye, but Papa sleeps like a baby in a pram, cheek on hands. One hears those vile machines and the whistling and thuds, and then one starts waiting for the next and counting the watcher-of-the-sky's steps overhead. I cannot bear to look out of the window. There always seem to be great fires ringed round. The All Clear goes when light comes, and at last one sleeps for an hour – and then one looks out on to the next day and there are no fires, and one cannot believe that so much can have gone on and so much yet be standing and unchanged.

There was a big row tonight between Papa and me undressing and in different stages of nudity. Our gun was banging away outside and the thuds were hideous to hear, and I said that we *must* go down to the basement. I had meant to all that day, and had taken precautions to stop argument such as 'I haven't got a suitable dressing-gown' by buying him a very suitable shade of blue alpaca with dark red pipings. 'I think you're too unkind,' I'd say, pulling off a stocking. 'We *can't* go down; I'm too tired. Besides it doesn't make any difference where you are.' I was beginning to cry and give in when the guns gave a particularly violent salvo and the look-out man popped his tin-hatted head in at the door saying excitedly 'You are advised to take cover.' This was a break for me and it settled Papa, who then donned his Tarnhelm outfit with the slowness of a tortoise, and down we went. I had arranged with the management that if I achieved my purpose we could have two rest-beds in the Turkish bath. So there we slept in hygienic comfort and, to my mind, greater security. The dynamo makes a nice *Enchantress* or Clipper noise, so that you hear the bombs less, and our own big Hyde Park gun doesn't blow your head off as it does above ground. Still we are encouraged by its bombast because we feel it is some kind of answer and the noise is said to exhilarate. [. . .]

1 October
Our first funk-hole, the Turkish bath, is said to be a death-trap, so we are in the re-constructed gymnasium. Eight nice Little Bears' beds behind screens, all the camels, horses, bicycles and rowing-sculls removed. Unfortunately it has a hollow wood uncarpeted floor, three swing-doors with catches on them and the room is treated as a passage. I never get a wink, but Papa is the proverbial log. The second night a great improvement took place. We had sheets, a table and a lamp. No one else had a lamp. There was a carpet to muffle the many fewer footsteps. Conversations are conducted in whispers that take me straight back to childhood and to you – Sir George Clark asking Major Cazalet if he knows what the time is etc. No one snores. If Papa makes a sound I'm up in a flash to rearrange his position. Perhaps Lady Halifax is doing the same to His Lordship. Between 6 and 6.30 we start getting up one by one. We wait until they have all gone. They each have a flashlight to find their slippers with, and I see their monstrous forms projected caricatureishly on the ceiling magic-lanternwise. Lord Halifax is unmistakeable. We never actually meet.

HILDE MARCHANT
A Journalist's Impressions of the Blitz

At the corner of the street a little general store had been broken down. It was the sort of shop that sold everything from floor polish to hairpins. The grocer was digging there. His apron hung on the bedroom door above him, blown to rags but still hanging on the hook. His credit was a heap of bills under the smashed counter.

He was rescuing tins of pineapple, salmon, milk, peaches and neatly stacking them on the pavement. Some had been blown open and were mashed into the ground. As I talked to him he unearthed a dusty card of aspirins. He jumped out of the hole and yelled across the street.

'Hey, Alan, your mother might like these.' Then he turned to me and said, 'Might be useful. His mother's expecting. A bad time.'

Life circulated round this little store. People came up to the grocer and asked if he had a tin of soup or a packet of cheese or a tin of milk, and as he handed it out to them he said quite solemnly, 'Put it on the account.' It was a game he was playing with himself, for the accounts were somewhere in the hole, and he was not even bothering to make a note of the tins he gave away. [. . .]

The next day, they sent me to look at Madame Tussaud's waxworks that had been hit in the back. It was the only rather numb laugh of the grim week.

Heads, arms, legs and torsos were strewn around the Hall of Tableaux. In one gallery models were heaped on the floor in agonising and painful positions, some with their heads at the side. A workman was picking up the arms and legs and sorting them out in stacks of left and right, and putting all the heads together in a neat row. Flying glass had stuck into some of the models' faces and a girl was picking it out with large tweezers. Hitler's nose was chipped and Goering's magnificent white uniform was covered with black dust. Mary Queen of Scots had left her head on the executioner's block and her body was blown across the room into the Tableau of Kings and Queens.

Walking through this damaged history it was impossible not to find significance in the survivals. Queen Mary sat regal and undamaged and Queen Elizabeth was still ordering the end of the Spanish Armada, even though her coronet of jewels was a little cock eyed. Napoleon was blown to pieces and I picked up pieces of Caesar's wax laurels in the far corner of the hall. [. . .]

At the street corner a Ministry of Information van was broadcasting instructions to the people . . . 'Boil all water to avoid typhoid.' Hospitals offered injections, and, sensibly, many of the people took them.

'Keep away from the centre of the city between two and five this afternoon.' The Royal Engineers were dynamiting the buildings.

Addresses were called out where hot food, blankets and first aid were available.

The people stood around listening to the voice, occasionally asking when bread was coming into the city, did typhoid injections make a child sick. There was no clamour. Just sullen resentment at the inconvenience. They had patience because they were too weary to be angry.

In one battered area I saw a shelter sign and went down to see how the shelter had withstood the bombardment. It was dark inside and a friend who was with me switched on his torch. At the end of the concrete trench the beam picked up four faces, greenish faces, so still that they looked dead.

There was a man, a woman, a boy of about fourteen, and a child of ten. We said:

'What are you doing here?' They didn't answer, and I saw the woman and child had half a pork pie in their hands. They began to eat them very slowly, with both hands to their mouths.

We talked quickly for about a minute, but still they did not answer. The man, who was blinking in the light of the torch, said very slowly:

'Don't move us out.'

We reassured him and asked why he wanted to stay there in the middle of the day.

The woman looked at me and said:

'We want to be here first for the night . . . we want a good seat tonight . . . it was crowded last night . . . my girl had to sit on my knee . . . we want a good seat.'

I stayed with them while my friend went out to find a helper. Though it was three in the afternoon this family had not been out all day. They had not eaten, and when the eldest boy went for the pork pie they said they had kept his seat. The benches at the side were empty.

A woman from the WVS came down to persuade them to go to a rest centre, but the woman whimpered and said someone would take their place. So we wrote out slips of paper with 'Reserved' on them, and she took them for a meal. They were bomb shocked. They stumbled down the street. [. . .]

One day something quite fantastic happened. As we looked at the flats, suspended in mid-air, one of the bedroom doors opened and a young man put his head round. He stepped into the room and went carefully over to the cupboard and began to take suits from their hangers. It was as if, by some strange X-ray, we were looking through the wall of his flat into his home, for the young man was quite at ease taking the clothes from the cupboard. Once he looked out into the road and shouted to someone below:

'Which of these two?'

And the man in the road shouted back and the man made up his mind. He put several suits over his arm and then walked back to the bedroom door, opened it, walked into the corridor beyond, then carefully shut the door behind him. He had done it all so smoothly and naturally, as if there was nothing strange about walking into his flat on the third floor, with the back wall all blown away.

101

SYLVIA TOWNSEND WARNER
Bombs in the Country
November 1940

The house is full of feathers because when the incendiary ate up the bed it loosed great quantities of stuffing from pillows and eiderdown, quantities of which are still floating around like unwieldy gossamer. And with wet feet and cold hands and mouths full of down we exclaim to each other (through the down): Isn't it lovely to be home? Everything's so comfortable! [censored] morning we were got out of bed at [censored] bombs falling sufficiently near to wake me. If a bomb wakes me, it can be assumed that it is too close to be disregarded. When no more fell we wondered if we would make tea, then we decided we would go out in to the garden. Oh it was so lovely to go out of the house, which wore, as all houses surprised too early do, a rather surly and dishevelled expression, into that sweet night air. The sky was marbled with flat pinkish clouds, exactly like the pattern that sea makes of sand at low tide. The little river, heavy with rainfall, went by with its full hushed spinning-wheel voice; and I said to Valentine, being full of platitudes and great thoughts as one is if one wakes up too early, how extraordinary it is that one feels this profound difference between things like bombs, which one can only partially assimilate to one's experience, and things like a cloudy moonlight sky and the naked boughs of an apple tree, which are commonplaces, and part of one's ordinary being. For all its violence, war is papery-thin compared to a garden with apple trees and cabbages in it. Even when it's forced down one's throat, one can't swallow it. Whereas one goes out and eats great mouthfuls of cabbage and apple tree and moonlight. In fact, I shouldn't be surprised if in the last analysis it turns out that the horror of war is tantamount to the horror of boredom; it is the repugnance one feels to being compelled to attend to things that don't interest one.

Afterwards this lovely late moonlight turned into a sunrise with the eastern landscape banded with grey and faint golden vapours, and in the western sky a terrific tall navy blue raincloud with a rainbow climbing up it, and the elm-trees like gold inlay, and the postman coming up the drive shaking off the rain like a cat and saying that all four bombs had fallen quite close, and fallen in fields and done no harm to any one. So perish all warlike heroism: for it is undoubtedly heroic to go out on bombing raids, it is even more dangerous than going out on a horse to kill foxes. If more deeds of heroism could just fall flat there would be more hope for humanity. It is interesting how almost all working class people seem to know this without having to bother to hold it as a theory. They have almost endless fortitude, but whenever they get involved in some act of obvious or showy bravery they instantly begin to disinfect it by saying it was a bloody nuisance, or that they would never have done it if they'd had time to think, or that they've never felt such a fool in their lives. This is so marked in the eighty per cent of our population that the remaining gentry percentage have more or less to follow suit, though they very rarely achieve the true grumbling note of the working class hero malgré lui. But the essential difference goes much further when you come to think of the spectator. Working class spectators of the brave acts pour on as much disinfectant as the performers, and say that they never saw Bert run so quick, or that Alf was unlucky from a boy, always getting mixed up in things, or that his trousers will never be the same again. Gentry spectators just can't or don't attempt this, they'd as soon part with a trump.

BEATRICE WEBB
Nights of Battle, Days of Peace

20 April 1941 3 a.m. [Passfield Corner]
These last two nights have been the most fearful of the war. The Battle of Britain is raging round us. Tonight continuous bombing and gunfire have shaken the house. A huge fire has lit up Aldershot and Farnham to the east; whilst gunfire and flares light up Bordon and the south coast. Mrs Grant is cowering downstairs in the kitchen; I find Sidney reading, but glad to have a cup of tea. Neither he nor I are perturbed; Annie wanders up and downstairs, looking out for fire bombs. I tell her that the Germans won't waste any on us in a non-built-up area; and anyway if a fire bomb falls on the house and gets through the roof, we should hear it. Meanwhile, last night, London has had a terrific attack. [. . .]

The nights of battle and days of peace are the strangest sort of life the British people have ever experienced. Just as I feel that we and our generation are, through old age, on the verge of non-existence, so do I envisage that the present-day Great Britain and her ruling class are doomed to disappear within the next few years. Our little island will become subordinate – either to the USA and the Dominions or to Germany, or to the USSR and its new civilization, creeping over the world. As we happen to believe in the *rightness* and eventual success of Soviet Communism, we are not despondent about the future of mankind.

Chapter six

CALL UP

By 1941 it was becoming clear both that production needed to be expanded dramatically and that employers were still reluctant to hire women. Under pressure from its Women's Consultative Committee, the government was forced to act, and in December 1941, for the first time in the history of this country, introduced conscription for women. This was the biggest single change that the Second World War brought to women's lives. A new world was inaugurated, with new rules and categories and terms: registration, essential work orders, reserved occupations and the definition of the mobile woman. Once called up, a woman could choose between the Services, Civil Defence, the Land Army and industry. Part-time and voluntary work were also a feature of conscription, the rules of which had to accommodate the traditional shapes of women's work and responsibilities.

Strong feelings about the conscription of women spilled into the press in the second half of 1941 and the beginning of the following year. Conflicting imperatives and advice – the good of your country versus the good of your family – clashed on the pages of magazines. Women reporters collected material for inspiring accounts of British women at war; they were joined enthusiastically by the popular J.B. Priestley. His illustrated book *British Women Go To War* came out in 1943.

During the course of the war nearly half a million women joined the Services, and many millions more put on uniforms to work in the Land Army and Civil Defence, on buses, trams and railways, in hospitals and canteens. The uniformed woman became one of the war's strongest images. She often appeared in advertisements, not just for the war effort but for products from floor polish to face powder. Not universally beloved, however, she also came top of the Daily Mail poll of wartime grouches.

As with work, so with uniform: the war might force women to adopt the ways of men, but those ways must then adapt to the ways of women. Literally, in the redesign of the ATS uniform to make it more fashionable (but 'khaki is a colour detested by every woman and makes a well-developed girl look vulgar' according to one *Times* correspondent), and imaginatively too. The new Wren rating's hat won the highest seal of approval when it caught on as a stylish shape among women generally, and versions of it in different colours filled high street shops.

Uniform for women was not just a matter of clothes. 'Whatever happens, remember to wear lipstick because it cheers the wounded' was the advice to ambulance drivers in France. Uniform could mean many different things to its wearer: a rite of passage, a sense of belonging and worth, a challenge or a threat. 'Problem: how to obtain the right degree of femininity and still look efficient' wrote one woman as she struggled with her hat. Problem solved, thought some observers, by each woman wearing her hat at a different angle. Uniform need not mean uniformity.

CORRESPONDENCE IN
TIME AND TIDE
Women's War Service

20 September 1941

Sir: My daughter's case must be typical of many, though not every young girl has the pluck or the wit to cut the knots that bind her in a false position.

She was married at Christmas to a young Lieutenant and was able to find quarters in a quiet country village near his unit and to see him at frequent intervals. The call for her year came; at her interview ('a most incompetent affair', she called it) she opted for hospital work of which she had had some experience. No summons came for her; no suggestion of what she ought to do. She immediately began making independent inquiries for some hospital which would be glad to take her as a war probationer.

Far from offering encouragement, the Colonel, the Major and the Captains all assured her husband that it was 'absurd' for her to 'go before she was fetched', while the Colonel's wife and the Major's wife and the Captains' wives, with all of whom she had been on the happiest terms of friendship, tried to convince her that her eagerness to serve was 'foolish panic' and that she must not let herself be 'overwrought'.

She is a courageous, independent young woman; her answer to all the mischievous advice of her elders was: 'if the country needs the 1919s* it needs *me*, and if it needs me, I'm off.' In defiance of her entire circle she packed her boxes, found her job and is radiantly happy in it. She joined her husband on his next leave in the proud consciousness that she was doing her duty, as he his.

But is it fair to put a young girl to so severe a test?

Comb out the residential hotels and boarding houses throughout the safe areas and release the less courageous but willing young women whose seniors are advising them to wait till they are fetched. Comb out in particular the nests of camp-following parasites who are neither running houses nor rearing children, but living for jaunts and dances and cocktails at the expense of junior officers who are hard enough put to it to meet their mess-bills.

I am, etc.,
A PROUD MOTHER

18 October 1941

Sir: Several letters have recently appeared in your paper attacking officers' wives (though why 'officers' and not NCOs' or any other wives I have been

---

* Women born in 1919.

106

unable to discover) for not taking up full-time war service. I should like to say a word in defence both of myself and of those much maligned women whom one of your correspondents describes as 'playing bridge and knitting and gossiping and perhaps salving their consciences by doing a morning a week at a First Aid Post or a canteen'. I have found most of them willing, even anxious, to work, but held back by the surely quite natural desire to see as much as possible of their husbands before they are sent abroad or perhaps *killed on active service*. Many of these wives have children to look after, most of them are living under very difficult conditions in abominable lodgings on small pay and nearly all of them do far more than your correspondent's 'morning a week' in the way of voluntary service. One of the chief difficulties in the way of their obtaining work is the short time their husbands are stationed in one spot. I myself volunteered to work for three weeks at a time in a forestry camp whilst my husband was at sea only to be told that they didn't want 'temporary labour'. Most of the semi-permanents *do* work, and I have found that those wives whose husbands go abroad get jobs almost at once, if only for the emotional relief of having 'something to do'. This also applies to war-widows.

The women's services? In theory a wife is given leave when her husband gets it, but it does not always work out that way. For example, often the first notification a naval officer's wife has that her husband is getting leave is a telegram telling her to meet him some hundreds of miles away in a few hours' time. How can a WREN, WAAF, AT, etc. get away in time to catch the next train north, south, east or west? She can't, and if she misses it, those precious days of re-fitting or boiler-cleaning are wasted and they won't occur again for some months. In fact, leave in all branches of the services, even the Army at home, is so subject to sudden postponements, cancelling, etc., that it is almost impossible to arrange these meetings.

So, although I am now looking for a job myself, I remain unashamed to sign myself.

A CAMP FOLLOWER

('A Camp Follower' seems to hold rather peculiar values. We know that the whole question of man-power is deeply exercising those responsible for our war effort. We have been told time and again that our workers are responsible for as essential a part of our war effort as is our Navy, our Army, our Air Force. We know also that we have not got nearly so many of them as we need. Yet our correspondent seems to find it quite natural that married women should put their desire to see as much of their husbands as possible before their duty to their country in its hour of grave need. If the men who are being sent overseas to fight were to take the same line, if they were to say that most of them are willing, even anxious, to fight for their country, but are held back by the surely quite natural desire to see as much as

107

possible of their wives, would it not strike 'A Camp Follower' as being a curious and even possibly a slightly regrettable point of view? – EDITOR, *TIME AND TIDE*.)

EDITH SUMMERSKILL MP
Conscription and Women
1942

In December, 1941, a National Service Bill was introduced into the House of Commons which might in other days have created a Parliamentary storm of the first magnitude. It was unprecedented for it proposed to conscript the women of the country. And yet it passed all its stages in record time, and is now on the Statute Book. [. . .]

The periodic upheaval occasioned by war reveals that women have individualities of their own and are not merely adjuncts of men. They have aspirations and ambitions which become apparent in war time, because only then can they enjoy a real freedom to achieve at least some part of their heart's desire. But for the Crimean War Florence Nightingale would no doubt have continued to be the dutiful daughter of highly respectable parents. Her unwomanliness was deplored by her mother who believed that a lady should be satisfied with the shelter of her father's home until she exchanged his roof for that of her husband. It was scandalous that she should wish to nurse dirty soldiers. Women who did that were inviting trouble. And no doubt the grandfathers of those who whisper about the morals of the woman in the Services today opined that no respectable woman could become an army nurse and still preserve her chastity. [. . .]

Fears have been expressed that communal feeding and crèches herald the disintegration of family life after the war. Some of the worst features of home life are certainly threatened, to the dismay of the domestic Hitlers who revel in the petty dictatorships which they have established. The freedom which women are enjoying today will spell the doom of home life as enjoyed by the male who is lord and master immediately he enters his own front door. I hope that communal feeding has convinced us of the stupid waste of fuel, food and labour entailed in millions of families each day cooking their meals on millions of separate gas stoves. It must at least have shown the housewife that she is not indispensable, and that on occasions the family can feed well and cheaply, while she takes a day off to spend as she thinks fit. There is a curious belief which is shared by most men that women instinctively love cooking and washing up. A perfectly cooked meal is certainly an achievement and a woman may well experience pleasure in producing a savoury and appetising dish. But I have never known ecstasy induced by washing up.

ETHEL MANNIN
Non-Co-operation

When the time came, in July of that year, for me to register with my age-group for national service I did not do so. If they wanted me they could come and get me; as a pacifist I was not prepared to do war work, and if the refusal meant prison that, anyhow, would be an experience I had not yet had, and though I did not expect to like it any better than Reginald had it would anyhow be interesting and provide background material for a novel.

Nothing, however, happened, whether because the authorities overlooked the matter, or because they thought it not worth their while to bother with such an obvious trouble-maker, I shall never know. The authorities were sufficiently interested at the time to intercept my mail – and Reginald's. We were on 'the list' of mail set aside for 'inspection'. A friendly postman had tipped us off about it, though we were aware of it sometime before then, for our letters ceased to arrive by the morning post and when they did arrive, several posts later, bore the obvious signs of having been unofficially opened. [. . .]

In spite of my policy of non-co-operation over national service I did, however, volunteer for fire-watching, not under any moral compulsion but because it was rumoured that it was going to be made compulsory, and whereas I had no objection to doing it voluntarily – though I regarded it as quite futile – I had the strongest possible objection to compulsion. I applied at the post and was signed on, then, having taken a course of training, that is to say crawled round a smoke-filled hut on all fours and listened to a discourse on how to manage a stirrup-pump, I was issued with a tin helmet and allotted duty days. I understood that when I was 'on' it was my duty, as soon as the siren sounded, to put on my tin hat and run up the road to the big house which was the local firewatchers' H.Q., take a disc with the letter F imprinted on it in white paint from a box in the porch and run back home with it and hang it on my gate.

Low-minded friends thought this frightfully funny, for some reason; one of the most literary of them laughed until the tears ran down his distinguished cheeks. 'Why an F, Ethel?' he gasped. 'Why hang it on your *gate*?' F-Freddie, I explained, F-Firewatching. [. . .]

I hung up my F with the best of them, but inevitably there was a night when I was caught napping. There had been a 'lull', and on a night when I was supposed to be 'on' I had gone to town. It was so long since I had hung up my F that I had forgotten, on that particular night, that it was my night for F-ing, as my friends called it, and there was, of course, an alert before I got back.

STELLA ST JOHN

from *A Prisoner's Log, Holloway Prison in 1943*

The prisoners are usually amazed when you say you are in for conscientious objection to war.* On the whole they are very tolerant about it, some even being sympathetic to the point of saying, 'Good luck to you. I don't hold with this war, but I wouldn't get put in here for it.' Others merely look at you as if you were mad. I only came across three women in the whole time who were really antagonistic about it. None of the officers showed that they were much opposed to us. The chaplain was the most antagonistic to me. He had no use whatever for the pacifist position and thought it anti-Christian. He did not hide the fact in private conversation or chapel service. The Methodist minister, although not a pacifist, was very sympathetic. Some of the officers thought that we should be separated from the criminal offenders. We did not agree.

---

* Stella St John was sent to prison for six weeks in 1943, for refusing to be directed into war work.

MARGARET GOLDSMITH
Conscription and Women's Pay

I have noticed one very interesting economic result of conscription, though this has nothing to do with the pay in the services. I was first made aware of this development through the case of a young woman who was employed with a number of others in a large scientific organisation, the work of which is now of national importance. The salaries paid by this organisation to their trained women research assistants was always shockingly low, but the work was interesting and before the war there were plenty of applicants for employment with this firm. Then came the call-up. The first girl to be summoned to the labour exchange was quite pleased; she rather wanted to join one of the services, to 'be a part of her generation' as she precociously put it.

The official at the Labour Exchange asked about her qualifications. The girl had a good science degree from London, as well as a knowledge of languages. The woman at the Labour Exchange was puzzled:

'Well, are you a clerk, or aren't you a clerk?' she asked. 'According to your salary you are a clerk, and therefore your occupation is not reserved, so you must go into industry or the A.T.S., but according to your qualifications you might be most useful in special scientific work with the W.A.A.F.'

So the young woman went into the W.A.A.F. to train for a special job.

Actually the work with the scientific firm in which the girl had been employed was equally useful, but the Labour Exchange, having orders to call up 'clerks', had whisked her off before anything could be done about it.

Her employer was extremely annoyed, and stormed down to the Labour Exchange. The situation was awkward for him.

'Miss X is essential to my work, and to the country,' he said pompously.

'Well, she can't be,' the official at the Labour Exchange told him blandly, 'or you'd pay her more.'

The irate employer went back to his office and, to avoid further controversies with the Labour Exchange, he raised the salaries of his other scientifically trained 'clerks'. His sentiments as he did so are unknown.

ZELMA KATIN
On Being Measured for my Conductress's Uniform

Now we were hurried to the clothing store, where a tailoress measured us deftly for our uniforms – jacket and skirt, trousers and overcoat. This, so far, was the most exciting part of our initiation and we all felt we were getting somewhere at last. It's extraordinary what a profound part in your and my psychology a uniform plays. [. . .] I think we were looking forward to donning our uniforms not only because of appearances' sake but because we wanted to be set apart from or above the rest of our sex. Then in addition there was that blessed quality about a uniform: it makes physical defects seem insignificant.

HILARY WAYNE
Dressing Up

We were marched to the Stores to be fitted out, and very lavishly fitted out. To people feeling the coupon pinch and wondering where the next pair of stockings was coming from, it was miraculous to be handed four pairs. The kitbag which was given out first was, indeed, soon overflowing with underwear of excellent quality, khaki shirts, ties, sweater and gloves. Then cap, tunic, skirt and greatcoat were tried on and critically inspected by an officer before they became one's own. Then to the 'Haberdashery' counter for studs, shoe-laces, tooth-brush, hair-brush, comb, button-cleaning equipment, shoe-brush, field dressing and housewife. Then two pairs of shoes. And the only thing to disburse at the end of this orgy of acquisition was a signature as receipt. It was difficult to manoeuvre the overflowing kitbag back to the barrack-room, a considerable distance. I have never mastered the art of carrying a kitbag. It is always too heavy to hoist on to my shoulder, and if someone else did it for me it felt top-heavy and as if the contents would pour out in a shower. I found the only way, though it was unmilitary, undignified and unhygienic, was to drag it along.

I think some kindly AT helped us on that first journey. I know that the dressing-up was a very exciting experience and that it was most interesting to see the other twenty-four change from civilians into soldiers.

What effect does uniform have on those who wear it and those who do not? There is no doubt that 'dressing up' helps soldiers, as it helps actors, to play their parts. I think we not only looked different, we felt different. For one thing, I personally felt less self-conscious. I had rather dreaded sleeping with a number of women, but the very numbers and the fact that day and night we were all dressed exactly alike gave me the comfortable feeling that, whatever happened, I could not be conspicuous.

LESLIE WHATELEY
Smoking in the ATS

During March 1944, at the request of my senior officers, I issued an instruction regarding where auxiliaries must not smoke in public when in uniform. I had received various complaints and criticisms, all in the same strain, as to the bad impression created by auxiliaries smoking while walking in the street, sitting in a bus or standing on a station platform. I agreed with these criticisms, for to my way of thinking such habits looked unattractive and unfeminine in civilian clothes, and in uniform worse.

SHIRLEY JOSEPH
All Very Unsettling

War is a strange thing. The grander the uniform the more important your job must be. Values, ideals, and morals get mixed as if in a cocktail shaker. The result, for a time, is stimulating. In the shaking-up process girls who before the war were doing menial work – or what they regarded as menial work – found that they were welcomed into houses with as much enthusiasm as a conquering hero, just because they happened to wear a uniform. It was all very unsettling. The uniforms would have to come off one day.

BARBARA CARTLAND
Wedding Dresses for Service Brides

I thought the WRNS uniform very smart, the WAAF passable, and the ATS hideous. I was in the warmest sympathy with the auxiliaries who complained that they wanted to be married in white. As they had an issue of only fourteen coupons a year with which to buy handkerchiefs, it was obviously impossible. I wrote personally to Chief Controller Knox and to Air Commandant Trefusis Forbes (then Director of the WAAF) and had replies to say they had both tried to get concessions for brides, but the Board of Trade was adamant.

A year later, at a meeting of Welfare Officers in London, at which we met for the first time the new ATS Controller, Mrs L.V.L.E. Whateley, the matter was raised again, and I suggested that, if we advertised, people might be induced to sell their wedding dresses free of coupons. The Dowager Lady Loch, a local Welfare Officer for West Suffolk, remarked:

'Mrs McCorquodale must have a touching regard for human nature if she thinks she can get people to part with dresses without coupons.' Everyone else looked limp, said it was a pity, but what could we do if the Board of Trade would not change their mind? etc., etc.

I thought of the brides I had admired – of Margaret Whigham, who was mobbed by her admirers outside the Brompton Oratory when she married Charles Sweeney; or golden-voiced Mary Malcolm, wearing a medieval head-dress, as the bride of Sir Basil Bartlett; of dark, romantic Lady Pamela Berry; of Rosamund Broughton in white satin on the arm of dashing Lord Lovat; of the fair young Duchess of Norfolk in shimmering silver lamé, and I thought of the ATS brides in their ugly, ill-fitting khaki uniforms. Of course they wanted to look lovely and glamorous on what is the most thrilling day of a woman's life. It is the one day in which they are the centre of attraction and when everyone's attention is focused on them.

And most important of all, clothes do influence a woman. Everything connected with the wedding regalia is traditional, the veil, the white dress, the bouquet, the wreath, all have their place and meaning. It is a moment of surrender, of giving one's life and happiness into another's keeping. It is difficult to feel soft, gentle and clinging in woollen stockings, clumping shoes and a collar and tie.

I was determined not to be defeated. I advertised in *The Lady* and bought two very pretty wedding dresses, one for £7 and one for £8. Both were spotless and might have come straight from the dressmaker's. Both had their wreath and veil complete. I sent them to the Chief Controller as a gift and suggested that it would be easy to get others. In reply I was asked if I would buy privately wedding dresses for an ATS pool at the War Office.

The Service bride-to-be could apply through her Company Commander for a wedding dress which was lent to her for the day. Afterwards it was returned cleaned and refurbished to be ready for the next bride of the same measurements.

I agreed to buy the dresses and got to work. I advertised in *The Lady* and in the local newspapers. In all I purchased over 70 wedding dresses for the War Office and about 40 or 50 for different RAF Commands and stations which worked under a different system, but who also wanted wedding dresses and wanted them urgently.

It meant a great deal of packing and unpacking, it meant going to inspect dresses in all sorts of places. I always knew that a wedding dress meant a lot to a woman, but even I was surprised at how much they were prepared to sacrifice for it. In mean streets, in proverty-stricken houses, a tired, down-at-heel woman would show me a lovely dress which must have cost her at least £15 or more. Sometimes when they showed me a photograph of their wedding it was hard to recognize the radiant girl in white as the same woman who stood beside me. How many dreams had been unrealized, how many hopes dashed, how many tears shed since the day that photograph was taken.

Yet not one of them regretted that expensive, useless dress.

'I hate to part with it,' they said to me, 'but it's only lying in the drawer and I'll be glad of the money.'

I was limited as to the sum I could give for the dresses, not more than £8, but sometimes I gave a little more out of my own pocket because I understood that those dresses were made of more than satin and tulle, lace and crêpe de chine; they were made of dreams, and one cannot sell dreams cheaply.

But we got heartily sick of wedding dresses in my house before I had finished. My maid helped me by pressing and cleaning them, and finally she said:

'I know one thing, if I get married, it won't be in white. I never want to see a white wedding dress again as long as I live.'

The brides, however, were pathetically grateful. For one day at least a girl who was never meant by nature to be 'a fighting unit' could forget the war, her uniform, her camp, her duties, and be a woman. A woman lovely, glamorous, and enticing, a woman to be wooed and won.

Chapter seven

THE WOMEN'S SERVICES

The women in the Women's Land Army (WLA) and the Auxiliary Services – the Auxiliary Territorial Service (ATS), the Women's Royal Naval Service (WRNS) and the Women's Auxiliary Air Force (WAAF) – were fewer in number but much more visible than the huge numbers of women working in factories.

Controversy surrounded them. Should they fight? This sensitive issue was handled carefully in the Conscription Act: 'No woman should be liable to make use of a lethal weapon unless she signifies in writing her willingness to undertake such service.' Women were not directed to the front line of battle, but the definition of the front line might not be clear. ATS women on Anti-Aircraft batteries certainly had their hands on the trigger, and parents sometimes made 'an awful row about it', according to the Director of the ATS, Leslie Whateley. Her policy had to take public feeling into account: 'Officers were instructed never to allow anything that would cause public outcry. Girls on the batteries were all volunteers, but if their parents objected they were posted elsewhere.' Parents also worried about the living conditions provided for daughters away from home for the first time: hastily erected huts or improvised billets could be cold and primitive, and supervision inadequate.

Typical invitations to women to 'Serve in the WAAF with the men who fly' or to 'Join the Navy and free a man for the fleet' underlined the servicewoman's role as handmaiden rather than gun-toting Amazon. Her job would often be menial – the clerking, cooking or cleaning that she might have been doing anyway, but there were good opportunities for training and development, and a wide range of jobs on offer.

Women were outspoken about the Services and the Land Army. They brought a fresh eye to Service life. 'This is tripe', wrote one woman about a new Army regulation. They deplored the class-ridden anachronisms, but they welcomed the training and the chance to broaden social and educational horizons. Above all they appreciated the friendship which, for many women, was the best aspect of the war.

PHYLLIS CASTLE
A Week in the WAAFs

We were going to be made into 'good Waafs.'

Accommodation at the Grange wasn't fancy. It comprised – for fifty-five of us plus staff – three bathrooms, three W.C.'s and not one looking-glass. We slept on three-piece pallets called biscuits, and straw, sausage-shaped pillows. We kept our clothes in airmen's wooden boxes. The wretched things were painted grey and their most notable characteristic in the blacked-out semi-gas-lit gloom, which was all that we were allowed after dark, was a miraculous invisibility.

We were made to march over the innocent English countryside like young Prussians, and when we got rather out of rhythm negotiating a twisting down-hill loose stony bit of lane with hedges entwined with black-berry brambles overhanging just the height of our faces, we were loudly abused by the Senior Section Leader and commanded to whistle 'Hang out the Washing on the Siegfried Line' to keep us in step. [. . .]

There were eight of us in our room. There was a Cambridge girl, an elementary school teacher, an art student, two Harrods' shop assistants, a child of eighteen fresh from finishing school and presentation at Court, and an amusing tough collar-and-tie type who'd created records on the motor cycle, could take automobiles to pieces, and held a pilot's licence. The general atmosphere inclined to heartiness, especially when the flyer was about. [. . .]

Discipline and unquestioning obedience are, of course, first principles in the services. Orders are given with an air of God from a burning cloud, and, however impossible and preposterous, have to be carried out. Personally I was rather charmed by this. Such good exercise for the faculty of inventiveness, I thought. Discipline was rigid. I mean that. As one of my superiors pronounced over me: 'You can't be late in the services, there's no such thing – it simply doesn't exist.' (I'd just arrived half-an-hour late.) Life in the Waafs was going to be a cross between boarding school and prison, I quite saw that.

Our lectures were truly diverting. An officer would appear in the morning and talk about etiquette in the services. You were allowed to wear a pin under your tie in the army, but not in the Air Force – never in the Air Force – it simply wasn't done. That very afternoon another officer, lecturing on rations, would tell us that white bread was better for you than brown, and that fruit was an unnecessary element of diet. But we would hardly be listening to these peculiar pronouncements, we would be gazing – transfixed by the charm of the thing – at the pin under her tie.

118

ELSPETH HUXLEY
WAAFs in the Operation Room
1942

Round the big map sit the WAAF plotters, in their shirt-sleeves perhaps, each one armed with a long stick like a billiard-cue. When everything is quiet these plotters sit round the table, reading and writing, and knitting socks. Each girl wears earphones clamped to her head. Then you'll see an airwoman suddenly put down her knitting, lean over the map and push a counter from one square to the next. That's an enemy bomber approaching at 15,000 feet from the sea. Up above, the Controller speaks a sentence into a telephone, and a few minutes later a light comes up on a board on the wall: a fighter patrol has taken off to investigate.

The plotter moves her billiard cue again, and the counter approaches closer to our coast. Someone else on the bridge above makes a move now – a WAAF telephone operator moves a switchboard plug, a message goes back to Command, and a few minutes later the siren wails in some coastal town. For that was the birth of an air-raid warning, in an Ops. room many miles from the raided town, and it was a WAAF officer who gave the word that sets the sirens going.

And so it goes on, twenty-four hours out of the twenty-four. WAAF plotters work in four-hour shifts, night and day. They live a queer, keyed-up, underground existence on duty, and off-duty the same sort of station life as the men around them lead; sleeping thirty to a bare wooden hut probably, eating in messes with hundreds of others four good hot meals a day; a bit of PT and drill, dancing at the NAAFI, the station cinema, say, twice a week. Their job doesn't look difficult to learn, but they've got to be alert, quick, and 100 per cent reliable. One slip, one careless move, may let an enemy aircraft through, and then others will perhaps pay with their lives for that one small mistake.

CONSTANCE BABINGTON SMITH
Aerial Photography

I myself was much looking forward to seeing some German aircraft, because I was intensely keen about aviation and had been writing for *The Aeroplane* for some years before the war. But the first aerial photograph of an enemy airfield I ever saw was a disappointment and shock. It was a busy fighter base in the Pas-de-Calais, and I had to try to count the aircraft; but even under a magnifying glass the Me 109s were no bigger than pin-heads, in fact rather smaller. My heart sank, and I thought 'I shall never be able to do this'. A bit later, however, we had an aircraft test which was more to my taste: we were given some good clear photographs of a dump of French aircraft which the Germans had written off at Merignac, near Bordeaux, and had to identify as many as we could , with the help of some recognition silhouettes. I thoroughly enjoyed myself, but was rather worried because when I took my list to Kendall there was one aeroplane I hadn't been able to name. Kendall smiled. 'No,' he said, 'nor can I.'

We started by looking at single prints, but were soon trying to use a stereoscope, that apparently simple optical instrument which presents exaggerated height and depth – if the 'pair' of photographs below it is set in just the right position. There were not enough stereoscopes to go round, and I realized that a 'stereo' was something important and precious. In time I borrowed one. It was an absurdly uncomplicated little gadget, like a pair of spectacles mounted in a single rectangular piece of metal, supported by four metal legs that held it a few inches above the photographs. I stood it above a pair of prints as I had seen some of the others doing. I could see two images, not one, and there really did not seem much point. It was much simpler to work with an ordinary magnifying glass. I edged the two prints backwards and forwards a bit – still two images, and then suddenly the thing happened, the images fused, and the buildings in the photograph shot up towards me so that I almost drew back. It was the same sort of feeling of triumph and wonder that I remember long ago when I first stayed up on a bicycle without someone holding on behind. From then on interpretation was much easier.

BARBARA PYM
A Wren's Diary, 1943

Wednesday 7 July
Well, the Nore Training Depot is a big North Oxford Victorian Gothic house, that looks like a Theological College – actually it was a school. I was in time for Tea Boat – afterwards changed my ration books etc. and got sheets. There was a lot of queueing and I felt a little low and strange – but not very. I have a cabin – Beehive XI – which I share with a girl of 19, my own class and quite nice. She has a long rather melancholy face and I can see her when she is older as an English gentlewoman – one of her names is Mildred. There are about fifty new pro-Wrens – most of them in teens and early twenties. I don't think there are really any of our kind of people, though there are one or two pleasant ones.

Making up a bunk is difficult, especially when you have the lower one and it is fixed against the wall. You must do hospital corners and the anchor on the blue and white quilt must be the right way up.

Monday 12 July
We had Divisions and squad drill out on the grass in a fine drizzle of rain. AFS men and other Wrens drilled near us. It is quite fun except for the hanging about. I had a slight feeling of desolation, coming to myself a little and thinking but what am *I* doing here and why on earth am I standing out on the grass drilling with this curious crowd of women.

Monday 19 July
Too Many Women. Has this ever been used as a title? It would do for my life in the Censorship or this Wren life – squashed among them in the queue for breakfast. [. . .]

Tuesday 20 July
Today we were kitted. We were taken in lorries to Chatham at 8 a.m. – a great herd of us – I was standing in a mass of suitcases, lurching all over the place as we drove very fast. My hat is lovely, every bit as fetching as I'd hoped, but my suit rather large though it's easier to alter that way. I have also a macintosh and greatcoat – 3 pairs of 'hose' (black), gloves, tie, 4 shirts and 9 stiff collars, and two pairs of shoes which are surprisingly comfortable. After that we had to get respirators. One girl and I got left behind at the clothing store so had to hurry through the barracks – on our way we came across a little company of Greek sailors being drilled – in Greek. Service respirators are a good deal more comfortable than civilian – we went in the gas chamber. Then had lunch in the WRNS mess.

It all sounds quite simple written down like this, but it's a long dreary business and we all looked very tired and fed up as we sat (or lay) in dejected groups in the WRNS fo'c'sle – I wished I was out of it all – but suddenly, drinking the dregs of a cup of indifferent coffee my spirits began to lift and when we got back I was quite excited – I packed two large parcels of civilian clothes and sent them off. At 4.30 we had a lecture by a Padre, but all the time I wanted to shorten my skirt and there seemed to be so much to do.

Wednesday 21 July
It felt funny being in uniform – more like fancy dress than anything, but I don't look too bad. Hair is a difficulty. I think I must have mine cut.

Sunday 1 August
We had Divisions and I couldn't swing my arms properly so Third Officer Honey had to move me. Gradually people will begin to discover what a fake I am – how phoney is my Wrennish façade. My Wren façade – no that makes it quite different. We had the service outside this week – it was much nicer, though singing was a little difficult as the harmonium accompaniment dragged rather. After that I went to the Regulating Office and made out my list for Monday. I am going to try hard to be really efficient – it doesn't come naturally to me, no use pretending it does, but it will be good for me to learn to be.

Sunday 3 October
I am reading *A Room of One's Own*. Most delightful and profound – if I had the time I would write an essay about life in the WRNS.

Officers – pay them the respect due to their uniform but otherwise assess them as people.

On Being Yourself, and how you cannot be *too* much yourself or the life wouldn't be endurable. On Friday evening I was having supper when Marion Booth, a very attractive looking MT driver came and sat by me and we talked about German and Rilke and the necessity of hanging on to the things that matter – painting for her, writing and literature for me and music, of course. This is important, otherwise you will lose yourself completely, as you do in the first week or two. '. . . it is much more important to be oneself than anything else.' So Virginia Woolf. I wonder what she would have made of service life.

A WREN
On Duty in Plymouth

A seventeen year old Wren writes to her father:
I am pretty sleepy at the moment as I was on duty last night and we didn't get to bed until 2 a.m., and our first trip was 6.30 this morning.

We were doing liberty trips all night out to the destroyers in the Sound. The last trip at midnight was the worst. It was blowing pretty hard, and we had to take eighty men out and many of them were not sober. Before we had even started four of them went over the side. Luckily it was moonlight so we had no difficulty in fishing for them with a boathook. I just saved a fifth from going over by catching him by his gas mask, just as he was disappearing. Luckily there was a sober A.B. up with me in the bows, and between us we managed them. It was a terrific experience, and I think I must be pretty hard boiled as it didn't worry me at all. None of them ever get fighting drunk. You have just got to treat them all like a lot of small boys.

HILARY WAYNE
Class in the ATS

Before I joined up I took my voice for granted and I suppose I did not give the question of Class a thought from one year's end to the other. Unlike the lady who put a notice in *The Times* thanking her friends 'high and low' for their sympathy, I dislike the idea of social barriers between human beings so much that it is a temptation to ignore their existence. But they exist very definitely none the less, and almost immediately in the ATS voice and class consciousness were thrust upon us.

I once had in my possession a folder issued by one of the Women's Services, setting out the different occupations open to recruits. They were divided into two classes – S. (Specialised) and G. (General) – and although I know that no such thing was intended, the folder gave us the impression that the categories labelled G., which included cooks, orderlies, messengers and so on, would absorb the socially lower entrants. From then on we privately adopted the convenient, less offensive and to others unintelligible classification 'S.' and 'G.' to differentiate those whom a former generation would unblushingly have labelled upper and lower classes respectively. I shall use these abbreviations here.

In the ATS the Gs. greatly preponderate, and although I have eaten, slept and worked most harmoniously with them, although I have liked the great majority and I know that they have liked me, I discovered that, more's the pity, there is between the classes in this country a great gulf fixed. When I have deplored the cleavage, people have said, 'Education will change that,' but there is more to it than education.

True, the first and most obvious advantage of the S. over the G. is the educated voice. It at once proclaims the privileged camp. I remember a girl saying admiringly of an officer, 'She speaks lovely.' It seemed to me strange that she recognised her own shortcoming and was apparently powerless to deal with it: but this I found to be the rule.

When I was working in the kitchen at the Training Centre I came in the course of a hunt for cleaning utensils into the vegetable room and a rather hostile group. To my enquiry as to whether they had a broom to lend me they chorused nasally, 'Naow, we haven't.'

The devil made me mimic them: 'Noaw, we haven't!'

I shall never forget the reproach: 'You needn't copy us, Mrs Wayne.'

I felt very ashamed and I apologised. I think they deserved a gibe of some sort, but I was usually ultra-careful not to widen the gap between us. [. . .]

I hold no brief for any particular brand of voice or accent; I only record that those who speak lovely and those who don't speak different languages, and for absolutely free and equal intercourse among numbers it is essential that people speak the same language. Education may level this up, but it will take a long time.

But there is a still more potent obstacle to unrestricted social intercourse, and that is background. It must be realised that from the earliest days the lives of the G. and the S. run on completely different lines. They live in different houses, go to different schools, eat different food – the amount I spent on milk, butter and eggs alone when Hazel was young would probably have fed many a G. family: in a word, the standard is utterly different and – most vital cleavage of all – so far from being waited upon as the Ss. are, it is the Gs. and their ancestors who for generations have worked for and waited on the Ss. This has produced a relationship whose roots go back, I imagine, to the days of vassals and serfs. Satisfactory social intercourse must presuppose a more or less common background; otherwise nearly every subject is taboo. Travel, country houses, books, pictures, music, good food, opera – in a word, all the best things and the environment which takes them for granted – are outside the experience of the G., and therefore to converse about them is impossible and even to speak of them seems swanky. [. . .]

Of course, the Army system does nothing to help. The aloofness, the pomp and privilege of the officer, practically always S., emphasise the social gulf between him and the private soldier. This is not the case in the American and Canadian armies, where officers and men are on much more free-and-easy terms and the men are correspondingly happier and more contented. One is reluctantly forced to the conclusion that the majority of Ss. in this country do not want to bridge the gulf, to share their privileges.

The ATS, I think, had a rare opportunity to try to make new standards, to show a burning desire to destroy artificial barriers. But its slavish imitation of the men's Army, with even less access for the G. to commissioned rank and privilege, shut out all hope of a fresh outlook. And we had the same insistence on petty detail and petty restrictions and a disregard for the larger questions of comfort and contentment. It is very significant, I think, that the great men – the Wingates and the Montgomerys – prefer to discard privilege and identify themselves with their men. We had an officer of the same calibre. Pay Parade was almost a sacred rite in the eyes of most officers: even a whisper in the waiting ranks outside the office was angrily quelled, and a tunic button undone called forth a frowning rebuke. I shall never forget my surprise when our new officer paid me – I was the last to be paid because I had been issuing savings stamps – without my hat on my head and with no salutes. It was she who refused to allow furniture to be removed from the Sergeant's room to make her own more comfortable, and it was she who, after we left Riverford, turned our room into a cheerful and attractive recreation-room for the girls and presented them with her own radio. To her, too, we owed the gas-ring in the kitchen.

It was interesting to consider whether there were any characteristics more inherent in the G. than in the S., and the result was much what one would imagine. The G. is far quicker and more capable at practical work. Now that there is so little domestic help, the S. has learned to cook and dust and sweep, and although I think she has made a very good show at it and has gained self-respect and usefulness in the process, the G. has had a long start. I can tell an S. by the way in which she takes up and handles a broom. It is the way of the amateur. The G. has a completely different technique. Her quickness and vigour are amazing. She will wash and iron her clothes, shampoo and set her hair with admirable speed and competence.

Conversely, she does not theorise. Hers is a world of action, not speculation. Even on the subject of a 'picture' or a film star it is almost impossible to start a discussion; you like or you dislike, but you do not delve.

Again, no doubt because they have for generations been the under-dogs, the Gs. are in our opinion too meek. They may grumble at bad conditions,

125

but they accept them. The creed of the S. is rather 'Those who don't ask don't get,' and she will agitate for something better and usually get it. This attitude shocks the G. She carries self-effacement to extreme lengths. Sooner than ask for help she will risk injuring herself by over-lifting. This trait may have been encouraged by the lack of chivalry in her own class; the men at the Barracks were more willing to help us, and the S. accepts help readily because she is used to it.

At Riverford there was a high percentage of S. girls in the Motor Transport Section, and it was illuminating that they had a far pleasanter and more comfortably equipped billet than ours. People get what they'll take. [. . .]

Communal life is not everyone's taste, and the herding of the sexes is very conducive to narrowness, nerves and 'cattiness'. There was much home-sickness and loneliness – Hazel* and I were constantly envied for being together. The woman soldier does not know the compensation of belonging to a regiment with its traditions, comradeship and pride. She is merely attached to a unit, without any guarantee of permanency. To girls used to independence and freedom the rules and regulations to which they are suddenly subjected are most irksome. Discipline may be good for the soul, but the adult mind prefers it diluted with common sense. And common sense does not flourish in the ATS.

It is not common sense to object, as our officer did, to our having anything but our pay-books in our pockets and forbid the carrying of a bag to take the glasses, compact, handkerchief and purse which were the minimum necessities. When I asked her what we were to do with them, she said we must carry them in our left hands! It is not common sense to issue regulations days ahead in winter that 'gloves but no greatcoats will be worn' on Church Parade, and to let people freeze in consequence. It is not common sense to allow the wearing of civilian clothes on 24-hours' leave and forbid the comfort of it in the evening when work is done. In short, it is not common sense to make of a community of sensible girls and women a constantly supervised and chivvied boarding-school.

---

* Hilary Wayne's daughter.

VITA SACKVILLE-WEST
from *The Women's Land Army*

We have grown tired of hearing the Land Army described as the Cinderella of the women's services; it has a sort of self-pitying sound. But this, in many ways, it really is. Not for the Land Army are the community existence, the parades, the marchings-past, the smart drill, the eyes-right, the salutes – or very seldom. For the most part its members work isolated and in a mouse-like obscurity. Their very uniform seems to suggest a bashful camouflage of green-and-fawn to be lost against the grass or the stubble. It is seldom that the Land-girl emerges into the streets of great cities; when she appears in public at all, it is in the village or the little country town, for by the very nature of her occupation she is rural, not urban. Yet often in her previous occupation she has been urban enough. She has been a shop-assistant, a manicurist, a hair-dresser, a shorthand-typist, a ballet-dancer, a milliner, a mannequin, a saleswoman, an insurance-clerk. She has worn silk stockings and high-heeled shoes, pretty frocks and jaunty hats; has had plenty of fun, being young and gay; has done her job during the working-hours, and then at the end of the day has returned to her personal life among friends or family, entertainment or home. At a moment's notice she has now exchanged all that; instead of her silks and georgettes she wears wool and corduroy and clumping boots; her working-hours seem never definitely to end, for on the land there may always be a sudden urgent call; she lives among strangers, and the jolly atmosphere of homely love or outside fun is replaced often by loneliness and boredom. She gets up at an hour when other people are still warmly asleep – and although dawn in spring or summer may be a moment one should be sorry to miss, a dingy wet morning in the winter before the light has even begun to clear the eastern sky is a very different story; she goes to bed with aching muscles after a dull evening, knowing that next morning the horrible alarum will shrill through her sleep, calling her back to her damp boots, her reeking oil-skin, and the mud and numbing cold outside. All this she has done, and is doing, so that *we* may eat. Nor has she always done it under the threat of a compulsory calling-up, but often voluntarily before her age-group was reached.

'Why did you chuck your good job before you need?'

'I just couldn't bear to see other girls in all sorts of uniform and feel I was doing nothing but sell shoes in a lovely shop.'

Whenever one is dealing with human beings in the mass, some very odd and unforeseen factors emerge. They are most revealing, and demonstrate how much at fault one was in any preconceived estimate of how people were likely to react in given circumstances. Thus it was astonishing to find that one-third of the Land Army volunteers came from London or our large industrial cities; and astonishing to note the tragic disappointment shown by those who could not be accepted for country work because they were more urgently needed elsewhere. This surprising fact does suggest that there are many townspeople who feel they would prefer the country, in complete contradiction to the popular view that the youth of today is wedded to the cities.

MARGHANITA LASKI

Our Auxiliary Women

1939

When we first heard that we were to take two land girls for training, speculation was rife. Miss Brown, the farm manager, who had had grievous experience of agricultural pupils, paying enormous premiums and apparently uninterested in agriculture, was deeply pessimistic. My brother had a wild hope that at least one of them would be a platinum blonde. I patiently expected two strapping typists whose refined voices would gradually be transformed into uproarious holloas.

It had been unanimously decided that we wouldn't have the girls living in the house. 'It would be bad for them,' we explained to each other. 'They'll have eventually to go and work for farmers whose living conditions will be totally different from ours, and it would be only kind to introduce them to that sort of thing right away.' So we arranged for them to stay with the gardener, who lived with his wife in a red-brick bungalow without electric light or running water, but 'much, much better,' we said, 'than anything they'll have to put up with later on.' We even wondered a little if we hadn't been too kind, and if they wouldn't be better off in the corrugated-iron shack of the hedger-and-ditcher. Finally we insisted firmly that we weren't responsible for their morals, 'but,' we added apprehensively, 'one does hope there won't be any trouble with the men on the place.'

The first girl arrived with her mother and the Nonesuch Blake. (We had a moment's delight at the thought of a ploughman's mother insisting on inspecting his sleeping-quarters.) This girl was seventeen years old, would have gone to Cambridge if it had not been for the war, was decisively

128

gentry. The mother wore high-heeled shoes and admirable tweeds. She announced to Miss Brown that the car would be sent on Saturday to bring Brenda home for the week-end, and seemed to have no cognisance of the fact that an optimistic Government was paying twenty-five shillings a week for her daughter's services, and that cows have to be milked on Sundays, modern methods of breeding having as yet failed to achieve bovine recognition of the Sabbath Day.

We left Brenda to Blake and the gardener's wife and sat down to wait for the next. My brother was still uneasily hoping for his platinum blonde, but the rest of us wanted no more than a strong uneducated wench of something over twenty-five.

The second girl arrived in the course of the afternoon, and both were invited up to the house for tea. There had been considerable discussion over this, some of us enquiring whether such glimpses of *le higlif* mightn't tend to unsettle them, others retorting that it was Only Once and that we could lend them some of the sixpenny Penguins we'd finished with.

There was no doubt about it, Dorothy was even more of a shock than Brenda. She said she was sixteen, but she looked an undersized twelve. Her mousy hair was tied back with a pale blue ribbon – 'Oi'm growing it ter look loike Greeta Garbo' she explained. We sat back weakly while she poured out a continuous flood of explanation.

'What Oi reely wanted wus ter be a spoi,' she said, 'but Oi couldn't find out 'ow ter set about it. Oi uster be in service, and then Oi went to a *fête*, and there was a tent with a lady in it taking names of girls fer the land. My, Oi wusn't 'alf sorry for 'er, because no one went and enrolled. So Oi goes in and enrolls, and they puts me down for a medium uniform, three soizes they 'as, small, medium and large. They puts me down for a medium' – she was about four feet ten, and small in proportion – 'Oi allus did loike the idea of working on a farm. No, Oi 'aven't reely bin in the country before. Oi come from Southampton. Oo, moi Dad, 'e's going ter be that angry when 'e foinds Oi'm 'ere. But moi Mum, she allus lets me do jest what Oi want. You go, she sez, and Oi'll settle yer Dad. Moind yer, 'e moight come 'ere after me, but Oi wudn't let 'im ketch me. Oi'd run away.' She bounced vigorously on the sofa, and the chocolate-box bow flapped up and down.

'Do you ride?' asked my brother of both girls indiscriminately.

'Oh yes,' replied Brenda, as one might say 'Naturally.' Dorothy began, 'Oi've allus wanted ter roide. Oi'd loike ter be a cow-boy, tomboy, moi Mum uster say. But Oi'm scared of 'orses, though not so bad as of cows. But there, Oi'll have ter git used ter them. Moi Dad says –' and on she went, her pallid face lit by every facile enthusiasm of the moment.

At last I said, 'Would you both like to borrow some books?'

'Oi'm that fond of reading!' cried Dorothy readily. I took them into the library. Brenda was soon absorbed in the shelves. Dorothy said to me, 'You choose one fer me. 'Ave yer got one about spois? I don't want no politics nor jography.'

I found a book called *Secret Agent*, or some such title. Dorothy said eagerly, 'Does it give any 'ints?' and I, with the book open at a conversation between Ludendorff, Hindenburg and von Mackensen about strategic considerations on the eastern frontier, unkindly said, 'Lots.' To salve my conscience I pressed on her a book about cowboys, published by a firm strangely calling themselves The Wild West Club. Brenda had taken *The Hunting of the Snark*. I smiled at her, then the girls went off and I returned to the drawing-room to find the discussion in full swing.

General opinion, I found to my surprise, was distinctly in favour of Dorothy. Brenda was felt to have behaved unfairly in displaying undeniable erudition and gentility. There was an uncomfortable feeling that she ought to have been asked to stay in the house, which found expression in such phrases as, 'Do that girl good to have to rough it.' and 'She'll soon get her airs and graces knocked out of her.' My impression of the normal sadism of women to girls going to, coming from, or at the University was fully confirmed.

Dorothy, it was agreed, was the right sort of type – *i.e.*, class – to make a success of farm-work. The opinion was, however, unanimously held that both girls were far too young to go farming, and that we didn't know what the Government was thinking about to send us mere children.

Personally, I was desperately sorry for Brenda. I saw her in the B.B.C. joviality of the gardener's family, sitting silent for lack of any conversational bridges, dubbed stuck-up and rude in the absence of any possible understanding. She was too young and too unsure of herself to seek for common ground. But I privately backed Brenda, Breeding and Blake, and felt strongly that when it came down to it education would tell.

Alas for my hopes! Next morning Brenda had left. Faced with the threshing machine she had remarked that she had meant to come to a farm where there was a real shortage of labour, and that as we had plenty of men, and in any case the work didn't appeal to her, she'd like to ring up for the car to come and fetch her. Dorothy, it was reported, was displaying great eagerness and doing splendidly, apart from a certain naïve inability to recognise the connotation of such simple words as 'shovel' and 'fork'.

So we are left with Dorothy, who is gradually learning to snap names and farm implements. Inquiries among neighbouring farmers has revealed that no one wants any land-girls ever. We train Dorothy diligently for a job in which no one is going to want to employ her, and for which she is physically unsuited.

And the family is finally and irrevocably convinced that too much education unfits a girl for life and only results in making her unbearably superior.

E.M. BARRAUD

P for Prisoner

For two months – with intermittent breaks on account of bad weather – we were threshing, and we had the help of six Italian prisoners of war. At first there was a very natural atmosphere of armed neutrality on both sides; we were unconsciously thinking of uncles, brothers, friends still out in North Africa; they were remembering their comrades – we were both remembering we were enemies. Gradually the mere fact of working together through the exigencies of the day's demands began to thaw us out. One of the men made a sparrow trap with three little slips of wood and a bit of board. David and I went and examined it, drew Stone's attention to it. Grudgingly he came to have a look at it, stared a moment, then smiled. 'Cor,' he said, 'I'm made 'undreds of them time I wer a boy,' and indeed I discovered all the village boys know the trap very well. Differ the ways of countries never so much in their more sophisticated aspects, in these simple things there is a common denominator which gives one hope that the day may come when war between the peoples of different nations will be as unthinkable as war would be nowadays between, say, Yorkshire and Lancashire.

Apparently the gangs of prisoners were sent out in alphabetical order; the surnames of all our men began with a P. They were not, therefore, all from the same unit. Two were from the crack Bersaglieri regiment, now armoured: one was an artilleryman, from a mountain unit operating on skis; the other three were infantrymen, from different regiments. They were all captured in the first few days of our advance from El Alamein, and they were all unreservedly glad to be out of the war.

Our first efforts at conversation were single words about the work. None of them spoke any English, except a hesitating 'Good morning!' and none of us had a word of Italian, except odd words from musical scores, or the titles of operas – and somehow I did not quite see how I could work in such things as 'La donna e mobile', particularly as our old mare is anything out! I had hoped one of them might speak French, but we were unlucky. Nevertheless, I found my rusty French was a bit of a help, backed up by even rustier Latin, most of it ecclesiastical, and one of the men had a tiny dictionary which helped us over the worst patches. After a day or two we had exchanged the words for the job in hand – oats, barley, wheat, chaff, sack, hay, fork, straw and the like – and even managed to pick up bits of information about each other. And somehow one feels more human when names have been exchanged and one can call a man 'Carlo' instead of plucking him by the sleeve.

Carlo was the first of them with whom I exchanged words. He told me he came from El Alamein, was an artilleryman in a ski unit, that his home was in a little Lombardy hill village where he helped on a family farm, that after the war he intended to go to join an uncle in America, that his mother was displeased with him for allowing himself to be taken prisoner, and that his father was English! Carlo was short, thick-set, dark-haired, blue-eyed, slow to speak and yet his English was soon better than any of the others. The others were content to rub along with a minimum of nouns, but Carlo painstakingly filled in his gaps with verbs and other parts of speech. It was Carlo who made the bird trap, borrowing my knife, his own having been confiscated when he was taken prisoner.

Giovanni was a shop-assistant in Sienna, a tall raw-boned fellow, fair-haired and with grey eyes. Giovanni was a fanatic, quick tempered, yet good natured and friendly as a small child. This was my first impression of him, and because of it I was a little alarmed when David one lunch time actually dared to mention the war, and our continued successses in North Africa. Giovanni, squatting on his heels, looked at him earnestly. 'Victory Italy, good!' he said. 'Victory England, good! No interest!' All he wanted, he explained, was 'Finish guerra, go 'ome.' And after lunch, as he worked beside me, he haltingly found words to tell me, driven home with gestures, how friends had been blown to pieces beside him, how one man had gone out of his mind. Giovanni had no use for Mussolini and indicated forcefully just what he would like to do to Il Duce should opportunity ever offer. It was for Giovanni I braided up straw in the various patterns Stone has taught me. He was delighted with the results and placed them carefully in his haversack, telling me he would take them back to their campo and put them in what he called the 'presepio'. This puzzled me, and finally I decided he meant some sort of museum they had got at their camp, but Christmas came soon after, and in comparing notes with them about customs in Italy and England, the word kept coming up, and at last I discovered its meaning: Giovanni was going to use my straw braids as part of the decoration of the manger they were making in the camp chapel.

EX-LANDGIRL
Landgirls' Discontents
November 1943

I was in the Land Army for eighteen months and thank God I am out of it now. My fundamental reason for resigning was that as a result of the monotony, the deadly drudgery, the entire lack of intelligent instruction, the lack of money, the loneliness and the apathy which one inevitably fell into after a couple of months, I felt myself slipping into a moral decline. [. . .] The only outlet was to pub crawl or to pick up a nice-looking American soldier. Reading, somehow, or even attending a lecture, was a terrific mental effort after a physically strenuous day even if it was available. All one yearned for was having a good time. It seemed the only panacea for the drudgery of our daily life.

I admit all Land Army girls do not have these dead-end, deadly jobs, but I can safely say that the majority of them do. Surely it is up to the Land Army to direct these unspent energies into the right channels. But what do they do – officially – practically nothing. There are, it is true, such bodies known as Welfare Committees. I had the honour – as a Landgirl – to be asked to sit on one. One look at those women on that Committee was enough for me. They had no idea of the job they were tackling. They looked upon us, mentally, as the servant girl type. The Committee consisted for the most part of already overworked members of the County Committee, District Representatives (usually aged and charming spinster ladies not conversant with the facts of life, who once a month made vague and diffident enquiries as to whether we were getting a bath once a week and if we would like another pair of shoes) and, perhaps, an elderly clergy man's wife. They had no funds beyond the money which had been raised at a few dances got up by some hostel or other. They had no experience in welfare work; they were the type of woman who has no real understanding of the young girl of today or how to tackle the problems of wartime morale. On psychology, I can safely say they had never read a book.

The war has been on for over four years now, and I think, without prejudice, the Land Army is the most neglected of all the military and civilian Services and Organisations. In most cases the Land Army girl is doing a bigger job of work than many women working in factories or in the Services; she works longer hours and earns much less money; but, nevertheless, she is the most neglected. I have known young girls of 17 or 18 sent down from the north of England to farms in the extreme south-west of England, having never left home before. They were put in private billets (not hostels where they would, perhaps, have got some older girl to look

after them), with no supervision whatsoever, and I have seen them pick up
the inevitable American soldier with the inevitable pub crawling and hedge
crawling and all the rest of it following in due course. I consider it a
damned shame that no one cares what happens to the Land Army girl now,
or after the war.

Chapter eight

OTHER WAR WORK

By 1943 women between the ages of eighteen and fifty were being directed into war work. By then at least 80 per cent of married women and 90 per cent of single women were contributing to the war effort in some way, whether in a full-time, part-time or voluntary job. The Services accounted for much less than a tenth of these millions of working women: other areas, both traditional and new, made their demands too. More nurses and welfare workers were needed, to deal directly with war's bloody and painful aspects. A variety of exciting jobs beckoned adventurous young women and bored housewives, as the small selection in this chapter shows; and women took to their canal-boats, Tiger Moth planes and tractors with zest. Radio talks featured women describing their exotic new jobs: smashing up motor cars, harvesting nettles, organising baths for the troops and so on. Most women, however, would have to go into munitions, making weapons and aeroplanes for the war.

These women knew the war at its least glamorous. Shifts were long – a twelve hour working day was not uncommon. Factories were often difficult to get to and conditions in them primitive. Then there would be the rest of life to fit in: the shopping, housework, cooking and childcare arrangements. No wonder absenteeism was common. There was also opposition from employers and workers alike as women moved into hitherto all-male preserves.

Women had always done voluntary work, but never before or again on the scale it reached during the war. Many of the social services we now expect from the State were provided, indeed sometimes invented by voluntary organisations, and in particular the Women's Voluntary Services. Founded by Lady Reading in 1938, by the end of the war the WVS had a membership of over a million. WVS woman was easy to ridicule, the archetype of the bossy female beloved of cartoonists. It was easy too, to underestimate the hard work, the skill and care that went into schemes for evacuating, clothing, feeding, salvaging – for whatever the need of the moment was.

All these different contributions to the war effort had to be recorded and acknowledged. Women were commissioned to provide reports like Celia

Fremlin's *War Factory* for Mass Observation and Rumer Godden's description of WVS work in Bengal. The workers themselves were also keen to put their new experiences into words. Susan Woolfitt, for example, gives an enthusiastic and engrossing account of the year she spent on narrow-boats, carrying cargoes on Britain's canals. She was one of many women who wanted to describe the effects that the work had on them; and sometimes they found the work itself so fascinating that they wanted to capture its every detail.

BRENDA McBRYDE
Nursing in France 1944

The Resuscitation department formed one arm of a U-shaped arrangement of tents with the theatre as a bridge leading to a surgical ward. It was floored with a heavy tarpaulin groundsheet and stacked with trestles to support the stretchers of wounded as they arrived from the ambulances. Here the men were given intensive treatment for shock until they were sufficiently restored to undergo operation, after which they passed straight from the theatre to the wards.

At the entrance to Resus., was the treatment area, a table covered by a sheet on which were laid trays of instruments, syringes, sterilisers, etc. Upended wooden boxes provided shelves for medicines and dressings; splints were stacked in a clean dustbin, and large, wooden chests contained the transfusion apparatus. On the other side of the entrance was a makeshift desk which bore the Admission Book and an array of requisition forms for diets, dispensary, replacements and repairs, extra blankets, pillows.

Thirty casualties had been admitted into Resus., during the night, all but two of whom had now been operated on and transferred to the adjoining ward. The two sisters from the 81st who were going off duty now handed over these remaining casualties, and wearily made for breakfast and bed, leaving Audrey and me in charge.

The two men lying so still on their stretchers with eyes closed were from the 7th Armoured Division. Both had been badly wounded in an abortive attempt to take an enemy pillbox. They had lost a great of blood but were now beginning to respond to the transfusions which had gone on all night. We were registering their blood pressures when one of our own surgeons from the 75th, Major MacPherson, a Canadian, came in.

He raised sandy eyebrows towards us. 'You settled in all right?' He felt under the grey blankets of one of the stretchers for a pulse and bent down close to the soldier's pale face. 'We'll get you to the theatre presently, son. Fix up that leg. OK?'

The soldier, who had a huge gunshot wound of thigh, made an almost imperceptible movement of his eyelids. He was swinging between reality and unconsciousness. We went to the desk to check his transfusion chart.

'Give him saline next and we'll do him first on the list.' Major MacPherson sighed and lowered his voice. 'I'm not looking forward to operating in that tent.'

With Sister Agate in charge, he would not even notice that the theatre was a tent.

'Sir.' George Easton, the Resuscitation orderly attached to the 81st, stood at the tent entrance. We turned at the urgency in his voice. 'Convoy of wounded on the way.'

'Inform Lt. Colonel Harding, i/c 75th Surgical Division,' Major MacPherson said sharply and went to the door as a string of ambulances went by on their way to Reception.

The taking of Tilly-sur-Seulles on 18th June had been a great victory for XXX Corps. Now, five days later, they were meeting stiff resistance in the high ground south of Tilly. This battle was being translated to us in a grim toll of casualties.

We entered the names of many famous regiments into the Admission Book that day: the Staffordshire Yeomanry, 4th Wilts, Dorsets, Green Howards, and East Yorks, men of the 7th Armoured Division and 50 (Northumbrian) Division. Most of their proud uniform, stiff with blood and caked in mud, had to be cut from them. We sliced the tough boots with razors to release shattered feet. The stretcher bearers came again and again until every trestle was occupied and the floor crammed so that there was barely room to put a foot or kneel between the stretchers. Audrey and I accompanied Lt. Colonel Harding and Major MacPherson as they went from one man to the next, assessing his condition and setting up transfusions.

In the trauma of that first day, everything I had learnt during four hard years of training suddenly made sense. My hands had a sure and certain skill and my brain was unflustered as I replaced dressings over gaping wounds, gave injections of morphia and the new wonder drug, penicillin, charted blood pressures. I began to see, for the first time, that the disciplines of the training school were a necessary part of the whole. That tent, full of men, reeking of blood, was where I was needed. These men, whose clammy bodies overpowered me with the nauseous sweet smell of shock were my fulfilment, since they could no longer help themselves.

LENA K. CHIVERS
Night Duty

5 August 1944
The latest convoy of wounded at our casualty clearing station in Southern England had been settled in bed. The men who had been to the operating

138

theatre were back in the ward, the dressings had been finished, the plasters fixed, the first round of medicines and drugs administered. The screens were put round the bed of the Fighting French Commando who seemed likely to die.

Blood was slowly dripping into the veins of four of the men. The field ambulance cards tied to the bedrails of two soldiers were marked 'Gas gangrene test positive'. You could smell that without looking at the cards; it is a smell you can't confuse with anything else – a special sweet and evil stench, less sweet than the smell of death, more penetrating than that of stopped-up drains.

I started to tidy up. We had undressed the men quickly and left their uniform on the floor by each bed. If it was not badly soiled you folded it up and put it in the lockers, but if the articles were torn or blood-stained you emptied the pockets and put them in a pile for the orderlies to carry away.

I started by Sergeant Davies' bed. I thought he was asleep and I was very quiet with his things. It must have been raining in Normandy – you could tell he had been lying on his side in the mud. I took the flat, wet cigarettes out of his trouser pockets – and his shaving things, a comb, a small steel mirror and half a dozen boiled sweets. I put his wallet and his pay-book and the crumpled photo of his wife on his locker. He opened his eyes as I moved away with the uniform. 'Nurse', he said, 'couldn't I keep my rat? Could you cut it off for me?'

With his uninjured arm he pointed to the divisional insignia on the sleeve of his tunic – a jerboa or desert rat, the badge of the Seventh Armoured Division, which had been nicknamed the 'desert rats' in North Africa.

'I had the same one in Tobruk,' he said. 'He brought me luck. I cut him off my tropical uniform and sewed it on this lot. I shall want him next time.'

I cut the stitches with my surgical scissors and put the badge on the locker. 'Thanks, Nurse.' And he started to tell me why the Seventh was the best armoured division in the British Army.

But there was no time to listen. The ward had to be made tidy quickly. Boots and tin helmets had to be tidied together under the beds, and the rest either inside the lockers or in the pile in the corner. It was getting to be quite a big pile – black berets of the Armoured Corps, tunics of the glider troops with their badge of a blue winged horse on a dark red ground, or the parachutists' badge of a white parachute with pale blue wings, often the red shield and blue cross of the Eighth Army, and several times the ribbon of the Africa Star, the shoulder flashes of Commandos, of Royal Marines, of the R.A.S.C. . . .

There seemed plenty to do during the night. There were some four-hourly drugs to be given, and fomentations, and drinks, and pillows to be changed around. Men with new plaster splints found it difficult to get comfortable. You often had to put a pillow or a sandbag in a most unexpected place to give a man relief. Sergeant Davies insisted on telling the man opposite why he would never even consider serving in anything other than the 7th Armoured Division. But the man opposite who was in the Lincolns, just turned over and snored.

We had rather a bad night with Evans. He was a South Wales miner, who had volunteered at the beginning of the war and managed to get himself into the Royal Engineers. We had sent for his wife because he had been put on the danger list. They had taken his foot off that afternoon. His wife just sat and smiled at him and then when she couldn't smile any more, she went into the kitchen and cried. Every time this happened one or other of us made her a cup of tea, and then she went back to him and smiled again.

After midnight everybody seemed settled. Although I had been on night duty for a long time there always seemed something strange and almost theatrical about the ward at these quiet times in the early hours of the morning. Perhaps it was the look of the place – the shaded lights, the two long rows of beds with their bright blue counterpanes, some of their silhouettes looking freakish because of the bed cradles and the bed blocks; and then the men were lying in such a variety of positions, often with their limbs stuck out at queer angles in the plaster splints or sometimes slung on to frames and hung with weights and pulleys; the light caught the glass flasks of blood which was still dripping slowly into the four bad cases. They were asleep and completely unconcerned about what was going on. The pile of dirty uniforms lay in the corner like the discarded costumes of a crowd of players.

THE DOWAGER MARCHIONESS
OF READING
Women's Voluntary Services
1945

The flood tide of 100,000 enrolments which nearly swamped all Centres in September, 1939, dropped gradually to a low level record of 12,000 enrolments in January, 1940, to be raised to 20,000 in one month by the invasion of Norway and 61,000 by the fall of France. Out of this army of women, many of whom had no experience either in administration or in the practical duties they were expected to perform, the staffs of WVS Regional Offices and Centres fashioned an implement of Civil Defence which proved infinitely flexible, so that it could meet any local emergency in the way best suited to overcome it, and yet consistent enough in policy and organization to merit the confidence of the Central Government and the Local Authorities. There were no precedents for a voluntary organization working under the orders of Local Authorities and yet controlled by a national headquarters in close touch with the Government, but this very lack meant that there were practically no restrictions on what such an organization could do. When the urgent necessity for increasing the provisions for the welfare of serving men during the first winter of the war led WVS to open canteens in places where the appropriate organizations lacked personnel and equipment to do so, the Ministry of Home Security ruled that WVS could properly undertake *any* work, arising out of the war, which might be asked of it by a Government Department. Since then WVS has worked for almost every Government Department, but hardly ever did a new undertaking start at the suggestion of Headquarters; almost always it has been found necessary and tried out in some Centre first, and as the experiment proved itself so was it adopted nationally.

The German delay in opening an attack in the west, whether by land or air, made the development of WVS follow an unexpected course. Evacuation and not ARP dominated the work during the first year. Evacuation called into play every faculty most strongly marked in women, quick intuition of difficulties, a gift for improvization in domestic planning and a pride in the improved appearance of children placed under their care. A million and a quarter mothers and children moved into the country districts in September, 1939, and, without the devoted help of volunteers, most of whom were WVS members or worked in close co-operation with WVS, the scheme could not have achieved even partial success. Failures are always more vocal than successes and the difficulty of absorbing some types of evacuee into private billets needs no description – we have all heard enough about them! What we are more likely to forget are the thousands of cases in which volunteers, working as Assistant Billeting Officers, found homes in which evacuated children settled happily, if not on their first arrival then after tireless efforts had found the right combination of temperaments.

The clothing of evacuated children whose parents could not send them adequate garments absorbed most of the energies of WVS during the first winter, and it was this urgent need for clothing which first led the American Red Cross Society to send goods for the relief of civilian distress to WVS. Their representatives visited England during the early part of 1940 and found that WVS was everywhere in touch with the needs of the evacuees as well as possessing a central organization which could collate the results of local experience and estimate future needs. In August, 1940, the American Red Cross appointed WVS to be their distributing agents for all goods that they were sending to Britain for the relief of civilian distress and, since then, WVS has distributed on their behalf goods valued at many million pounds. This steady flow of supplies from the United States was amply supported by gifts from organizations and private donors in the Dominions and Colonies of the British Empire and from sympathizers in all free countries. [. . .]

If most forms of WVS work started with evacuation they found their apogee in the heavy raids. Outside London the majority of Rest Centres were staffed, wholly or in part, by WVS while members worked tirelessly in Clothing Depots, Emergency Feeding Centres, Administrative Centres and Information Bureaux which brought help to the bombed-out. The members of the Housewives Section, with their minimum of training and their maximum of common sense, brought a feeling of self-reliance and mutual help into almost every street. Mobile canteens, many of them bought through the Civil Defence Canteen Trust which was inaugurated, at the suggestion of WVS, in November, 1939, were the first line of defence in emergency feeding. When the provincial cities became targets for concentrated attacks, these canteens were called in support from all over the country and their teams made long journeys, over unfamiliar roads which were sometimes frozen, or blocked with bombs, to a rendezvous at dawn in a stricken city. Here they worked day and night, feeding firemen and rescue squads who could not leave their work even to go in search of food, and people who had either lost their homes or all means of cooking in them. [. . .] The influence upon our national life of the million women who, through WVS, have learned to take a wider view of their duties as citizens will be considerable. There are three essential characteristics of WVS work: –

First, that WVS has been able to tackle anything and, when one need passed, to switch its resources of trained woman power on to the next job without alterations to a rigid constitution, whether the change was temporary, like the rush of issuing ration books, or a permanent change in the emphasis of the country's needs, and has thus never wasted that most important raw material of war effort, the intelligent service of volunteers, on stand-by duties.

Secondly, without distinction of religion, class or politics WVS has given a sense of responsibility to women who had never thought of influencing the life of the community beyond their own doorsteps. They have found happiness in helping, not only their neighbours during emergencies of peace or war, but also the stranger within their gates.

142

And thirdly, they have also learnt something of the intricacies of Local Government; in fact, WVS, through the work it has done, through the integrity of service it has given, and through its readiness to try and help in a really orderly and sympathetic way, has become the hyphen between official-dom and ordinary human beings. A working woman once said that volun-tary public service had been the prerogative of the wealthy until WVS brought it within the scope of all. That contribution must not – and will not – be lost.

NELLA LAST
The WVS Canteen

Thursday, 28 August 1941

There was a ring and Mrs Thompson, our canteen head, was at the door. She had come to tell me that we will have the two new American mobile canteens any time now, as well as our own Jolly Roger, and also a 'first grade' canteen for the soldiers. She wants me to give an afternoon and/or evening as advisory cook. She says I'll not have to work really hard, only overlook and give advice on economical and tasty oddments. Mrs Diss, who has taken over as head of WVS, had sent her. It's what I've always wanted to do – I am realising more each day what a knack of dodging and cooking and managing I possess, and my careful economies are things to pass on, not hide as I used to! She stressed the point that I would not have hard work to do, and I said, 'I'll do my share like the others.' But she said, 'Mrs Diss said you do more than your share at Hospital Supply, and it's too bad to ask you to do more.'

When she had gone out, my husband said, 'You know, you amaze me really, when I think of the wretched health you had just before the war, and how long it took you to recover from that nervous breakdown.' I said, 'Well, I'm in rhythm now, instead of always fighting against things' – but stopped when I saw the hurt, surprised look on his face. He never realises – and never could – that the years when I had to sit quiet and always do everything he liked, and *never* the things he did not, were slavery years of mind and body. [. . .]

Friday, 26 September 1941

We managed very well at the canteen, considering we were fresh to the place and there is a shortage of crocks etc. I prepared salmon paste and sardine paste, and a boiled tongue was brought in. It was all sandwiches or pies this afternoon – it's at night that there is a run on cooked bits, like sausage and mash or eggs and chips. It will be a grand place when we get going, for there is a nice room for reading and writing, a billiard-table and dart-board, and servicemen are encouraged to bring their wives. I will try and cook oddments at home, and think up fresh recipes to keep the menu list attractive. We are giving good value: a plate of tomato sandwiches (four slices off a loaf, spread with marge and butter), two large cakes and a breakfast cup of tea came to 8d.

Friday, 3 October 1941
They are a grand lot on my shift at the canteen. They say, 'Just tell us what to do and we will do it,' and then scurry and hurry round. I'm very lucky to have such good helpers. I've shown one woman how to make potato cakes, and another says she is going to practise making waffles at home, ready for next Friday.

I get many a chuckle at myself nowadays – no hiding away my dodges and strict economies as I used to. Instead, I broadcast 'how little fat', or 'how economical' my bits and bobs of recipes are. And Gran's old recipes are going the rounds. Her piccalilli and chutney are pronounced 'marvellous'. I had no time to copy out a recipe one day, and hurriedly pushed my old tattered recipe book in my basket, to do it at the Centre. I got on with my job, and when I went into the office, a chorus of 'Would you mind me taking a recipe for . . .' greeted me. It's childish of me, I know, but it gives me such a warm feeling to find I've anything people want. I've not a lot to give, and I do so like giving.

JOAN BRIGHT ASTLEY
Women at the War Office

Women were expendable in the War Office in those early days as they sat at their typing-tables, guarded by lady supervisors, with eagle eye and scratching pen, who noted their movements and checked as to whether 'Colonel B. has had Miss K. recently', or whether some other girl should have the dubious privilege. None of us, no female, was allowed to carry the red-lettered 'Top Secret Officers Only' files; it was a daunting experience to me at the time of Dunkirk – when even the tea-trolley stood silent and the jokes had ended – to be asked by a furious brigadier: 'Can't you *read*?' as he pointed at the 'Top Secret Officers Only' file in my hand.

FRANCES PARTRIDGE
A Cook Leaves

11 May 1941
When Joan brought in the green tea this evening after dinner, she gasped and said, 'Mrs Partridge, I want to leave and do war work, as Tim's being sent abroad.' I went with her into the kitchen, where she told me that he was going in about three weeks' time, and she felt she couldn't bear it unless she was hard at work all day, so she had been to an aeroplane factory in Newbury to see if they would take her on. I didn't know how to show her how sorry I was without upsetting her more, her white face and breathless voice were so pitiful. I came back to the sitting-room so struck by Joan's tragedy that I felt on the verge of tears, and neither R. nor I could read or think of anything else for some time. Here was something absolutely good (Joan's relation with Tim) and it has been struck, and is crumbling away so rapidly that she has to try and drown her misery in the rumble and crash of machinery. And of course it is the happiness of not one but hundreds of Joans and hundreds of Gunner Robinsons, thousands, millions I should say – of all nationalities – that is to be sacrificed in this awful pandemonium. R. went to talk to her. We were both too upset to read.

The ducklings were put out this morning in a run on the lawn and we spent some time watching them. Our life gets more domestic and agricultural and when Joan goes it may get more so. If only I could cook!

VERE HODGSON
A Munitions Procession

September 1941
Cath and I went to see the wonderful munitions procession lining up in Hagley Road. It was to attract women to the factories. All firms sent contingents in marvellously coloured overalls – on lorries containing parts of Spitfires etc. with the words: We Made These.

There never was such a talkative procession - they chattered like magpies all the time. One lorry had elderly women. We are all between 60 and 80 . . . we are still working - why aren't you? How happy they all looked. They insisted on a lorry being provided for them, otherwise they said they would walk - but left out they would not be. There were some wonderful Tanks - the fastest in the world. It was a mile long, with a donkey to finish up with!

AMABEL WILLIAMS-ELLIS
Factory Work

In two big steel-mills and in a third factory where they worked in brass there were women and girls in every department, except at the rolling-mills and furnaces. In the steel-mills there were 5 or 6 men to every woman, but these two factories were so big that there were over 2,000 woman in one firm. Plenty of them worked with the red-hot metal too; and in the brass-works 'hot pressing' was done by women waited on by young girls.

A long bar of brass as thick as a woman's forearm had been cut into six-inch lengths. Besides Mrs Knowles (in a dark bib-and-brace suit over a pink satin blouse) stands a gas oven on long legs and with an open front, the licking flames giving out an intense heat. This oven is fed from behind by Florrie, who fetches the short brass bars and rattles them down a hopper. With a long pair of tongs Mrs Knowles takes one of the bits of brass - its once-sharp edges blurred because it is nearly white hot. She puts it under the green-painted hood of the press and pulls a lever, which brings the mould stamp heavily down. She leaves the metal in for a moment (the work has its own special rhythm); then, as she releases the press, the rough

146

form of what will be the nose of a shell tumbles, still burning hot, into a hopper below. There is a row of these presses, and the noise is so loud that it is impossible to talk. Mrs Knowles' face gleams with perspiration. Now and then she moves for a moment out of range of the heat to get a drink from a jug of water.

INEZ HOLDEN

Night Shift

It was strange the way the talk could go on. We worked on nine and a half hour shifts for six nights a week; it was true we had one hour each night off for a meal, but it was difficult to get any food; then, it meant a long wait at the food counter, fetching plates backwards and forwards from the cooking stove to the benches where we sat to eat. No one spoke much during the one-hour break. Many of the workers were tired when they reached the factory; we worked all the time we were there, and yet conversation crept in – cut-up scraps of conversation between the times of fixing up a machine, counting pieces of work and waiting for a new drill or tap to be fixed in the machine. But even in prisons, where there are more difficulties, the chatter gets through; words are sent out from the side of the mouth in chapel between the snatches of hymns. [. . .]

A young day-shift engineer who had just come off Home Guard duty was talking to Nan at one of the lathes near the end of the centre work bench. She had been laughing as she worked and listened to his talk, but now her face wore an ill-at-ease expression. The Home Guard boy was leaning over the machinery like a caricature of a drunken guardsman breathing down a barmaid's neck, and then suddenly Nan slapped his face, quick as a cat at play. Nan's slap was not a hard hit, but it was a boomerang blow, so speedily sent and quick to return that it was difficult for the boy to be sure that Nan's hand had ever left the lathe. He went on talking as if nothing had happened, but the memory of the slap stayed like a brake on the back of his mind.

CONSTANCE REAVELEY
The Machine and the Mind

When I began to work a capstan, I enjoyed it greatly, though it was a strange transition from a don's life. I tried to analyse this pleasure, and seemed to become aware of a number of heterogeneous gratifications. I felt a strong sense of virtue in carrying out repeatedly and exactly the simple processes I had been taught, the small child's smug satisfaction in obedience. I liked the sense of safety, of being looked after, when my machine was set for me and I had nothing to do but pull the levers and turn the wheels. It was flattering, and gave one a sense of power, to have so intricate and expensive an instrument under one's hands, and I loved it for working for me. I was a little surprised at first to find that I didn't resent getting my hands messy with the brown oil that lubricated the machine; the release of the inhibition against dirt gave a faint sense of illicit freedom. I liked being allowed to destroy something, that is to grind away parts of the solid bar which was to be made into a screw. I even more enjoyed making something, the little screw which fell into my hands as the parting-tool finished its work. I liked reaching certain figures in output, 20, 50, 100, 120 and so on. Substantial output was pleasing in itself. When I was cutting away one small surface, I sometimes omitted to flick over the lubricant; the thought came that if I were a dentist, and let my tool get heated in that way, I should hurt someone; this gave me an agreeable sense of power. As I got more accustomed to the job I enjoyed conforming my movements to a rhythmical pattern; rhythm is economical of time as well as delightful. I have no idea whether these primitive sensations are common. They faded out as I got more used to the work. It is not easy to get working people to analyse their own minds, especially in relation to their everyday experience; I could not find out what other people felt.

I was not left on a capstan for long, but was moved to a grinding-machine. I enjoyed this too; a certain deftness was needed, and some judgement. I enjoyed improving my speed, and the shining silver of the ground surface. As the novice's pleasure in simple performance wore off, I became interested in other matters. I watched the life of the factory. I thought a good deal went on that ought to be more widely known about and understood. I thought I would write to the Bishop, and urge that young men in training for Holy Orders should work for six months or so in a factory (or a mine or a shop) to get an insight for themselves into the way people live and work; the young are generous enough for anything when once they get an idea into their heads. Again, it seemed to me that the girls I knew at the works needed a better literature to feed their minds. Fiction, like poetry, should be an interpretation and criticism of life; the stories they were reading were nothing but wish-fulfilment fantasy, and they got sick of them. I thought I would write to the head of a women's college, and suggest that a girl who wanted to write, and would work in a factory for a few months, could produce stories for factory girls about factory girls, which would give them a lot more interest than anything there is on the market for them at present. And if the stories were illustrated by an artist who had spent some time in a factory, factory people might begin to feel that their experience is part of the common life; I must get in touch with an artist.

I did none of these things. There was no time. I realised that if you have ten hours a day for thinking of things to do and only two or three very weary ones for doing them, you either become accustomed to unfulfilled purpose, to fantasy-thinking uncorrected by experiment in the real world, or else you give up making plans.

Like many other people I chose the second alternative. I was getting very tired. I found at this third stage that the time passed in day-dreaming and brooding. It is very difficult to remember or analyse day-dreams. They seem to be at the mercy of emotion and your emotions seem to be much influenced by the way you spent your last leisure; you remember what you said and what he said, and invent long conversations that never were and never will be; more brilliant than real conversations, of course. Or if your leisure had very little in it, your mind wanders forward. If you are very tired, you may become preoccupied with grievances, or imaginary grievances; will the charge-hand refuse to give you an early pass, or will he put you back on the machine you most dislike? When you are tired, which is most of the time, your thoughts repeat themselves as your machine repeats its process; you can't disengage yourself from them. You are imprisoned in your own imagination for hours on end, tied to some idea which has associated itself with the succession of the job. Nothing happens to break into the helpless cycle of these thoughts.

I went and consulted a tool-maker friend of mine and his wife. I asked them whether this fatiguing and sometimes unpleasant repetition of useless thoughts happens to evey one who works a machine. 'No,' they said, 'you have an active mind. Many women haven't. They don't think of anything.'

CELIA FREMLIN
Lack of Interest in Working for the War Effort

It is felt by the management that one of the big problems of this type of factory is that the work seems superficially to be so remote from the war; that it is not of obvious immediate use, like making bullets and shells. They feel that lack of interest in the work is largely due to this – that the girls do not feel they are contributing directly to the war. And a good deal of trouble has been taken to emphasize and publicise the importance of the work for the war effort.

As far as the machine shop is concerned, however, evidence goes to show that some of this anxiety is misdirected. The trouble there is not that the girls do not realize that their work is important to the war, but that the majority of them are so little *interested in the war that they do not care whether their work is important to it or not.* As in so many country places, to the women at least, the war is simply a thing that happens, like a thunderstorm or an earthquake, and victory is similarly a thing that will happen. All that can be done is to hope that it will happen soon, as one hopes for fine weather. The idea that anything one does or doesn't do oneself can possibly have any bearing on it all, comes very slowly.

This attitude to the war was illustrated by a small study of newspaper reading in the canteen. Every day for a fortnight at the end of February, an observer brought a copy of the *Daily Mirror* into the canteen and handed it round among immediate neighbours (about a dozen usually had some kind of a look at it), and noted down afterwards all the items in the paper that had attracted any comments of any kind. During the whole of this period there was a total of not more than four remarks about the war news at all, and these were of the briefest. Here is a typical set of reactions to looking at the paper – the particular day being February 26th, the day when a Cripps speech was headlined all over the front page:

'What's your birthday, Peg?'
'June. First half of June. What's it say?'
' "No great excitements, but a pleasant, easy-going sort of day." '
'(*Laughs*) Easy-going! I work till eight o'clock, and don't get home till half-past nine! Good thing they say there's no excitement, anyway.'
'What's yours, Lil?'

And so on, until the birthdays of most of the girls within hearing have been accounted for. Then they start looking at the other pages:

'Isn't that a nice one? Look, the Queen talking to someone in a factory. It's nice, isn't it. It flatters her.'

150

'What's that about the ATS pyjamas? They don't get no coupons, do they, in the ATS?'

'It says they can get them without now, or something. I wouldn't mind being in the ATS, would you? Better than here.'

Interest flags, and there is no more talk about the paper. One girl goes on looking languidly up and down the middle page until one of the men from another table comes and borrows it.

This negative attitude to the war is to a large extent characteristic of all country districts, but it is even more strongly marked among factory workers like these than among the rest of the population in the area. For, paradoxical as it may seem, life in a twelve-hours-a-day war factory makes one feel further removed from the war than one could in any other type of life.

AMABEL WILLIAMS-ELLIS
Hostels and Girls

Each hostel holds a thousand women and girls; there are four, five, sometimes seven, hostels in a group; there are four or five such groups in England and Wales, perhaps more – there is official reticence regarding that, on security grounds. Everywhere the routine is much the same, for the factories work night and day and three shifts of human beings must minister. The girls climb into a row of waiting 'buses, clock in at the factory, work, eat during the brief factory break, climb into their 'buses again and back to the hostel for another meal, rest and bed.

It was with the expectation of finding something rigid, mechanical, even monstrous, and tolerable only as a war necessity, that I went and looked at seven such hostels, staying three days in one of them. There would, of course, I knew, be a certain decency (the large numbers allotted to 'welfare' was a feature), and some attempt would be made to amuse the poor conscripts. A fellow-visitor had similar anticipations. 'Till a cum a made sure t' place must be a barracks wi' so many! Many a time, puttin' t' dinner on t' table in Bradford a near cried thinking of our Maudie alone in such a place!' Invited to stay and to see for ourselves, Mrs Hawks and I entirely revised our opinions. There are hostels that I have not seen, but of the seven (in two different parts of the country) that I have visited I can report that they are the nicest of clubs, that they represent real and varied experiments in communal living, and that the atmosphere is comparable to that of a summer-school or of a well-organised one-class cruise.

The source of hostel atmosphere is twofold. In the first place, each of those visited had been handed over for administration either to the Workers' Travel Association or to the Co-operative Holiday Guild, that is to people used to having to please and amuse their public, but also with a sense of social responsibility – some of their public have always wanted to enlarge their horizons. Men as well as women do this work. In the second place, first-rate architects with a real cultural background have been responsible for lay-out and decorative detail; architects, moreover, with the soundest and most modern views on plumbing. The war forced an austerity on the architects that they (and I) enjoyed: but, had the hostels not been a war-time measure, no doubt a little of what one might call 'Sickertism' would have pleased the residents. Residents agree that the hostels are bright and pretty, that the chairs are comfortable and the little bedrooms for two beautifully planned. The state of the light-coloured decorations and curtains after six months of use (three-shift use) show that they have been, on balance, approved. (Experience is that people are not so reasonable and responsible in their care of material objects unless they like them.) Girls and women have come, or been drafted, to these hostels from all over the place and, had this interesting social experiment not been a by-product of war, it would have been interesting to see whether some of the home-sickness of most residents' first weeks could have been prevented by the actual framework within which the life of the place moves.

One homesick girl from Belfast spoke as if she were in a sense impatient with herself at not being able to take more advantage of many things the hostel had to offer. It was hard to be precise as to what was the matter; the other girls just said she would 'get used to it.' What was it, besides her familiar friends, that she missed? She could not put her finger on it, but remarked that, though the food was nice and there was plenty of it, she couldn't have a cup of tea just when she thought she would, and that, though all the buildings were kept so nice and warm, there wasn't a fire to poke. In peace-time this could have been remedied, not by the administration but by the architects, which might, or might not, have helped her. The size of the place and the many contacts were a relief to some. A London woman of about fifty (small, rather drooping with a singular look of sadness and resolution) told me that just now she could not stand either her own home or someone else's. She had been widowed by the last war and left with a little boy of two. This only son had now been eighteen months in Africa. 'Always been plenty of time for something to happen between his writing and me getting it. Time passes best here.'

152

MOLLIE PANTER-DOWNES
War Work for Wives

31 January 1943
Wives of all sorts of men come within the scope of the new Bevin regulations, which are to take effect shortly. These, in addition to providing a close check on possibly slippery female labor by insisting that employers notify the Labour Exchange when a woman worker leaves them, will direct all childless married women under forty-five to take part-time jobs within a reasonable distance from their homes. Housewives have been, oddly enough, officially designated one of the 'unoccupied classes,' but it looks as though the days of many of them are not going to be so very leisured in the future, divided as they will be between household chores and office or factory. Tapping this last great reservoir of female labor is the follow-up of a recent drive to make it harder for women not only to get out of war service but to choose what form their service should take. Girls who are affected by the new call-up of nineteen-year-olds can no longer decide that they look better in Navy blue than in khaki and act accordingly, for they are being put willy-nilly into whatever service is shortest of recruits. It has also been ruled that once a girl joins a service, she cannot duck out after the fortnight probationary period because she finds the service life doesn't suit her. The effect of the demands Mr Bevin has made on the personnel of retail business is already visible in some of the shops – notably in one on Regent Street where customers in the neckwear department were seen the other day timidly selecting purchases with the help of a commanding, white-haired dowager in a velvet train.

ZELMA KATIN
First Day on the Trams

At 3.30 I awoke suddenly, my eyes rimmed and my head dull. I was troubled with uncertainty. Was it I who was going to dress up in conductor's uniform, run down to the tram depot in the blackout, shout 'Fares please', punch tickets, and chaff other conductresses in a canteen? Was this woman in navy blue myself? There must be two 'I's': the original 'I' is a married suburban woman who once studied botany in a university college, speaks with a southern intonation, confines herself to her house, and belongs to the petit bourgeoisie. She must have indulged in a burst of dichotomy and procreated another 'I' – an aggressive woman in uniform who sharply orders people about, has swear words and lewd jokes thrown at her, works amid rush and noise, fumbles and stumbles about in the blackout, and has filthy hands and a grimy neck.

MARY DE BUNSEN
A Hen among the Eagles

I was rung up and asked to get in touch with a firm of aircraft dealers. It appeared that they wanted a ferry pilot, and somebody had recommended me.

Trying to disguise my enthusiasm, I telephoned to them at once and expressed my willingness to collect a couple of Tiger Moths from Manchester and fly them south to an aerodrome which I will call Stoney, to be dismantled for export.

I went to Stanford's to try and get the 4-mile-to-inch Ordnance Survey maps of the North Midlands, and was told that aviation maps were no longer on sale to the public. So, just for fun, and knowing that it would be quite futile, I went to the Air Ministry and was ushered into the presence of the OC Maps (I do not know his official title). He listened patiently while I explained that I was an unattached civilian, suddenly called upon to fly what would doubtless prove to be a circuitous and complicated route, beset with balloons, Heinkels and all sorts of unknown hazards, and that it would tend to minimize the confusion I should cause in the process if I could be provided with some sort of adequate map.

He shook his head sadly. Now if I were another department of the Air Ministry, or an official body, it would be quite different; but there existed no mechanism whatever by which an aviation map could be issued to an unattached civilian. I should have to chance the balloons. [. . .]

The Tiger Moth was standing out on the tarmac, painted bright red with silver wings, creaking and straining a little in the wind and looking as tigerish as even a mild and biddable aeroplane sometimes can. I remembered with disfavour the liveliness of small biplanes in gusty weather.

Inwardly I was experiencing all the usual symptoms of stage fright, while outwardly playing the part of the Experienced Old Hand. [. . .]

The Tiger Moth left the ground somewhat prematurely on a strong gust of wind; but, finding itself in the air, was good enough to remain there while I held the nose level to get up a bit of speed. I watched the air-speed indicator and climbed at a safe 75 miles an hour through a very bumpy layer of air. They told me afterwards that I appeared to be chucked about a good deal in the first few hundred feet. At about a thousand feet, things quietened down a bit and I looked round to get my bearings. The weather was squally, with a chance of thunder and excellent visibility, except in local rainstorms, when it was liable to shut down to under a mile.

Manchester, true to tradition, was enveloped in a yellow, smoky haze, filled with monstrous floating shapes: the barrage balloons I had regarded hitherto with such affection and which now took on an unfamiliar and menacing aspect. Heavy clouds hung over us and a rainstorm hid the southern horizon. Beneath me lay the cemeteries which are a permanent reminder of the transitoriness of life to all who enter or leave this aerodrome on wings.

I crossed a canal and arrived over Altrincham, from which radiated the usual network of railways. It was essential, in order to check up on my doubtful compass, to discover which was which; but on my 10-mile map they were small and difficult to identify. I started circling, and focused all my attention on the map; but every time I fixed my eyes upon it, the aeroplane tried to stand upon its head, and had to be retrieved from some unconventional attitude.

I set out eventually along a railway which, though uncertain, appeared to agree with my compass course. I verified it finally by referring to a fairly large-scale motor map, which was not very helpful about railways, but clearly marked two small but unmistakable reservoirs.

Without any further difficulty, I arrived, in about half an hour, at Stoke-on-Trent, which was shrouded in the usual industrial haze blended with the outskirts of a heavy shower. Here it was necessary to get on to a new bearing, and, once again, to find a railway line or other identifiable landmark on which I could check for drift. Somebody must have taken the aerodrome away and hidden it, because next time I passed that way, on the second ferry trip, it was right there, staring me in the face. Anyway, this time I started off with insufficient evidence along the *wrong* railway line, and when I had discovered this, made my first mistake. I should have retraced my steps to Stoke and tried again. But time seemed all-important, and I was perhaps too conscious of the existence of the Observer Corps, for whom I was doubtless providing a sort of field-day. If I turned back it might upset everybody's calculations. It felt better to appear to be going somewhere definite. So I went on. [. . .]

155

All at once a gigantic mare's nest of an aerial obstruction reared its ugly head on the horizon. I remembered a once-famous Notice to Airmen which drew attention to the presence, in the neighbourhood of Rugby, of a group of X wireless masts X feet high, and after enlarging on their size and number, concluded naively with the words, 'These constitute a danger to aircraft'.

'If that,' I reflected, 'does not constitute a danger to aircraft, I will eat my hat. This must be Rugby.' It was. I was found. What is more, after being lost for the best part of an hour, I was within about three miles of my intended course.

It was at this juncture that I was aware of a curious sensation in my throat; a sort of intermittent vibration accompanied by a buzzing in the ears. Suddenly I discovered the cause of it. I was singing Christmas carols. I was happy; I had been lost and was found, and God was in his heaven and all was right with the world.

I soon got on to the country covered by my large-scale map, and after that it was plain sailing. I had seen a few aeroplanes, too far away to identify, and once a Blenheim flashed underneath me much too close, clearly demonstrating the effectiveness of camouflage. I altered course and flew round a couple of opaque rainstorms. The clouds broke up gradually and sun flooded a suddenly friendly and welcoming countryside. Cloud shadows lent life and movement to the rolling grasslands. Below, grasshoppers were chirping and larks singing, and I, had I his voice and opportunities, could have outsung the lark. The violent bumps of the early part of the flight had given place to a gentle rocking lullaby. These moments, when engine noise and vibration are drowned in a vast inward peace, are the joy and solace of the pilot.

My watch showed two hours in the air, and there before me lay my destination, and my troubles were seemingly over. It remained only to get down – a simple matter.

The one element in the flight which had so far given no cause for anxiety or complaint was the aeroplane. She had been a perfect lady, had humoured my harshness, and responded willingly to my lightest touch. Losing height gradually at half-throttle, I opened up again at 1000 feet for a preliminary circuit. I had been expressly told that failure to circle for identification might mean that I should be shot at. But perhaps she smelt her stable and was in a hurry to get down; for the engine only picked up on two cylinders and the whole contraption felt like shaking itself to bits. I made an attempt to stagger round, just to fulfil the regulations, but the aeroplane had decided otherwise, and so I put her down very hurriedly in the middle of the aerodrome, making one of those accidentally perfect landings which would be so impressive if one could succeed in bringing them off every time.

I taxied in, and was received at the point of the bayonet by a detachment of grinning soldiery, who allowed me to alight on production of my identity card, which was in my handbag in the luggage locker. Happy and rather dazed, I went off and drafted a telegram to my employers: 'G-AFZD delivered Stoney this morning, returning Manchester for G-AFYA.' One day I should write the saga that lay behind that bald statement. For the present let them take it for granted, as I hoped they would. Honour was satisfied and I should have something to tell my grandchildren.

'What did you do in the war, Granny?'
'Why, dears' (casually), 'I was a pilot.'
'Oh, *tell* us . . .!'

Dreaming new dreams, and with an older one fulfilled, I took the train back to Manchester.

SUSAN WOOLFITT
Work on a Narrow Boat for Inland Waterways

One of the clearest impressions I have of those early days is of the exhilarating feeling on waking up each morning, *longing* for what the day would bring forth. For five years life had been a matter of just getting through the day as best one could; rations, mending, fuel restrictions, queues . . . all the innumerable irritations that made up the daily round. Now that was all a thing of the past; there was very little waiting about and so far no signs of rules and regulations . . . instead there was a permanent rush, activity, a job to be done under my nose, here in the boats; a question of ropes, tillers, judgment of eye and hand, movement, novelty and excitement.

For it *was* exciting – it was thrilling and I was enjoying every second of it, even though I was being clumsy and ignorant and inefficient. It was all new: sights, sounds, people, drill, clothes, food . . . the whole pattern had changed and I felt as though an enormous double window had been flung open, allowing me to breathe in great gulps of fresh air, while away in the distance a huge and unknown country lay at my feet.

Another thing, which other housewives will perhaps understand, was the perfectly blissful sensation of being bossed about by someone else, for a

157

change! Thinking for the family all day and every day in war-time left you more exhausted than you knew, till you got away from it. It was really heavenly to be given orders and not be expected – in those early days – to think for myself or make decisions for other people. [. . .]

Have I made it plain what a wonderful job this was, what a superb piece of escapism, while yet doing war-work? There was no time in a beginner's mind for anything but the work on hand; so much learning left no energy or mental space for speculation, no matter how important it may have seemed a month before. Not for us was the misery of listening to the news four times a day and pondering the result of a reported battle; of standing in queues for food; of doing all the housework without domestic help; of trying to keep up one's personal appearance on forty-eight coupons a year, and of all the other little fidgeting things that had got many housewives so completely down.

In case I sound very unpatriotic, I would point out that we *were* conscious that the war was still on, and that in our own line of country we were doing what we could to help win it. If in so doing we could also escape from it what more, short of victory, could anyone ask?

I went home for a week's leave at the end of this trip feeling as if a tornado had blown through my body and mind, tearing away all the cobwebs with which I had been hung for years, and leaving me revitalised and vibrating with life and new hope.

My friends thought I looked very dirty; they were right, I was filthy; my hands were a disgrace and a tribulation, my hair looked as if the mice had been in it, and all my movements were big and clumsy and my table manners appalling. I had put on a lot of weight and my eyes had a great many new, and grimy, lines round them from being constantly screwed up and looking into the distance, and I suspect, though nobody was unkind enough to say it, that I was frightfully hearty.

What the outside world could not see were the pictures in my mind, which will always be there; the warmth in my heart which comes from feeling that you fit into something; the delight in using my whole body to do my job and not only my feet and hands; the comradeship that I had found, the comradeship of people all doing the same difficult work and sharing the same hardships; and finally, the pleasure of resting my tired body in the knowledge that soon I should be going back to start it all once more.

NAOMI MITCHISON
Tractor Driving

Tuesday 15 April 1941

Lachie was taking over Jo [the horse] and the harrow, to go over the field wherever the cultivator had passed. Duncan had done about half [with his tractor]; I went over and he showed me how to work it, and went round with me a couple of times. Then said he must be going, asked if I thought I could take it on. Of course I said I would, though I was doubtful really; but I felt a nasty kind of pleasure because Anne, anyhow, wasn't able! But the first round had jolted me about, so that I almost pitched out; my skirt kept on working up past my knees, and I was always bruising the inside of my knees on the steering wheel; it was like nothing so much as steering a ship in rough weather. The hints were supposed to be filled in, but they were awfully rough to cross. At first I was rather frightened of the slope at the bottom but soon found that the tractor didn't run away. It was a job to turn, one had to make a wide circle usually over the cultivated part. It rocked, and sometimes gathered clods; then I had to back, to get them out of the teeth of the cultivator. Once I stopped the engine accidentally, by not accelerating enough on the slope up. [. . .]

It was grand, though, after a bit, when I decided I wasn't going to fall out after all, and had got reconciled to the bruises, and used to the feel of the engine. The tractor was so powerful, and it was fun making a new break, judging how to turn and so on. I got it all turned over, and then undid the cultivator and turned the tractor, which now bounded along, down the grass edge of the field . . . Lachie picked up my notebook which I had dropped and was about to run over and gave it me, grinning. Gingerly I got out of the gate and turned down the drive. There was no horn, but I was making a lot of noise. I got on to the road and into the top; one is much higher up than in a car, able to look over hedges. I pulled my skirt down and chugged along and wished people could see me, I was so pleased. Several did – the doctor shook his fist at me, he always thinks I'm doing rash things.

DIANA COOPER
Making Camouflage Nets

The making of camouflage-nets seemed to have no appeal for war-hands, with its 1s. 6d. an hour and no music while you worked. This curious and useful task had dumped itself on the top floor of the Army & Navy Stores, so there I clocked in for the full working day. There were erected large open frames of wood like Gobelins tapestry equipment, on which tarred nets were stretched. To each frame were allocated two women, face to face through the trellis, both supplied with foliage-coloured strips of canvas. We would thread and knot them in roughly symmetrical patterns. I began as a time-worker opposite a calm middle-aged lady who, as the long hours ticked peacefully away, told me much of her past life and her aspirations. Older than me, she was far nobler. As war-effort she had resolved to learn Esperanto and hieroglyphs that, thus armed, she might be ready to follow the invading armies across the sea into countries where, not knowing their vulgar tongues, she could still be useful. The rest of us were a bit cretinous, dregs in fact, without zest or much morale.

Efficiency at the hand-destroying job was quickly learnt and I put myself on to piece-work. With no union this was allowed, and oh, the difference in production! The three or four of us on piece-work brought our sandwiches and pots of yoghourt and ate our snacks gaily enough on a bank of bogus woodland. Half our time was spent dodging bottle-necks, pursuing nets and strips that held us up by not appearing when they were wanted. We naturally turned out twice as many 'camouflages' as did lethargic 'timers' who gave most of the day to queueing up for cups of tea or the lavatory, and to snatching ten-minute breaks for a fag on the balcony, generally falling into a watch and thence into a weakness.

DOROTHEA RUSSELL
Music for All

One day in 1940 a friend told me that the Air Force men from the Canal on leave in Cairo usually returned before their leave had expired because Cairo was a hateful place and there was nothing to do there. He said: 'You have done nothing for these men.' Having opened the first Welfare Club very early in the War I was rather piqued and said that I thought we had done a lot, but he replied: 'Nothing but food, lunch and beer, buns and tea; these are intelligent men, they want something for the mind.' So I said: 'All right, I'll do something.'

It seemed to me that we had to give men what they could not find already in Cairo, and that was quiet, and something to occupy their time. Men did not want to sight-see or to walk the streets all day or go to variety shows every night. The existing clubs, except for one excellent library, were all overcrowded and mostly (including my own Tipperary) trying to be as cheap as possible. I planned to have a centre entirely cultural and high-brow, with classical music its main attraction and with all the amenities of a first class London or provincial-town club under one roof on which a man could base himself for the day.

I believed that men wanted comfort and homeliness combined with attractive surroundings and above all quiet and space, and that they would willingly pay for this. An entrance fee would keep out the merely curious. And it was to be for all ranks, men and women, and their guests. There was a great deal of opposition to this in the more conventional army circles, but I knew what this would mean, especially to Imperial and Colonial troops, and eventually I was given a free hand. I called the club 'Music for All.'

At first, the Executive Committee of the Co-ordinating Council, which had the spending of the British Colony's War Fund, turned it down. They said it was a lovely idea, but quite unpractical, it would never work, they could not subsidise such a club for a mere couple of hundred men a week! (nearly a *million and a half* have been through 'Music for All', and over 3,000 men have visited it in one day). They said I could not find a building, that I could not get an audience, nor the musicians, nor, they added, could I possibly run it. They would have to get a first class man out from home on a large salary! They simply hated to disappoint me but it could never be a success.

I did not despair, but the more I thought about it the more sure I was that my scheme was what was wanted and that if only I could get the money it would succeed. I cast around to see from where the finance would be forthcoming, but I am not one of those people who can persuade others to put up money for their schemes. I returned to the charge and this time decided to try General Auchinleck. I knew that if I approached him in the ordinary way he would be bound to refer the matter to my own masters again, so I asked him to dine one night and got him so interested that he told me to send my scheme and budget in to him, and a fortnight later I received a letter saying he had given orders for the necessary credit. I asked for £5,000 and spent £20,000.

Mrs Besly (who has worked with me since September, 1938) and I went ahead on our great adventure. To start off, we had the most extraordinary piece of luck, for I heard of the one utterly perfect room in all Cairo (holding 730 seats) and within three days of seeing it we had taken it at a large rent and surrender price, for we had to buy out a cinema. Then our troubles started. Everything that could go wrong went wrong, prices doubled, materials became unprocurable, transport non-existent. After seven weeks of gruelling work, gutting, building, furnishing, painting, we were due to open with a Palestine Orchestra concert at 6 p.m. on November 19th, 1941. At midday there was still scaffolding up to the immensely high ceiling and not a chair in the place, but we were ready and led off with a great splash.

For months we had a most anxious time. Our day began at 9 a.m. and generally ended at 11 p.m. for in the beginning we had to be there all day and to attend to everything ourselves. Gradually a staff was formed and trained mainly out of complete amateurs. The only exception was the Musical Director, first a distinguished local musician, later an Air Force man, Clifford Harker, formerly sub-organist of Newcastle Cathedral. We started with only our big Music Room Lounge and a temporary kitchen; we began with a concert every night and a trio which played twice a day, and we went on from event to event till we now have four musical as well as many cultural programmes every day. No one wanted to run our lectures for us till at last the Acting Dean of the American University, Dr Worth Howard, took them over; someone organised chess, someone bridge. Eventually we began a small tentative library in a corner of the Entrance Hall; now this has a large room to itself and has 1,100 books out at a time. My old friend Monsieur Groppi (famous name in Cairo) took on the restaurant at his own risk, and was a staunch supporter through a most anxious and difficult time, telling me not to worry if the restaurant lost money for he would still carry on.

No one can imagine the worry and the anxiety. We were really working in the dark for no one had any experience of such a centre. Were we on the right lines? Was this really what men wanted? Was I right, on insisting on my opinion in the face of the disbelief of almost the whole of the Welfare Council? We felt our way as to what was suited to what day, to what time of the day; the stationary people in Cairo liked one type of thing, leave men another; so many factors had to be carefully balanced. You cannot please everybody and one of the things we had to learn was when to ignore complaints and requests, and when to pay attention to them. We stuck it out in spite of losing £500 a month for the first two months – in spite of the long faces of my Council who used to come and tell me I must have variety, I must have dances, I *must* make it pay. Keeping going in this difficult time was complicated by the extreme fatigue of long hours and much responsibility. Daily returns were scrutinised, analysed, losses were cut, large expenditure embarked on and debt incurred. £20,000 on overheads, over and above running expenses, has all come out of takings up to date. Trial and error succeeded trial and error until at last we arrived at what was really wanted. Tremendous encouragement from the men themselves kept us at it; letters that I shall never forget came to us in the office telling us what 'Music for All' meant to many of them.

A man can spend the whole day here for 7½ d. Once he is inside he goes where he will, listens to what he likes. He pays only for his bath, food and library books. We can pack the hall holding 730 people for gramophone or live music programmes, for a musical lecture, for Chamber music for which at first we could hardly get an audience. Many men have told us that they did not know what classical music was until they came one night out of curiosity, eventually to take out a subscription ticket and to come many days a week. People have heard Britten, Stravinsky, Hindemith, for the first time in 'Music for All.' Many men had never heard an opera until something took them to one of our gramophone opera evenings, and we sometimes have such crowds for these performances that we have to close the main doors two hours before. We have proved that this is the kind of thing people hunger for, that you must not talk down, that you can afford to be very highbrow, and that if you are, you will be a great popular success.

JOYCE GRENFELL
Entertaining the Troops

Jerusalem, Sunday, October 7, 1944

To No. 16 Gen. Hosp. after lunch. Two TB wards. It was good. Hard work in the first one for sound as there were constant alcoves and pillars and one was continually having to move so that they could all see and hear – if possible. Hosps. are my dish all right. I really do know how to do this part of the job, I think. But if only there were more *time*. We could have spent the whole day in each ward talking – telling them about home. One man, from Edinburgh, asked about food. I said it was better there, much. Which is true. He asked me if I was saying so to comfort him – 'propaganda?' or if it was really true? They are wary out here and worried too. Many of the men I sang to yesterday have less than a year to live. They have all been told. No sign of depression, only a rather agonising wideness and clarity of eye that unbuttoned me. A young sailor, a Geordie, sat cross-legged on his

163

bed leaning forward so's not to miss a trick and when he laughed he slapped himself and rocked. Another got such giggles at 'Ernie' that he pulled the sheets over his head to control himself. A surging of feeling pours over me about the whole thing and I wish I knew and could do more. The way they thank one afterwards is undoing. Scotch scones for tea and a visit to a nice depressed Welsh officer from Bangor who said he'd listened in to me. In the last ward, lit by the low sun and therefore lovely to look at, with the men lying and sprawling on red-blanketed beds in a white ward, zinnias burning in bowls at intervals and a dusty green of olive trees seen through the window – in the last ward there was a very young Indian lying alone in a little room at the end. He made a beautiful design – lying on a very white bed hung with snowy mosquito curtains, his lovely face and long boy's arms dark in contrast. He smiled a gentle smile and spoke in perfect English to say it had been 'so nice'. [. . .]

Poona, Saturday, December 9, 1944
Did four shows yesterday. TB officers at midday, surgicals at 2, neuros at 3, and TB other ranks at 6.30. I'd forgotten how heartbreaking this job can be unless one disciplines oneself and keeps things quite clear in one's mind. The first impact here yesterday was a bit much. The last show of the day was in an enormous TB ward. Most of them were able to move up to one end and it wasn't bad for sound. They were a very tragic lot and I was haunted by their unseen homes and families. No sentimental stuff in there. [. . .] Except a request for 'I'll be seeing you'. One can't – or I can't – bear to sing songs like 'Someday' or 'All my tomorrows' to people who have no future.

CLEMENTINE CHURCHILL
from *My Visit to Russia*

It was in the autumn of 1941 that the British Red Cross Aid to Russia Fund was started. The might of the German armies, intoxicated by their victories in Europe, had been flung in wanton aggression against the Russian people on June 22 of that year. We in Britain were filled with admiration at the heroic resistance put up by the men and women – and the children even – of the USSR. We were shocked by the stories of the desolation and misery brought to the brave Russian people by Hitler's hordes. The calculated cruelty and barbarism of the Nazis were carried to new excesses in the invasion of Russia. We wanted to flash a signal of friendship and comradeship across the wastes of subjugated Europe to these men and women in their bitter ordeal. Above all, we were eager to do something practical to relieve their sufferings. Our hearts were with the Russian soldiers and with the civil population of the over-run territories. We knew how grievously the hospital facilities must be taxed. We thought of the numberless wounded lying on the battlefields. When we heard that medical supplies were running short, that doctors and nurses were working until they dropped with fatigue, we guessed what that meant in terms of human suffering.

It was in this mood that the idea of a special appeal for Russia's needs was born. I was proud, indeed, to become founder and head of the Red Cross Aid to Russia Fund. The British people saw in this Fund an opportunity for expressing their emotions of admiration and sympathy for the Russian people in their struggle. By Christmas, 1941, they had contributed £1,000,000. By the end of last year (1944) the Fund exceeded £6,000,000. It is now over £7,000,000.

It represents a great act of practical friendship which must surely affect the relationship of our two countries for many years to come. Friendship is a creative and life-giving quality, and throughout my visit to Russia I was conscious of the wonderful kindliness of feeling towards us which the operations of this Fund has evoked.

Many people in Britain may have looked upon my journey to Russia as the climax and culmination of the work of the Aid to Russia Fund. To me it is only a beginning. I do not mean from a monetary point of view, but as the beginning of a closer relationship between the Soviet Red Cross and the British Red Cross Society. I feel that this is a priceless foundation on which to build for the future. People draw very close to one another through the communion of suffering. Men and women in London and the other blitzed cities of Britain felt a swift, instinctive response to the ordeal of Leningrad and the agony of Stalingrad. We saw how human nature could transcend all the obstacles of different language, different customs and geographical distance when Russian cities and British cities were linked together in a common valour of resistance to the same implacable enemy.

RUMER GODDEN
Every Monday in Calcutta

Every Monday night you may see a queue stretching far out of the doors of a certain RAF canteen in Calcutta. Every Monday night the canteen counters are cleared, except for the urns of tea; everyone is waiting.

Towards half past six a car appears and draws up outside the canteen; from it a lady and Indian servants in white get out and begin to unload trays, plates, bundles, baskets, everything for a cold supper she has brought to serve two hundred men; this is a supper such as she would serve herself to honoured guests in her own house; it is served on her own crockery by herself and her own servants at her own expense in her own way.

The men start to file past the counter when she has set it out with flowers, silver, and bowls and dishes of the beautiful food. The supper begins with cold chicken and ham pie, sliced tongue, sliced beef, potatoes stuffed with cheese, or egg, or tomato; with several kinds of salad and celery; with French rolls and butter. Next there is apple tart and whipped cream or cold coffee soufflé. As the canteen cannot serve food entirely free, a nominal sum of An 1 is charged for a helping. After supper this lady makes coffee in a giant Percolator and sends round with it cream, cakes, éclairs, meringues, cigarettes, and chocolates, while, from a selection of her own records, a gramophone concert is amplified to fill the whole room.

The evening lasts from 6.30 to 9.30 when she packs up and drives away to return again next Monday; and this has been going on since 1942 – every Monday night.

MARY TREVELYAN
Welfare Work with the Soldiers
Belgium 1944

My work is to be in charge of the programme at this hotel, a peace-time luxury hotel called the Hotel Albert 1er, but already known to thousands of soldiers as the Albert. Three times a week four hundred soldiers arrive at the Albert, and four hundred are leaving at the same time, so that we have 1,200 guests in the course of one week. [. . .]

All the men who come here seem quite blissfully happy and are full of praise for what they call 'the wonderful organization.' They immensely appreciate small touches, such as lovely flowers in the lounge, or the tea-time orchestra which plays for three hours daily, or the way the waiters in the dining-hall call them 'sir' and light their cigarettes for them. It is a long time since they have been able to live as individuals, free to do what they like and treated as persons, not as units in a crowd. [. . .]

We are working out some very definite views about sympathy. It is impossible not to be moved by these men and you'll perhaps think I am becoming very sentimental, but all the same I don't believe that we really help them by giving them too much sympathy. Coming here and stopping suddenly, as they do here, has certain dangers, not least because in so short a time they have to go back to the nightmare. Very often a group will pool their experiences for our benefit, as we sit talking over a cup of tea in the evening and we find ourselves surrounded by white-faced men and boys who have lived for months very close to death. I am beginning to find that a small remark as to their toughness, a hint of admiration, not given seriously enough to embarrass them, will make a whole group stiffen up again. I am putting this very badly, but I believe that is one of the small ways in which we can try, in a very amateur way, what I call mental rehabilitation. If we sent them back feeling sorry for themselves, and heaven knows they've every right to be that, we should make things harder instead of easier. Since they are in the thing and are determined to see it through, then they've got to be helped to go back to it with as stout a heart as possible.

Chapter nine

WATCHING, WAITING, PRAYING

In terms of the number of people who lost their lives or were wounded in the Second World War, British casualty figures were low. But that did not lessen the anxiety of all the mothers and wives, sisters and friends. Separation was a fact of war, and there would always be worry for whoever you were separated from, as well as sadness for their absence. The new friendships which women said they enjoyed during the war could be supportive, but in public women's responses to wartime tension tended towards the stiff upper lip, the 'I Cope' which was the FANY motto. Kind offers of sympathy might be rebuffed as women wanted to keep control of their emotions: 'One can't afford to break down often,' observed Clara Milburn as she waited to hear about her son's fate after Dunkirk. Hearing that her husband had been shot down, Esther Terry Wright brusquely rejected the landlady's kind gesture: 'I did not feel that it was her affair at all.' Emotional release had to be temporary and private. Women remarked on the increase of crying in the darkness of the cinema.

Anxiety about the well-being of others was not the only thing which made the war difficult for women to think about. A nation at war must think aggressively, and this does not come easily to women. How to think about the enemy, how to think about forgiveness: these problems exercised women during the war. In this chapter Sybil Dobbie and Margaret Lane contemplate the mothers of dead German and Italian airmen in their 'stricken homes'; Betty Miller meditates on the extraordinary relation we have with our enemies in times of war, and Dorothy L. Sayers concludes her thoughtful essay, 'Forgiveness is a difficult matter.'

Women are supposed to be peace-makers, and Lily Montagu firmly rejected the urge towards hatred and revenge in the aftermath of the raid on her synagogue. With the failure of peace-making, however, many women were troubled by feelings of guilt. They had failed to keep the peace, and were involved in the processes of destruction. Vere Hodgson, a welfare worker attached to a religious community in Holland Park, expressed these feelings when she imagined 'all our ancestors looking down reproachfully saying: "You have failed your trust" '.

168

Words could comfort, offer support, provide expression, give consolation. Special wartime prayers for women were published; poetry and prophecy were popular. Public utterance sometimes came more readily than more personal intimate expressions of feeling. Although women are generally supposed to be better at expressing their emotions than men, women too arrive at a point where words fail. Helen Waddell wrote a beautiful epitaph for her nephew, but the letter of condolence to her sister began with the words 'I can't write.'

CLARA MILBURN
Waiting for News of a Son after Dunkirk

Friday 31 May (1940)

The longest day ever! Every time the telephone rang one expected news. Mrs Carter came in at 10 a.m. to say that she had heard through Major Cox that two days before our men of the 1/7th Battalion Royal Warwickshire Regiment were safe. We were so happy to hear this, but later, on ringing up one and another, we found each had heard something of the kind and no-one seemed to set great store by it. So our spirits went down and down and the day wore slowly on. We worked in the garden and, lest we should not hear the telephone, we gave our big bell to Mrs Biggs at the telephone exchange next to us to ring for us while Kate was out. After supper a walk with Twink in an endeavour to calm and compose oneself in the tranquil fields, so rich in their late spring growth.

Saturday 1 June

Still no news . . .

Wednesday 5 June

A glorious day with a strong cool breeze to temper the heat. We decided to spring-clean the hut in the garden and there came across the little car Alan made and the box of motor trial trophies put away at the beginning of the war. This, on top of a restless night, was too much altogether, and to cry a bit relieved the tension. Mrs Gorton came then, full of sympathy, and her embrace set us both weeping. But it was a case of pulling oneself together. One can't afford to break down often.

Thursday 6 June

Still perfect hot weather. I never remember such a lovely spell, and the mornings are just grand.

The telephone rings at intervals all day with rumours and snippets of news from one or another, but nothing definite about our boys. As we sat down to dinner tonight, very tired and thirsty after digging and hoeing, Mrs Cutler rang up. She is just an acquaintance in Balsall Common whom I knew through billeting. But she said: 'Mrs Milburn, I am going to Olton Monastery tomorrow and I am having candles lit and prayers said for the safe return of your son'. Surprised and touched, I could scarcely answer properly before the voice said 'Goodnight'. The kindness and sympathy everywhere is wonderful. After dinner a rest and then, as we were about to continue our gardening, Harry and Ethel Spencer came, and she and I

170

talked of Nevill and Alan, both thinking of them as our 'little boys' – mothers always do – and wiping away a tear or two. How drawn together we all are these dark days. Tonight, as they left, we all kissed each other like brothers and sisters. It is good to have so many real friends. [. . .]

Friday 7th June
When I was writing a few notes this afternoon I heard Twink bark and a voice called out 'Can I come in?' It was Mrs Winser. She soon told me that they felt they had real confirmation now that Philip is killed, and I felt how splendidly brave and calm she is. So we talked a little together about our boys and she has the feeling that the dreadful anxiety is over and that it is even comforting to know the worst.

Cooper from the garage reports that a man named Smith in Alan's platoon saw him near Dunkirk, but one wants to see the man and hear his story. The 1/7th seem to have held the line against great odds before the real evacuation took place. And so the days go by with hopes rising and falling, the telephone ringing and still no definite or genuine news.

Saturday 8th June
Tales of the gallantry of Dunkirk are still pouring in and the thought of the beach and the men on the open sand dunes waiting, waiting to embark, perhaps for 24 hours and then to be told they will have to wait another 24, is haunting to the imagination. The stories of bombing and machine-gunning are so terrible, with no cover for the troops.

Sunday 9th June
I was up early for church, but disturbed by the very kind questioning of one and another.

A message from Harry Spencer about a man of the 1/7th Bn. R.W.R. at Meriden sent us dashing over there just before supper to get news of Alan from him. The woman from a small shop brought him to talk to us in the car. He saw Alan a fortnight ago and was sure he was a prisoner. The man himself was in the evacuation, but said Alan was probably captured the day before King Leopold's capitulation – May 27th. We went back for supper and then Ethne Green rang up to say that Ivan Woodcock was home and reported that Alan was a prisoner of war and was surprised that we did not know this. Jack went round to see him and gleaned a little more of the same story. Though we dare not take this as authentic, somehow it seemed more hopeful and we went to bed and slept well, thankful for a quiet night. [. . .]

Monday 10th June
A telegram from the War Office arrived saying that Alan's unit reported him as believed missing. This may fit in with the story of the capture. Oh,

171

what a long and weary business it seems. Still we ring up other parents and wives and we are all just hanging on.

Tuesday 11th June

A letter arrived today from Major Cox describing the action in which he thinks it likely Alan and his colleague Purchas (who was wounded) and 40 men were taken prisoner. A farmhouse where Major Cox and his men were taking up station could not be vacated for a moment because of 'murderous machine-gun fire'. Later, after a counter-attack, they went to look for Purchas and Alan and for men who were placed earlier in a house 200 yards away. But nothing was to be seen of them at all, and so it was concluded that they had been taken prisoner.

One's mind seems numbed, and the last day or two I go on, keeping on the surface of things as it were, lest I go down and be drowned. Every moment Alan is in my thoughts, every hour I send out my love to him – and wonder and wonder. This queer unreal world, carrying on in some ways here just as before, with this gorgeous weather and summer heat heartening us, and yet most other things so sombre and heartbreaking. [. . .]

Monday 1st July

The raiders were over last night and I was glad we did not have them. A morning full of household jobs and oddments of tidying, washing and putting away – a typical Monday morning. Still longing to have some word of Alan. Everyone asks and still we say: 'No news.' Always is one thinking of him, wondering whether he still lives and, if so, whether he is well, where he is, what he does all day, what discomforts he is suffering. If . . . if . . . And so the days go by. Always one works and works and occupies oneself from morning till night, getting up at 7.30, breakfast at 8, seeing Jack off at the gates and closing them about 8.40, working in house and garden, going out into the village, walking Twink, once a week going to Leamington, sewing at Berkswell Rectory on Tuesdays, occasional WI and MU meetings, always something to do. [. . .]

Tuesday 16th July

About 5.30 I sauntered rather heavily off through the field at the back to take Twink for his walk. When I was well away, I heard Jack calling and saw him waving to me from the hedge. 'It can't be a telegram about Alan!' I thought, so I crammed that thought back and we met in the middle of the field. 'Kate has just had a telegram over the phone for us from the War Office. Alan is a prisoner of war,' he said. There and then, saying 'Thank God', we embraced each other for sheer joy at the good news. Oh, how delighted we were to hear at last that he is alive – and apparently unwounded.

Well, Twink and I went through the fields and then I came home to telegraph and telephone messages round to all the very kind friends who had so often inquired, or even shown their sympathy by their one expression and then their silence. Everybody has been so sweet and kind, it was almost too much to bear. Even the garage proprietor, Mr Cooper, said: 'We thought a lot of him.' After a very busy evening it is 11.30 and, with a heart full of thankfulness, I hope to sleep.

My darling dear, you are alive!

ESTHER TERRY WRIGHT
A Husband is Shot Down

Perhaps if he had known, S. would have come to the telephone, as I had always imagined someone kindly and discreet would do. As it was, when I rang at midday to see if David was feeling unsettled too, it was an airman who said: "'E's one of the one's o've come down.'

That is how it happens.

I tried saying that I was Mrs Lachasse, hoping for something better, because for all it was a busy morning, that seemed a bad way of breaking news; and so by degrees I found that David was in hospital in a place that sounded like the Highlands of Scotland. If I would ring again in an hour and a half they might be able to tell me more.

I was in the police-station ringing up. I tried to get a car, but no one would help. I told them at the garages that I had a husband who had been shot down, but that made no difference. I managed to find a willing driver at last, and I said I would ring again, then I went and told Mother; and we packed our things.

The little landlady peered up at me with a nervous grin and said: 'I'm sorry about your trouble.' I hope I was not short with her, but I did not feel that it was her affair at all.

I waited until the hour and a half had passed exactly, and this time they sent F. to the telephone. He had been at the party. He was someone I knew. He told me David had come down by parachute and was burnt. They had taken him to hospital and he had been on the table for examination, and that was all they knew. I said to F.: 'He's not going to die or anything?' F. said: 'Nothing like that.'

To leave the subject, I asked F. who else had been shot down. He said nothing, and I cursed myself for being gauche.

Much later on, an Army colonel who had seen it described B.'s end as graphically as anyone could have wished.

After quite a long time I decided that David might be alive, and might even go on living, for all the journey to him was so long. Nothing was very real on that long drive: it was like the morning after a sleepless night, when your senses are doubly alert and yet register very little. I had two packets of cigarettes in the car. Mother sat in front with the driver. Once we stopped and she bought fresh sandwiches, and while we waited for her, I told the driver what our journey was for. He listened to me, and then he told me how he had had to abandon the car that morning to a dive-bombing attack in a main street; and here they both were safe after all.

When we were getting near the hospital I asked Mother if she would mind my going in alone. If there was any drama about, I would see it through better by myself.

Mother had already decided that for herself. I left her in the car, and when she had what news there was, she drove away to find beds for us.

They put me in the master's office and left me alone. There was a letter on the desk addressed to me, and so I read it:

'*Dear Madam,*

'*I am writing to confirm my telephone conversation of this afternoon's date, stating that your husband, Pilot Officer D.W. Lachasse, is very ill in the above Hospital. You may visit at any time you wish to come.*'

On paper, the message was sinister. It did not cheer me at all. It took David from me, just like that, and made him a part of the hospital, and so a part of a government scheme, as the Air Force had never done. I had plenty of time to think things in that hot little office.

After a very long time, the master came in. I had expected something dignified; and here was a little bald North Country man with protruding eyes, and a grocer's confidential manner. I told him that I had seen the letter, and I waited. He said that David was very badly burnt, but 'nothing that won't get better,' he said. He seemed to be sizing me up. He told me how they had watched him come down by parachute that morning, and how the air had been so still that it had taken him twenty minutes to come. And how they had him on the table a quarter of an hour after he landed. I asked tentatively if I might see him. The telephone-bell rang before the little man could answer. Because I was listening acutely, I heard his voice change, as he said very quietly: 'Leave it to me.' He would turn round now and tell me that after all I had come too late. I wished it might have been someone else, and not this funny little man, and I was thinking how I would ask in a hurry if I might see one of the doctors, before he could get the words out and have it all over when, down the telephone, he began describing the morning's excitements: 'It was *hell on earth*!' he boasted.

He rang off at last, and now we went in the strong sun across the courtyard and round a pile of new sandbags into a cool corridor that they darkened. The master told me that we should be here for seven weeks. Then, it seemed an unbearably long time. And yet the implication that we should leave at all was cheering.

We found a doctor in the corridor inside standing as I knew by David's door. The master left us – so that I might be prepared, I knew. The doctor was immensely tall. He wore a navy flannel suit with a loud white stripe, and a bad tie. When he talked, he blinked down at me. He told me, as the master had done, that I should find David purple. I made lighter of that than I felt; and said that I had seen such things, because years before I had had a burnt brother in a lint mask. He said that his eyebrows were gone; and in the same mood of unreal brightness that had prompted my question to F. on the telephone, I made some fatuous remark about how proud he had been of those eyebrows. But successful conversation was surely not expected of me, and after all this, I was let into the room.

David was lying on the bed. The newness of his accident was a sensation in the room. He himself was something brand new and very real. I saw him just for a moment, his face and his arms purple with fresh dye, and very swollen. I thought he had no eyes; and I thought they had not told me that, but had left me to find out quietly for myself; and, curiously, how wise they were. Behind all this was David. I saw then, as I cannot see now, how we should manage his blindness. (The Irish colonel spat out later on, at his lunch-table, that without his eyes he would have been better dead.) The master was in the doorway, and I looked for his permission, and kissed David, and said the things I had ready to say. His lips were very red against the purple.

He told me how the hood had jammed and trapped him; and how after a long time he had remembered me, and got it open. N.R. said afterwards that it could not have been more than six seconds.

A nurse brought the wings and buttons and the buckle off his tunic. I made out a receipt for them and signed it; and she said it was all right and took it away. A wire came to say that I was on my way. There was a baby crying all the time. The sunlight was white and harsh outside the window. The baby cried and cried. After a time I got up and closed the window, and made the room my home.

AUDREY DEACON
A Wren's Diary, 1944

Monday 1 May.
Today I was sent for from Tidworth Military Families Hospital where
Terry[1] has been taken after an accident. When I arrived I found he had been
hit in the neck by a splinter from a PIAT[2] during a practice shoot. It struck
the carotid artery, and he lost a lot of blood. They gave him a transfusion,
but his condition was still serious. [. . .]

(After initially making a good recovery and going home to Plymouth on
convalescent leave, Terry was suddenly taken ill and had to be operated on
for a blood clot on the brain.)

Sunday 5 June
I went in on my way home: he was still not out of the anaesthetic. I rang
up about quarter past nine: Sister said his condition was critical and could
not well be worse, and asked me to spend the night at the hospital. I went
back again with Warick, and saw Terry for a moment. He looked rather
dreadful, with his hair shaved off, and his face very white. He was still not
conscious, but they said he was coming round from the anaesthetic. He was
breathing very heavily.

Monday 6 June
I slept in an empty ward – or rather stayed awake most of the time. Soon after
six I was brought a cup of tea, and then Sister came in and said he was worse,
especially during the last hour. I went down and saw him: he was terribly
white, and his breathing was terrifying – a kind of snort on the in breath and
a rattle on the out – quick and short, and very loud.

For a few moments I felt faint, but afterwards I found Sister and got her
to ask the RSO[3] to see him again. He told me that Terry's condition was
very grave. Sister rang up his home and mine.

I went back and dressed. Soon after that I was told that Warick had
arrived. We waited a little, and then Sister asked us to go to the ward. Then
she said 'I'm afraid he has just died.' He had never regained consciousness.

We came home then.

Everybody has been very kind. The SO[4] sent Joy out to say how sorry
they all were.

But it doesn't help. I just don't know how to start again. I had looked
to Terry for support and comfort for so long: absolutely everything was

1. Her husband of a year.
2. Anti-tank projectile.
3. Resident Surgical Officer.
4. Signal Officer.

bound up with him. He was so very sweet: he always understood, whatever I said.

MARY BROOKES
'Missing – Believed Killed'

On 18 November 1940 I received a telegram stating that the *Beaverford* had been sunk and that my husband was reported 'Missing – believed killed'. At that time I was living with his mother and sister at Weybridge and for many weeks we tuned in to Radio Hamburg at 7.30 each night. This was because the traitor William Joyce, nick-named Lord Haw-Haw, broadcast a daily propaganda talk in English, finishing with a list of British ships sunk by the Germans and names of survivors who had been picked up and taken prisoners of war. The radio reception was poor but we forced ourselves to listen to that detestable voice in desperate hope.

My Christmas 1940 was bleak and made even worse by a postal delivery on Christmas Eve of a returned batch of my own letters to my husband. These had arrived in Canada too late for him to have received them before the ship sailed for home. [. . .]

11.10.43 It was at this time that I finally had to come to terms with the fact that my husband had really died in the *Beaverford* sinking. This came about due to a newspaper article in a London evening paper being sent to me by a friend. We seldom saw any newspapers at this time, but relied on the radio or on the cinema newsreels to keep up with current events. The article described the last desperate fight and the sinking of the *Beaverford* as witnessed by the Captain of the last escaping ship of the convoy. Apparently the naval escort, i.e. the *Jervis Bay* had gone down gallantly twenty minutes after the initial German attack. The *Beaverford*, with its paltry few guns had kept the German raider at bay for five hours, enabling most of the convoy to escape before being sunk by a direct hit by the German raider.

The last official notification, 29/3/41, from the General Register and Record Office of Shipping and Seamen had stated that 'Warwick T. Brookes is supposed to have died on November 5 1940.' That word SUPPOSED had sustained my hopes, for never at any time had I been informed that, quite categorically, all the crew had perished. This news in 1943 had quite a shattering effect on my morale and I felt unable to consider further courses of any kind.* I was granted nine days compassionate leave and told to think about my future.

It was pure coincidence that during my leave I was invited, together with my husband's mother and sister, to attend a memorial service for the crew of the *Beaverford* at Downhills Central School, Tottenham. This was held because the ship had been adopted by the school and my husband had been in charge of correspondence between the crew and the children. Early in 1939 I had visited the school with him and met the staff and pupils.

HELEN WADDELL
On the Death of a Nephew
1942

My darling – and my darling Mollie who was his mother too –.

I can't write. He sits waiting on the settee in O.K.'s room, he walks into the Escargot, he watches O.K. make salad dressing, he stands in the hall getting into his overcoat, always that tilt at the corner of his eyelid, that far-back smiling.

. . . The wire came about the same time as the last news about Jack, we were still at the office, just about to go home. I did two things which have gone to *The Times*, but I am so scared you will hate them. The notice is just as Daddy wished, but I added two lines from the Greek anthology:

'Morning star among the living:
Evening star among the dead.'

Then I began writing a note to go under 'Fallen Officers' but the only way I could do it to make it effective seemed to me to link it with his friend. F.A. Voigt said that with one so young, it seemed to him better to dwell rather on the two comrades-in-arms, and somehow I thought Willie McGrath had no one to speak for him. Do forgive me if you think I have let you down.

---

* Mary Brookes was due to go on an ATS course.

MARGARET LANE
The Wreckage Wind
1944

We heard that the body of a German airman had been washed up some-where near Slyne Head.* Word went along the beaches, but the coast-guards were prompt and Slyne Head is difficult to reach when the big winds are blowing, so nobody saw the body taken up or knew what had become of it. It was only one of the many strange, useless or macabre objects which come in with the wreckage wind from the south-west. Perhaps a week after the news of the drowned man we heard that he had been buried in the Protestant cemetery. Nobody took much interest. The Protestant cemetery is a dead area, without character; nobody goes there, and you could spend years in the place without once seeing the derelict gates unlocked or hearing that the silent church had even been opened. The graveyard itself is only a handful of graves, with here and there is a for-bidding granite memorial to prove that Protestants have actually lived and died. Nobody ever cuts the grass; it is neglected; living attention is focused on the Catholic church at the other end of the village, and local funerals wind out to the ancient rabbit-rotten sandy graveyard at the edge of the beach. Looking over the stone wall one could hardly tell that the shaggy turf had been disturbed and another mound added, and soon the tough sea grass and the nettles together were covering the scars.

Some time later, when we were buying sago and bootlaces in the post office, a smart green motor car scattered the chickens in the doorway and a young chauffeur in foreign-looking uniform came in and saluted Mrs Doyle at her counter. In polite unnatural English he confirmed the name of the village and then begged to be directed to the Protestant cemetery. He had passed it, Mrs Doyle said, and she went outside the door with him and pointed. The car reversed, giving us a view of a massive muffled figure in the back seat, and slid smoothly away down the road by which it had come.

'That would be the German Minister,' said Mrs Doyle. 'That was a German uniform he was wearing.'

'Oh, surely that was a chauffeur, Mrs Doyle? Perhaps the Minister is the one in the back of the car.'

'Ah, not at all. That was a woman he had with him, a big, stout woman. Never fear, that was the Minister himself in his German uniform. He will be visiting the grave.'

Amused by our ignorance she showed her yellow teeth at us and retired into her lair behind the post office partition.

* On the west coast of Ireland, which was neutral in the Second World War.

Curious, we went into the sun-bright road and stared after the green car. At the cemetery gate the chauffeur had opened the door for a big man in a long overcoat, and now had reached a large white cardboard box out of the boot and was opening that, too. What could they be doing? We idled shamefacedly after them, wheeling our bicycles, turned down the rough track at the corner of the cemetery and came to a casual standstill at a gap in the wall.

Someone, perhaps the old woman from the cottage opposite, had unlocked the gate, for the big man and his chauffeur were inside, stepping irresolutely about in the rough grass with an air of distaste. The chauffeur carried a flat laurel wreath tied with a red ribbon in his left hand. Presently they found what they were looking for, and the chauffeur handed the wreath to the big man and fell back several paces. The man laid the wreath on the hummock, removed his hat for a second, put it on again, unbuttoned the breast of his overcoat and drew out a small flat camera suspended round his neck on a leather strap. The chauffeur strolled away and smoked a cigarette in the road.

The big man fiddled with his camera for a bit and held it up to his eye. Then he snapped up the leather case and went back to the car, buttoning his coat. The chauffeur trod on his cigarette and opened the door, and in a moment we heard it slam and saw the car slide off and grow small along the flat, white, narrow road and finally lose itself in the low-lying purple and green distance between the potato-fields and the sea.

When everything was quite still again, and we were fairly sure that nobody would see us, we climbed through the gap in the wall and went with a sense of guilt to look at the grave. I think we had a vague feeling that we should discover something; that there would be a card tied to the wreath, perhaps, with a name on it; that the diplomat with the camera must have left some clue to identify the nameless body beneath the grass. But no: there was nothing tied to the wreath but the red ribbon. Had these official visitors, then, known no more of him than we did?

We stood and stared at the grave in uneasy silence. How strange, how lonely, how cold to lie in the indifferent Protestant cemetery to which the sea has brought you. We are your mourners, alien, impersonal; we do not know you. We suppose only that you were young; that you were lost, and saw the strange coast with dismay, perhaps with horror; that you knew the coldness of its sea before you died, and were carried unresisting into the long weeds and the rocks, guided by the wreckage wind through the fringed barrier. Nobody will ever know your thoughts; and in some German home, eventually, that snapshot will arrive, bearing its routine message, and be slid slowly under the glass of a photograph on the mantelpiece – the photograph of a young man in uniform who may not even be you, but what difference will that make? He will be dead like you – you will have

180

that in common. The same symbol will serve to console any mother or wife. It will comfort them to have proof of your Protestant burial.

SYBIL DOBBIE
Air Raids on Malta

One day a small metal receptacle, tightly screwed up, came down on a little parachute during a raid. Round the edge of it was printed in English, 'We promise on our honour that there is no high explosive in this.' A guard was therefore immediately mounted near it and a summons sent to the bomb-disposal officer, but when it was opened up the promise proved to be true, for it contained only some shaving things, a spongebag, tooth-brush, one or two photographs and personal things, and the identity card of a certain German pilot shot down over Malta a few days before. There was also a note in English, saying, 'Please give these to Lieutenant – and tell him not to go flying again without his identity card.' It was a strange, almost schoolboyish gesture from the dour and serious-minded Luftwaffe. Only they did not know that their comrade had been killed in the battle.

In the course of my work I used to see a good many communications from the International Red Cross asking for information about German and Italian airmen missing after attacks on Malta. These communications proved more than anything else could do how many more planes were failing to return to Sicily than we had known, for very rarely could the missing men be identified. Occasionally it was known they had been killed. Such information as could be collected was sent to the Red Cross, but through the bare typewritten form one seemed to catch glimpses of stricken homes, of heart-broken, waiting wives and mothers. And one could imagine similar forms being sent to Germany and Italy and containing the names of British airmen. All over the world, in many languages, that cry is going up: 'Where is he? What happened to him? I could bear anything if only I *knew*.' The causes of war are national, financial, commercial, what you will. But the results of war, the pain and sorrow and bereavement, are international and universal.

BETTY MILLER
Meditations of a Fifth Columnist

Love your enemies is one of those precepts whose motive force, like a foreign currency, is instantly frozen in time of war. The State demands of us, an additional income-tax as it were, a ready and sustained flow of hatred. This emotional expenditure is required of us at a time when we are, in fact, and at other levels of consciousness, pre-eminently occupied with the thought of the enemy: actively, or through the youthful limbs of sons or brothers, seeking him out; searching him, body and spirit, in order to grapple with him in the passionate embrace, the bitter partnership of death. He is, in other words (and this is the reverse of the official medallion) closer to us, more intimately a part of our own being during time of war than at any other period in our relationship with him. It is when we are officially at war, therefore, that we are, unofficially, most susceptible to each other's influence. No longer a mere business or cultural acquaintance, already the illicit issue of our union – our mutual progeny of dead, our still-born – lie farmed out in their cemeteries: honoured by the living: by life, peremptorily disowned.

EVELYN UNDERHILL
Two War-Time Prayers

Let us so confess to God with shame our own great share in the guilt of war; our pride and possessiveness; our spirit of criticism and lack of generosity; our unworthy fears and suspicions; all that prevents the spread of love and the triumph of his peace; and let us ask for his forgiveness.

O Lord Jesus Christ, because thou hast taught us to love our enemies, we pray for all the German people. Change the hearts of those who rule them. Show them thy will, and turn their minds to justice, truth and peace. Have pity on them in all that they must suffer in this war. Especially we pray for all the children of Germany, to thee who didst become a child for our sake. Keep them by thy power and grant that they may grow up into a new world of peace and brotherly love; for thy Name's sake. Amen.

LILY MONTAGU
In Memory of Our Dead

As I left Whitefields* after our beautiful service on Saturday April 19th, a man pressed my hand in a kindly sympathetic way, and said, 'All right, Miss Montagu, we shall have our revenge!' If he meant that a Berlin woman who had given her life to some piece of work for nearly fifty years should experience my kind of heartache when she saw the outward shell destroyed in a few minutes, if he meant that another woman should see the place shattered which had echoed night after night for twenty-seven years with the joyous sounds of young people bent on recreation and education, and revelling in activity; if he meant this, then indeed he offered me a poor form of consolation. In memory of our dead, I would urge you to cast hatred out of your hearts, as hatred is destructive, and through hatred we lose our standards and aspirations. We love our country, our England, and insist that she must never do the dastardly things which the Nazis are doing today. If she does yield to the popular cries of revenge, she will have to lower her standards, until they cannot be distinguished from Nazi standards. Not so can our dear ones be honoured. By their graves, we dedicate ourselves to the uplifting of our thoughts and feelings, to the purification of our conduct, to the furthering of deeds of love, mercy and goodness.

DOROTHY L. SAYERS
Forgiveness and the Enemy
1941

Forgiveness is a very difficult matter. [. . .] Are there not crimes which are unforgivable? or which, we at any rate, find we cannot bring ourselves to forgive? At the present moment, that is a question which we are bound to ask ourselves. And it is here, especially, that we must make a great effort to clear our minds of clutter. The issue is not really affected by arguments about who began first, or whether bombs or blockade are the

* Whitefields Tabernacle, the London church where Lily Montagu held religious services after her synagogue was bombed and twenty-seven members killed.

183

more legitimate weapon to use against women and children, or whether a civilian is a military objective; nor need we object that no amount of forgiveness will do away with the consequences of the crimes – since we have already seen that forgiveness is not incompatible with consequence. The real question is this: When the war comes to an end, is there going to be anything in our minds, or in the minds of the enemy, that will prevent the re-establishment of a right relationship? That relationship need not necessarily be one of equal power on either side, and it need not exclude proper preventive measures against a renewal of the conflict – those considerations are again irrelevant. Are there any crimes that in themselves make forgiveness and right relations impossible? [. . .]

I do not know that we are in any position to judge our neighbours. But let us suppose that we ourselves are. [. . .] ready to greet repentance with open arms and re-establish with our enemies a relationship in which old wrongs are as though they had never been. What are we to do with those who cannot accept pardon when it is offered? And with those who have been corrupted from the cradle? Here, if anywhere, is the unforgivable – not in murdered citizens, ruined homes, broken churches, fire, sword, famine, pestilence, tortures, concentration camps and the enslavement of populations, but in the corruption of a whole generation, brought up to take a devil of destruction for the God of creation and to dedicate their noblest powers to the worship of that savage altar. If for the guilty there remains only the judgment of the millstone and the deep sea, we still have to ask ourselves: What are we to do with these innocents? [. . .] Forgiveness is a difficult matter, and no man living is wholly innocent or wholly guilty.

Chapter ten

LIVING THROUGH THE WAR

Losses at sea, in North Africa and the Far East meant that the middle years of the war saw many setbacks abroad. At home rationing arrived. Food rationing had begun in 1940, a complicated system of coupons and points which reached its tightest in 1942. People did not go hungry, but food could be monotonous and stodgy.

Clothes rationing started in June 1941, with the Board of Trade directing a patronising campaign at women. 'One of its officials,' wrote Mollie Panter-Downes for the *New Yorker*, 'goes on the air now and then in a dialogue with a young lady announcer of the BBC, in which he makes a point of such admonitions as "Cut your cloth according to your coupons" and "Never coupon today what you can put off till tomorrow." The young lady always acts as a stooge who has done all the wrong things, frittering away her precious coupons on nonessentials like bathing suits.' In 1942 'Austerity Regulations' limited shapes, designs and trimmings in order to save textiles, and Utility clothes were introduced to ensure that there was enough reasonable clothing at controlled prices. Home dress-making became popular – or perhaps necessary would be more accurate – and skirt lengths crept up. Waiting to meet her husband at the station at the end of the war, Diana Hopkinson caught a glimpse of herself in a long mirror: 'I saw that my petticoat showed at least three inches below my frock. Skirts had grown so much shorter since I had last worn it.'

British women recognized that, compared to the suffering on mainland Europe, their trials were small. For most it was a time not so much of severe hardship as of tiredness and boredom – 'that unspectacular product of war' as Hilary Wayne called it – and of the expense of an unusual amount of effort just to keep going. 'Nothing happens easily any more,' wrote Rebecca West.

Women were keen to chronicle all the large and especially the small changes of wartime life as they happened. Mollie Panter-Downes sent a series of fortnightly reports to the *New Yorker* throughout the war, superb 'Letters from London' which bring the daily details of war vividly to life.

Gertrude Stein's diary of life in Occupied France had to be kept hidden, and await the end of the war for publication.

Women recorded the shifts in domestic and social behaviour, usually with tolerance and sometimes with hope for the future, as Winifred Williams showed in her enthusiastic conversion to British Restaurants. Later accounts of wartime Britain might be more open about disaffection or crime, or more direct in criticising the way the country was being run. The writing of the time had the particular task of getting its writer and readers *through* that time. How it set about doing that is part of its meaning for us now.

NELLA LAST
The Changes War Brings to Women

Thursday, 14 March 1940

I reflected tonight on the changes the war had brought. I always used to worry and flutter round when I saw my husband working up for a mood; but now I just say calmly, 'Really dear, you *should* try and act as if you were a grown man and not a child of ten, and if you want to be awkward, I shall go out – ALONE!' I told him he had better take his lunch on Thursday, and several times I've not had tea quite ready when he has come in, on a Tuesday or Thursday, and I've felt quite unconcerned. He told me rather wistfully I was 'not so sweet' since I'd been down at the Centre, and I said, 'Well! Who wants a woman of fifty to be sweet, anyway? And besides, I suit *me a lot* better!'

Arthur said last time he was here that I had altered, and when I asked how, he said, 'You are like your photo taken a year last Christmas. It was quite a good photo except for the look in the eyes, which looked sad' – I've always had 'laughing eyes'. I notice the same rather subdued look in a lot of women's eyes. And yet we laugh a lot at the Centre, and I know I laugh and clown more than I've done since I was a girl. Perhaps the 'quiet look' is a hangover from nights when we lie quiet and still, and all the worries and unhappy thoughts we have put away in the day come and bring all their friends and relations!

Monday, 18 March 1940

As the account of the Fins' exodus came over the wireless, I looked round at my cushions, lampshades and rug with their uncounted hours of effort, at Gran's old tea-set in the cabinet, at my bits of brass and the bowl of golden yellow tulips, and thought of the anguish of mind it would be for me to crowd a few essentials on to a handcart and leave my bits of treasures. My heart ached for the Finnish women and such a WHY? seemed to wrap me round. I think my mind must be a bit limited, for I always seem to think – or try to think – of cause and effect, but the dreadfulness of the punishment meted out to Poles and Fins and Jews leaves me feeling so puzzled.

Sometimes I find myself admiring afresh my smooth panelled hall, my wide windows, my honey-coloured tiled fireplace, with a wonder which is like reverence that I can keep them, while other women – no different from me – see ruin and desolation to their loved homes. It's so *wrong*. The thought of all the suffering and loss makes me feel so little and futile, for it would take an army of workers and helpers to do much to help. I will be thankful when our airplane carrier goes. It's an ever-present care and worry in all our minds, for there is an unspoken fear that bombers will come to try and destroy it, and the spoken hope is that it gets away safely without being torpedoed or mined. [. . .]

Sunday, 29 November 1942
I listened to Churchill with a shadow on my heart. It's bad enough to think privately all that he said, without hearing it on the wireless – to see the long, hard and bitter road, to feel the shadows deepen rather than lighten, to envy the ones who think that Germany will collapse in the spring, to have in mind always the slave labour, the resources of rich Europe, to remember Goebbels' words that whoever starved, it would not be Germany. I thought of all the boys and men out East. How long will it be before they come home? It's bad enough for mothers – but what of the young wives? I felt my hands go clammy and damp, and I put my toy rabbit down. I looked at his foolish little face, such an odd weapon to be fighting with. I never thought my dollies and soft toys could be used in my war-time scheme of life. I don't envy people with money as I used to do, for most of them want it all for themselves; it's best to have a little gift of making things. Three and a half-ton bombs on Italy. I'm sorry it has to be. I like Italian people. I wonder what would happen if they revolted. I've read a lot of nasty things about the Fascists, and I wonder if there are a lot in comparison to the 'nice' Italians. [. . .]

Saturday, 5 December 1942
One of our helpers had a WAAF call for her, who used to be billeted with her before being moved into huts. She was such a nice refined girl, evidently well educated, and we chatted for a while. I said I hoped they had heating in the hut. She said, 'Ah yes, but not officially – we pinch the coal off a nearby dump.' We laughed, and then she went on, 'I'm rather shocked, really, at my attitude to other people's property – at the light "what's yours is mine" attitude of *all* of us – from coal to clean knickers, from handker-chiefs to stamps, and so on. If we haven't anything of our own, we just take someone else's!' It set me on a train of thought. I thought of all the good scrubbing-brushes and pan-brushes that had gone from the canteen, and the soap from the Centre.

One thing led to another, and I thought of other little changes, both in myself and friends. Of our slaphappy way of 'doing the bits that showed most', making beds soon after rising, without the turning and airing we once thought so needful: now, in my rush out on two mornings a week, they are lucky to be straightened. I saw pillow-slips and towels, even under-clothes, scrutinised to see if they were *quite* soiled – or would they do another day, or week? I saw myself putting on a dress, working all day at the Centre and then having neither time nor energy to change when I got in – just a quick wash, and a house-dress in a gay print, as I cooked tea. I thought of a stack of dirty crocks to tackle after tea, of pictures and furniture that were once polished every week, and now got done when I had the time. I wondered if people would *ever* go back to the old ways. I cannot see women settling to trivial ways – women who have done worthwhile things.

E. DOREEN IDLE
Social Life in the East End of London

Through the exigencies of domestic affairs certain social conventions have been broken down. Neighbours of either sex frequently throw in their lot together. A woman will live with her neighbour who is a small shopkeeper, looking after his domestic affairs; a man and a woman who work together during the day will also share their home arrangements and their shelter; those who are the sole remaining members of evacuated families pool their domestic resources. There are innumerable variations on this kind of association, and from what I have seen, they are extremely happy and successful, founded as they are on those qualities of neighbourliness which are only to be found at their best among the working classes. [. . .]

Shops now serve a more distinctly recreational function than before in the sparsely populated districts, for old women collect there, pull out the boxes and sit down for a chat, whether they have shopping to do or not. And I am told that the isolation and lack of local event during the summer of 1941 reduced topics of conversation to the rock bottom of monotony.

CORRESPONDENCE IN
TIME AND TIDE

Cigarettes – for Men Only

July 5 1941

SIR: While bicycling round the town this afternoon, I saw a placard in tobacconist's window, in fact three placards all screaming to the populace that Gentlemen only will be served with cigarettes.

Boiling with rage I returned to duty (in a boys' school where I teach the rising male generation) and entered the common room. Amid complacent laughter the masters told me that this action was not only legal but patriotic.

Hitherto I have suffered no disadvantage from being a woman, but today my eyes have been opened to the ignorant prejudices still abroad, but it would seem that often women themselves are to blame for taking them as a matter of course. I know many who do. The matron and I (both non-smokers but neither of us a bitch in a manger) hope to end this state of affairs here.

I am, etc.,

SCHOOLIE

(There is no official backing for an improvized tobacco rationing system which precludes women from buying cigarettes. Where individual tobacconists take it upon themselves to make this differentiation it is to be hoped that the local population will take steps to put an end to it with as much vigour as our correspondent. The practice is all the more unattractive for being Nazi-inspired. In Germany women *are* unable to buy cigarettes. The veto is a characteristic example of the position of women under the Nazi régime. – EDITOR, *TIME AND TIDE*.)

MOLLIE PANTER-DOWNES
Rationing

June 1 1941

Something unforeseen to the public was sprung this morning when the President of the Board of Trade came on the air to announce the imminent rationing of clothes, thereby ruining the Sunday-breakfast appetites of millions of women who regretted not having bought that little outfit they'd dithered about the other day. Sixty-six coupons are to be the basic ration for twelve months, no matter where you shop, which sounds all right until you realize that you must fork out, for example, seven coupons just for a washable frock and five for a sweater. To get a pair of pants, a man will have to turn in eight; if he's a Scot and fancies a kilt, he need part with only six. It was prosaically announced that the spare page of margarine coupons in the Englishman's food-ration book is to be used for clothing until the authorities get around to issuing separate clothing books, which should give couturiers an elegant shudder. No one quite knows how this is going to work out or how the officials plan to prevent a bootleg smock or two from changing hands quietly under the counter, but it is certain that this new step will mean the writing off of hundreds of small businesses which have bravely struggled along against the blitz and the disappearance of their best clients to the country.

The country is where millions of unmoneyed as well as moneyed Londoners usually count on going for an annual Whitmonday excursion, but this year a stroll to look at the sheepshearing now giving a bucolic air to Hyde Park is probably the nearest most will get to it. The usual jaunts to the seaside are impossible, even for those who can take the time off, because most accessible bits of ocean are in defence areas prohibited to casual tripper traffic, which, anyway, has been severely curtailed by the recent further cut in the gasoline ration. It is hoped by aggrieved civilians that something equally tough is going to be done about Army gasoline, which apparently isn't stinted, judging by the sorties of lorries sent on unessential journeys that a dispatch rider on a motorcycle could perform just as well at a fraction of the expense for fuel.

Motorists, gloomily counting their diminished gasoline coupons this month, were cheered by finding a memorandum from the Ministry of Transport tucked inside the book. It gives instructions for the immobilization of cars in the event of invasion. The magneto and the fuel-injection pump must be smashed with a hammer, and in case non-mechanical owners should stand gaping and wondering which of the silly-looking things to smash first, the pamphlet recommends gently that 'they should go to the nearest garage at once to find out.'

August 10
The classic English topic of conversation, the weather, has vanished for the duration and now would be good for animated chat only in the event of a brisk Biblical shower – of oranges, cheese, cornflakes, and prunes instead of manna. Everyone talks about food. An astonishing amount of people's time is occupied by discussing ways and means of making rations go further, thinking up ingenious substitutes for unprocurable commodities,

and trying to scrounge a little extra of whatever luxury one particularly yearns for. Nearly everybody now and then finds himself thinking of some kind of food to which in peacetime he never gave a second thought. Strong men, for instance, who normally wouldn't touch a piece of candy from one end of the year to the other now brood over the idea of milk chocolate with morbid passion. No matter how comparatively well one eats, deficiencies in diet lead to occasional empty moments which the individual mentally fills in to his own liking with filet mignon, plumcake, or a dish of ham and eggs.

Quite a lot of Americans in London, who earlier in the war irritably curbed a tendency of anxious families at home to shower them with things like tinned butter, are wishing they hadn't been so hasty. Since Americans here are not allowed to write home and ask for what they want, all they can do is pen effusive thanks for the delicious ham or whatever (which actually was never sent) and trust to their dear ones' sagacity to put two and two together. The official attitude toward food parcels is divided between reluctance to check these friendly impulses and a wish that precious shipping space could be left clear for bulk consignments, which would benefit the many instead of the few.

On the whole, the food situation, although it's far from good, is a long way from being desperate. The average number of calories which each member of the population consumed during the first year of the war was only one per cent lower than it was in peacetime and it is expected that it will be no lower this year. Those feelings of emptiness are more the result of turning rather suddenly to a thinner diet; obviously, a nation which once consumed a lot of meat and fats can't switch abruptly to vegetables and cereals without experiencing discomfort under the waistband. The urban poor come off the worst, owing to their distaste for such substitutes (the unshakable aversion of cockney evacuees to green-stuffs is the bane of many a communal feeding centre) and to their habitual partiality for deli-cacies like tinned salmon, condensed milk, and endless cups of tea, all of which are difficult or impossible to procure. The rural poor do a good deal better because they grow a lot of vegetables, generally keep a few chickens, and poach a rabbit or two when they're lucky. The more moneyed classes are able to buy trimmings to furbish up the dull, basic necessities, but anything substantial beyond those necessities is becoming increasingly hard to come by, money or no.

The shelves of, say, Fortnum & Mason are dazzling at first sight, but closer inspection reveals that the bulk of the displays consists of sauces, chutneys, and other condiments, which don't go far toward assuaging the appetite unless accompanied by a good slab of fish, flesh, or fowl. At the moment, fowls have practically disappeared from legal markets because poultry farmers prefer to sell at black-market prices rather than at the government-controlled figure. Fish is expensive, and the meat ration is such that a small family probably gets no more than a modest joint once a week. Horse-flesh is on sale, ostensibly for dogs, but possibly it appears incognito in many of the cooked foods which shops offer for human consumption. Eggs are rationed at the rate of one a week to a person and often turn up stamped with a cryptic blue hieroglyph which pessimists say is a Chinese character indicative of age. Vegetables are plentiful; Londoners dug for victory so manfully this spring that scarlet runners in every back yard seem to be trying to strangle the house, and for the time being there is a greater danger of being hit by a marrow falling off the roof of an air-raid shelter than of being struck by a bomb. Among unrationed foods, the following are likely to elicit a regretful no from one's shopkeeper: breakfast cereals, tinned and dried fruits, olive oil, tinned fish and soups, jellies, biscuits, lemons, lime juice, honey, chocolate, and macaroni and every other variety of pasta.

Now that marketing has become one long dialogue of queries and negative answers, the job of feeding a family is one which requires ingenuity, stamina, and endless time. The time factor has been sympathetically studied by the authorities in their drive to get women into line in the war industries. Some of the factories solve the problem by letting married women off for a couple of hours during the morning so that they can do their household shopping. In certain towns, food shops are trying out a scheme of reserving a proportion of their goods for war workers who can only get in late and would otherwise find everything sold out. The housekeeping difficulties of families in which both husband and wife go to work every day are simplified to some extent by the government-run chain of British Restaurants, of which there are now six hundred operating – two hundred and fifty of them in the London area – and about four hundred more under way. These restaurants, which were originally planned for bombed-out people and workingmen who didn't have the use of a works canteen, serve a good meal of meat, dessert, and a cup of tea for a shilling. The amount of meat served to customers at a British Restaurant or at a West End place like the Savoy is the same one-penny-worth a head, though the Savoy may add a few champignons.

Lately, there has been an acute shortage of beer, which is a big hardship to the workingman. Except in bars, hard liquor is equally difficult to buy. Often chagrined customers, after pointing wrathfully to displays of Scotch and rye in a shop window, discover that the bottles are dummies. The resulting skepticism about the nature of things sometimes has unfortunate results, as when a housewife stared coldly at a mound of lemons in her greengrocer's shop under the gloomy impression that they were hollow papier-mâché mockeries. She discovered later, after they were all gone, that they were part of a crate of the genuine article which had just come in that morning.

BRYHER

Camel Hair Coats

I opened the newspaper one April morning [in 1942] to find that the Zoo was offering to sell clippings from their camels' coats without coupons. [. . .] I dashed off alone at lunch hour. Eventually a man arrived, looking puzzled but otherwise affable. Yes, he assured me, they combed the beasts regularly to keep their coats from becoming matted and a firm had previously collected these combings, he did not know for what purpose, could it have been for brushes? 'I've got two sacks of Droms and five of Bacs.' He meant, I presumed, Dromedaries and Bactrians but how impolite, even in wartime, not to refer to his charges by their full names. [. . .]

'Had I a bag?'

In my enthusiasm I forgotten this precaution.

Well, he would see what he could do. He hailed a friend and left me alone with the animals. They ignored me. It seemed ages before he returned with a sack full of combings and then he actually helped me to find a taxi at the gate.

'Stinks, it does!' The driver slammed a window shut and we charged rather than proceeded decorously throught the empty streets to Lowndes Square.

'You can't keep that stuff here,' was Hilda's unenthusiastic reception, 'see if they will let you store it in the basement.'

'But it's camel and off coupons.'

Hilda slammed the door and it was only after much discussion that I was able to find a corner for my sack at the side of the baggage room. People would not realize that if conditions got worse I was a public benefactor. [. . .]

A resident at Lowndes complained about a curious smell in the basement, could it be the new gas? I got Mrs Ash to help me pack the clippings inside paper that we had drenched with disinfectant and posted them to Scotland. I heard no more for six months. Then without warning six skeins of rough and prickly wool, together with a startlingly small bill arrived with the morning post.

Our winter clothes were already thin with wear but I cannot pretend that the wool was a success. I shared it eventually with Osbert [Sitwell]. He had a coat made that he gave later to a gamekeeper, then doing night watches. I have always felt the cold terribly but my jacket was too hot even for me and I passed it on to a farming friend to wear during the lambing season.

MRS ROBERT HENREY
Piccadilly Circus, Easter 1942

The plinth of Eros was now covered with yellow and blue posters bearing the words: 'Save in War Savings.' Underneath the lettering were pictures of sailors signalling the message with flags.

I stood watching the throb of the Circus a moment from the steps of Swan & Edgar's. [. . .]

Behind us the big shop window had paper crocuses growing from green matting amongst the gloves and stockings. At the entrance to the under-ground, the newspaper sellers, with their backs against the square brick police shelter on the kerb, were crying out the evening papers. On the other side of the Circus, between Etam and Shaftesbury Avenue, and below the huge Guinness clock, the empty shop where, the preceding month, collections were made for Warship Week, was now taken over by the Ministry of Food to teach housewives how to make the best of the new national flour.

In another forty-eight hours the white loaf was to disappear until the end of the war. The significance of this momentous decision had not yet quite dawned upon the public. They had taken the white loaf for granted during two and a half years of war. Most of this time we were the only nation in Europe to enjoy this inestimable privilege. We could buy as much white bread as we liked while people on the Continent queued up for a black substitute. Some, like the Spaniards and the Greeks, had no bread at all. Even now we were not to be pitied, for the national flour, though no longer white, was to be excellent, though there was no telling what the future might bring.

Outside the shop where these lessons for housewives were to be given, was displayed a huge coloured canvas portraying an Atlantic convoy with the words:

'National Flour Saves Shipping'. [. . .] I turned into Rupert Street, which leads across Shaftesbury Avenue into Berwick Market. A big van stood outside the kitchen entrance of the Corner House, and a series of white-coated assistants were unloading tray upon tray of crisp, warm French loaves. They smelt good, and they were still white. It was the last baking.

195

SYLVIA TOWNSEND WARNER
The New Austerity
1942

I have just come in, wet as a water-rat, from carrying the washing to its local depot. No more vans coming to the door now, in this new austerity of petrol. One carries most of one's things, and also one carries bits of newspaper to wrap them in – unless one chooses to be perfectly natural and walk around clutching a nude fish. On the whole it all seems to save a lot of trouble and mental wear and tear. One can't visit, or be visited, that is very nice and makes one feel unusually warmly about one's acquaintances. House-keeping is child's play when one just buys what one can get. I don't at all object to being simplified, and personally I feel domesticity just slipping off me. It is a choice. Either one can let it go or one can intensify it. The people who intensify it seem to get quite a lot of interest out of that, too, and are as preoccupied as pirates. There is a great deal of release in hardship, people slide out on one side or the other, according to their natures.

For a long time we wondered what we should do when we had no more stockings, now we wonder how we shall keep our last pair of stockings up when there is no more elastic. Valentine has a theory that it can be done with little tabs of adhesive tape. It worries me, I must admit, a good deal. My work takes me much among clergymen, so I must have stockings and I must keep them up. Unless the church throws itself open to women, and I can become a dean and wear gaiters it seems to me I shall have to give up my work. Why my work takes me so much among clergymen is because it takes me into villages, where clergymen still abound. They are not even rationed yet, there is one to every village. The last one I saw combined being a clergyman with what is called being a village leader. That is to say, if his village were cut off from the world by invasion, he would then have to take charge of a lot of things like deciding whether cows should be milked or slaughtered, scorched cows policy, and whether Mrs Tomkins of the local first aid should or should not have priority over Mrs Bumkin of the local air raid precautions. When asked if he was village leader he hesitated before replying, and then explained that he did not care to spread the news as he had heard that village leaders would be the first people to be shot by the Germans, so naturally he did not want too many people to know about it. I thought this very nice and natural of him. It is becoming my belief that if our local villages were invaded, nobody would have time to notice the enemy, they would all be too busy taking sides over Mrs Tomkins and Mrs Bumkin, and storming the village hall, that is to say if the local first aid is in possession the emergency cooking squad will be storming it from one side and the

ARP personnel from another, and the boy scouts will be making their way in by the chimney and the home guards will be tunnelling in from below. There is not enough accommodation in our villages for all the things that are going on, or may be going on. Often, too, there is not enough personnel for all the various patriotic doings. I know many people who are in charge of so many different activities that the whole of their faculties will be absorbed in vetoing as one person what they wish to carry out as another. Valentine's mother is a case in point. In her ardour for service she has undertaken the charge of so many things that as far as I can reckon she will be essential in five different places at once; and as she attains terrific velocity, fells whatever stands in her path, and is permanently fitted with a screaming device like a German bomb, she will create incalculable havoc amid both defenders and attackers, besides spraining her ankle and getting very much out of breath. I often think that Mrs Ackland is the real reason why Hitler has not yet tried a landing on the East Coast. She thinks so, too.

It is very odd to look at all these poor consequential idiots and remember that war might at any moment make real mincemeat of them. Even under the shadow of death man walketh in a vain shadow. People often mention with surprise the flippant behaviour of animals in the face of death, how the live frisks over the dead animal and doesn't seem to know it's there. I don't know why they find it surprising, for in the next breath they are doing it themselves.

EDITH OLIVIER
Shopping Bag and Food Queue
1943

There are two phrases which will be for ever inscribed on the hearts of wartime housekeepers – Shopping Bag and Food Queue. Lord Woolton has decreed that 'man shall not live by bread alone', but I think he favours woman living by the Queue and the Shopping Bag. For it is no use getting into a food queue, or into a bus queue which will land you in one, unless you possess a shopping bag. Without that, you must carry home a miscellaneous collection of onions, cabbages, fish, and tea cakes in your pockets, for the salvage minister will not let you have any paper.

So every woman now owns a shopping bag, and she is jealously possessive about it. At first, these bags were brilliant and striking looking objects

197

– in vivid colours and jazz designs; but as the war years roll on, and cleaning materials grow hard to come by, they all decline to the same level of dusty duskiness, reminiscent of two colours fashionable in my youth – Elephant's Breath and Desert Sand.

On the morning when the ration cards for the new week come into effect, there is often a certain amount of well-mannered altercation as to whether or not a landlady and lodger may each borrow the other's bag. The winner of this friendly debate now hangs it on her arm, draws on a rather sorry-looking pair of Wellington boots, and sallies forth to shop. Other housekeepers are doing the same. The first two meet with cordial greetings, and proceed together up the road, talking about food. Another be-bagged figure is now seen approaching. The greetings become less cordial; and indeed they die away altogether, as it becomes clear that quite a number of women are on the same quest. They all hope to catch the early-morning bus to the market town.

Then begins the first queue. It is a bus queue, and queues of that breed are usually very friendly, but not so this early one. It stirs some of the evil passions of the human heart, for it is plainly about to develop into a food queue. Everyone wants to travel by this bus, so as to arrive in time to give its passengers the first pick of the market stalls, and there may not be seats for all. It is all very well for people who live at the extreme limit of the bus journey. There is certain to be room for them. But at every village on the road a little group is waiting by the post office. At first these groups are easily absorbed, but as the bus gets nearer the town, every cubic inch of space has been filled up, till there is no hope at all for people like ourselves, who live only a mile or two from the market. At last the bus appears round the corner. Futile umbrellas hail it, though these are obviously unnecessary, as the driver can plainly see the little crowd which now sways uncertainly into the road. He quickens his pace, and the bus rattles heartlessly by.

This common misfortune draws the rebuffed travellers together. They will no longer be rivals in that first picking over of the market stalls, so they have lost the angry sensation of a food queue, and are merely a defeated bus queue. They consult together. The tough ones resolve to make the best of it, and to walk. Others give up altogether and walk home; while the remaining few form themselves into a gaggle to gossip in the shelter till the next bus comes, an hour later.

VERE HODGSON
The Struggle for an Onion

17 September 1942
Such a struggle to get an onion. Tried the Old Pole (her greengrocer). None. Went to Mr Bybest – he had a few, but they were all booked. I took his refusal humbly, and bought a pound of carrots and a stick of celery, thinking sadly of the onion. I could see an idea was germinating in the man's mind, so lingered on. Finally I won without saying any more – a voice murmured: 'If you only want it for flavouring, I will let you have one.' Pouring thanks and blessings on his head I walked away triumphant. A victory indeed!

JANE GORDON
Sanitary Towels

We passed a woman proudly holding a navy-blue carton clearly marked Kotex.

'Women have lost all sense of refinement,' Rosemary announced, and added, 'That is most unladylike.'

I said: 'Well, considering those things have been practically unobtainable for months, and there has even been a question about it in the House, I suppose she thinks she is being very ladylike to find a box.'

WINIFRED WILLIAMS
At a British Restaurant
1942

Hundreds of men and women were standing on the stairs leading to the basement. They read newspapers, they chatted, they seemed strangely amiable. Well, I thought, viewing the lake of heads, Lord Woolton has got himself into a nice mess! He provides restaurants for the workers and they have to spend their lunch hour queueing. I shall be eating, if I am lucky, in half-an-hour, I thought. [. . .]

I was mistaken. We got through in seven minutes. I stood at the counter with my small wooden tray, and food was being piled on it in three surprising tiers. There'll be no empty seat now, I thought: but there was.

It was quite a pleasant place, too, with yellow walls and small square tables and shiny chairs. I sat beside two workmen who swallowed food and news simultaneously (steamed ginger pudding, the *Daily Herald* and the *Daily Express*): a pretty girl in pretty clothes joined us. Black coats and blue overalls seemed to mingle without being aware of their difference in status. This is a very democratic place, I thought, looking to see what my neighbour's paper was saying about Stalingrad.

Conversations were continuing everywhere. Apparently people treated the place as a club. [. . .] Soon the two workmen were piling their empty dishes on to the trays and taking them back to the counter. Everybody, I noticed, carried his plates and spoons there: apparently it was undemocratic to leave them on the tables. Well, I thought, Lord Woolton seems to be educating the people as well as feeding them.

And as I drank my penny cup of tea I was dreaming – of People's Restaurants of the future, when the war is over and won, of finely-decorated buildings with paintings hung on the pale walls, of a gay democracy eating delicious lunches at a price the poorest could afford. The Minister of Food has built something bigger and better than he knows: having once given restaurants to the people will he, when the war is over, snatch them for ever away?

And having thrown up thousands of fine civic restaurants throughout the land, I started building new schools and new factories, blocks of workers' flats, terraces of shapely houses, fine city streets. And why not? I asked myself, striding to the counter with my tray, looking at the vigorous faces of the workers around me. Why not? They will never again be able to tell us we haven't the cash. For a country that can finance this sort of war can pay for that sort of peace.

FRANCES PARTRIDGE
Beige World

24 August 1943
We joined a swelling stream of the citizens of Swindon, all following a series of notices marked 'British Restaurant', to a huge elephant-house, where thousands and thousands of human beings were eating as we did an enormous all-beige meal, starting with beige soup thickened to the consistency of paste, followed by beige mince full of lumps and garnished with beige beans and a few beige potatoes, thin beige apple stew and a sort of skilly. Very satisfying and crushing, and calling up a vision of our future Planned World – all beige also.

VERILY ANDERSON
Respectable Looting

The blitz had played some queer tricks with its victims. Into our garden had been blown a broken lawn-sprinkler, which we converted into a standard-lamp for our drawing-room. Beside it lay a linen-basket which we bent back into shape and painted a nice shade of crimson and cream. From other gardens, sometimes digging a little to unearth them, I collected curtain-rods and rings and coat-hooks and other things needed, but impossible to buy then, for moving into a new house. Donald was too law-abiding to relish this pilfering as I did, but he ceased grumbling when we had got our loot safely into the house. And he took an attractive pleasure in restoring it to a usable state.

A nursery fire-guard was something impossible to find in any shop. The day I stepped out of a bombed site with one in my arms, I walked straight into a policeman. I thought instantly of the notices saying that looters might be shot. The policeman shook his head in a disappointed way, as though he expected better of me.

'I know,' I said. 'I'm ready. You can shoot me.'

'It's not that, miss,' he said. 'I've had my eye on it to take home after dark for my own toddler.'

'Take it,' I said, holding it out to him. I knew now what thieves meant by *hot*.

'No, miss,' he said sadly. 'You got it first.' And he continued on his beat.

MOLLIE PANTER-DOWNES
The Fourth Christmas of the War

December 27 1942

It's now reasonable to suppose that this fourth Christmas of the war may be remembered as the one which brought the phrase "after the war" back into active circulation. Certainly one hears it being used far more frequently and confidently now than for some time past. People talk about the end of the war as though it were a perfectly matter-of-fact objective on the horizon and not just a nice pipe dream.

The recent holiday season, besides being the brightest as far as outlook goes which this country has had since the horrors started in Europe, is also likely to linger in the public's memory less cheerfully as one of the most expensive which ever bore down upon the pocketbook. The cost of all traditional garnishings which weren't price controlled, from mistletoe to food and drink, soared alarmingly during the last few days before Christmas. The toy racket tardily drew stern official attention, rather too late to do much good for parents who had already in desperation shelled out high prices for shoddy rubbish.

One of the gayer manifestations of the festive spirit has been the bower of tents and greenery which suddenly blossomed in the sombre, gutted shell of John Lewis's bombed Oxford Street store. This was a Potato Christmas Fair, sponsored by Potato Pete, a creation of the Ministry of Food's propaganda department to make starch-stodged Britons eat even more home-grown tubers and go slow on the imported wheat loaf. The show was visited on its opening day by Lord Woolton, by a baby elephant called Comet, who proved too heavy (perhaps from too much patriotic spud-eating) to be able to negotiate the wooden gangway down into the wrecked basement, and by hordes of the public who dutifully received hot baked potatoes from Father Christmas and signed a visitors' book beneath the vow 'I promise as my Christmas gift to the sailors who have to bring our bread that I will do all I can to eat home-grown potatoes instead.'

GERTRUDE STEIN
Life in France

During the Spanish-American war there were food scandals, and in the Boer war there were concentration camps where they had nothing to eat, and all that is natural enough. The concentration camps for the Boers excited us all, nobody knew then how everybody was finally that is everybody in Europe was finally not going to have anything to eat. There was famine in China even in Russia and there was famine in India and every one then in the time of the Boer war and before and after was very much excited about it but now here in 1943 not having anything to eat enough to eat, having what you can eat, buying eating black, that is black traffic, thinking about eating, everybody on the road bicycling or walking with a pack on their back or a basket in the hand, or a big bundle on the bicycle, hoping for provisions, somewhere in the country there would be an egg or something or something, and perhaps you will get that something. One day I was out walking, well naturally I had a basket and big prospects and hopes and I met a nice gentle little bourgeoise from Belley, and it was spring time and she had a very charming and quite large bouquet of flowers very beautifully arranged in her hand and I said what a charming bouquet of flowers, yes she said eyeing the bouquet carefully, yes, I have been in the country to visit some relations, and I had hoped, I had hoped perhaps for an egg, perhaps even perhaps for a chicken, and she heaved a little breath they gave me these flowers. They are very charming flowers I said, yes she said, and we said good-bye and went each one on our way. There are so many people in prison because they sell what they should not sell, and yet, well and yet, I met Roselyn I said you are looking very well, the restrictions do not seem to have had any effect on you, well said Roselyn, one finds things. Roselyn, I said, you indulging in black traffic, mais non, she said of course I would not, to find something is one thing, to indulge in black traffic is quite another thing. Explain the difference to me I said. Well said Roselyn, to find is when you find a small amount any day at a reasonable price which will just augment your diet and keep you healthy. Black traffic is when you pay a very large sum for a large amount of food, that is the difference. And she is right that is a difference and we all all day and every day go about and in every way we do or do not find something that helps the day along. As Madame Pierlot said, you do not buy now-a-days only with money you buy with your personality. Jo Davidson used to say that you always had to sell your personality, but now it is not a question of selling it is a question of buying by personality. Nothing is sadder these days than people who never make friends, they poor dears have nothing to eat, neither do the indiscreet, and yet almost everybody does eat. Almost everybody, almost, it comes hardest on middle-aged men, not women they resist better but middle-aged men, without wine and cheese, they get thinner and thinner and thinner. We women of a certain age, we reduce to a certain place and then we seem to get along all right, but the middle-aged men get thin, and thinner and thinner. Naturally those that had been fat. Oh dear me. [. . .]

It's funny about honey, you always eat honey during a war, so much honey, there is no sugar, there never is sugar during a war, the first thing to disappear is sugar, after that butter, but butter can always be had but not sugar, no not sugar so during a war you always eat honey quantities of honey, really more honey than you used to eat sugar, and you find honey so much better than sugar, better in itself and better in apple sauce, in all desserts so much better and then peace is upon us and no one eats honey any more, they find it too sweet and too cloying and too heavy, it was like this in the last war '14–'18 and it is like this in this war, wars are like that, it is funny but wars are like that. [. . .]

I had to buy a jar of jam.

You have to buy what you do not want to buy in order to buy what you do want to buy. That is if you have nothing to trade and a good many of us have nothing to trade. Of course if you are a farmer it is all right you have lots to trade but if you are not a farmer then you have nothing to trade. Once when we were in Bilignin during the winter we wanted to buy some eggs and nobody wanted to sell us any because all the eggs their chickens lay they wanted to eat themselves, which was natural enough, and Madame Roux said can we find nothing to trade that is not to trade but to induce them to sell eggs to us, at last we found something, and it was our dish-water. Madame Roux had the habit of carrying off the dish-water to give to a neighbour who was fattening a pig, and as there was very little milk with which to fatten pigs, dish-water was considerable of a help, this was in the worst days, '41–'42, in '43 life began to be easier, well anyway Alice Toklas said to Madame Roux, no we will not give away our dish-water, if the neighbour wants it she has in return to be willing to sell us a certain quantity of eggs. So Madame Roux went to the neighbour and told her she could have the family dish-water only under the condition of our having the privilege of buying from her a certain quantity of eggs, well she wanted the dish-water and we bought the eggs, but alas she killed the pig at Christmas, and everybody killed their pig at Christmas and so there was no need any longer of dish-water to fatten the pigs and so our right to buy eggs was over, we had not had the idea of making the bargain for longer. [. . .]

There are little things too, little like an inch on the end of one's nose, and that is tobacco. I do not smoke but Alice Toklas does and she has to she just has to if not well anyway she just has to. So when cards came in cards for tobacco and they only were giving them to men, women were not being encouraged to smoke not by the government and so what to do, well the tobacconist and I agreed that since they did not ask if you were a woman, you just inscribed yourself we would do so with initials and who would know, well that worked for a whole year and helped out by an occasional friend Alice Toklas did not do so badly and then the next year they had regular cards and they had to be regular no initials did not do and what could she do, we did several things but none of them quite enough. Alice Toklas found it very hard to bear, boys of eighteen had a right to chocolate and they had a right to cigarettes too, that did seem unjust, either they were too young or too old to eat chocolate that was not reasonable but as foreigners even if not yet enemies we had no right to protest, so we tried everything, and one way and another way we got a few cigarettes, here and there and in one way and in another way and friends brought some from Switzerland you could go to Switzerland then and come out again and there were some but not enough far from enough, and then a friend found a sergeant in the French army who would sell some that the army gave them and some more too and soon Alice Toklas had enough quite enough, and then we invaded North Africa and the French army was disbanded and the sergeant went away and it was a trying moment and then the Italian army came and that was fine, why the Italian army had so many cigarettes I do not know mysteriously the German army has not, but anyway whatever the way it was done the Italian army had them by the ton very nice little cigarettes they were too and the Italians loved to sell them, and everybody bought them and all the smokers were happy again. And then the poor Italians had to go away, just suddenly and and although everybody had a supply it was not a big enough one and something had to be done. In this part of the country tobacco was always grown, it has a climate that seems to suit tobacco one would not think so because it is mountainous and has a cold winter and a not too hot summer but it does seem to suit tobacco, and now everybody began to grow tobacco in their garden anybody and there were some who grew a very good cigarette tobacco and they were ready to sell us several pounds of it and I learned to roll cigarettes with a little machine everybody bought and mysteriously there was no lack of cigarette paper, everything is mysterious in this kind of war and that there is no paper but there is no lack of cigarette paper and so everybody and Alice Toklas was happy again. That is here, in other parts of France where tobacco will not grow they were not so happy.

Chapter eleven

LOVE, SEX AND IMMORALITY

Women's sexuality was a fraught topic during the war, a matter for public debate and difficult private decisions. The war added urgency and eroticism to sexual relationships; it heightened romance, sentiment and feelings of obligation. It also forced couples apart and brought lonely servicemen from overseas to Britain.

Wartime weddings reached a peak in 1939–40 and the birthrate rose dramatically from 1942 onwards. But illegitimacy was also on the increase, as were divorce and venereal disease. Charges of immorality were thrown at women in the services. Rumours spread, and parents worried about their young daughters away from home, either in the services or living in the huge hostels for factory workers. The government responded in 1941 by setting up a committee of inquiry under Violet Markham. This committee toured the country, and found no evidence to back up the allegations of immorality.

Women's magazines naturally preached fidelity and celibacy to the wives and girlfriends of men serving overseas, assuring them that these were important contributions to the war effort. In the name of this cause the magazines also – and more realistically – urged restraint upon those who had lapsed. Women were told to think very carefully about the 'untold harm' which could be done by 'wretched "confessions" '.

Lovers were among the most dedicated writers of the war, and the most prolific. Bill Cook and Helen Appleton exchanged 6,000 letters while he was serving overseas as an army chaplain. (They married in 1945 and published some of their letters in *Khaki Parish*, 1988.) They were exceptional correspondents, but many couples wrote to each other twice a week. Mavis Bunyan even wrote to her RAF husband twice within six hours of his departure overseas in 1943, and dispensed with paragraphing to make the best use of space in airletters and airgraphs. The private letters which women, fully aware of the censor's eye on all mail going overseas, wrote to their lovers and husbands were sometimes surprisingly uninhibited in their discussions of love and sex – an aspect of women's war writing not very visible in the public domain until some years later.

ZELMA KATIN
The Sight of a Girl in Uniform

To many people – perhaps because they suffer from sexual frustration – the sight of any girl in any kind of uniform, even Salvation Army uniform, at once suggests immorality. So firmly has this legend taken hold that bus and tram conductresses, because they come into contact with the general public more than other groups of uniformed women, and because each forms a working team with a man, are singled out for special blackening of character. Numbers of passengers believe that the last act of a conductress and her driver or motorman each night before going home is the exercise of sexual intercourse. When, occasionally, a conductress is seen misbehaving, her guilt is considered indisputable evidence of the state of morals in the industry. I have noticed the suspicion on women's faces when, passing me while the tram is waiting at a terminus, they observe me enjoying a cigarette with the motorman.

JOYCE GRENFELL
Easy to Get

Wednesday October 25th 1944, Beirut
Viola and I have been wearing our 'glamorous' ENSA uniforms for the journeys and they do save our clothes but not our faces. Whenever I wear the uniform I get the 'hi-babe' looks, approach and conversation with the soldiers. I never meet with anything but extremely friendly and easy manners when I'm in my ordinary clothes. Even though we turn our ENSA tabs under they seem to recognize the uniform and out here ENSA stands for the 'easy to get' and I resent it deeply.

MAUREEN WELLS
Immoral Englishwomen

4 March 1942

Mummy and I had a visitor yesterday. Catherine is the bossy WAAF officer daughter of one of Mummy's old school friends. She is a strong believer in free love for young girls and practises it. A year ago she fell most passionately in love with her commanding officer, a married man with a son of three, and they've been living together. She brought him down here once and I've never seen such a selfish, disagreeable-looking individual.

The next time she came she told me what a fool I was not to follow in her footsteps – wasting my youth etc etc. I brought up all sorts of arguments but she was firmly convinced in her mind that I was an old-fashioned boop, a relic from the Victorian era. 'My dear, I assure you that 75 per cent of the Waafs will never see virginity again, and what's wrong? The men must go with somebody and the authorities prefer that they go with the Waafs, who are medically examined, rather than the women of the town.'

I gave up. [. . .]

August 1943

The Yanks are saying that Englishwomen are the most immoral in the world. Marie Thornton met a young US Army air corps officer in a train the other evening and he saw her to Ashley House where she was going to stay the night. As they said goodbye he asked 'Don't you want to sleep with me?' After Marie's strong answer he said 'I'm awfully sorry, only you see I've been over here a month now and you're the first girl I've met who hasn't wanted an affair.'

PAMELA RUFFONI
Italian Prisoners and Landgirls

Autumn 1943. The mob of Italians were not wanted and only three came. We were stacking a hay-rick, three Italians, three girls, and then things started happening. Two in long kisses, and then the other two started larking about throwing hay which smothered the remaining Italian and myself. Hmmm good job I'm a little tough and have a few wits, anyway Rene came to my rescue. I thought everything appalling and disgusting, yet how sorry for those fellows I feel, prisoners for nearly three years, a girl on a haystack must be a very tempting proposition with no one around. I had been talking with the Italian who palled up with me, but I realized after this instance 'give an inch take a yard'. Even afterwards I could not refrain from talking to him, because I think he knew what I was, and in broken English said 'me like you, you serious.' But I can't get over the fact, him having a wife and baby, and giving me a picture of St Anthony.

JENNY NICHOLSON
Sensible People

Naturally with such a vast cross-section of British womanhood as there was in each of the services there were bound to be individuals whose standard of behaviour wasn't up to the average scratch. But service life didn't breed them. They arrived like that. Happily, behaving well was a good deal more contagious than the other thing, so once a brazen hussy found herself separated from her home-town gang of brazen hussies and among a number of sensible people, the tendency was for her to grow noticeably more subdued as time dragged on. It was certainly true to say that the women who entered the service like driven snow and were turned cheap and nasty by it were exceptional.

VERA LAUGHTON MATHEWS
Wrens and Contraceptives

At one station an innocent WRNS Officer asked in sick bay what these prophylactic packets were. She was duly informed by the Sister, who added that they were in great demand before a dance. The Officer, in telling me, said, 'My heart stood still because I knew the bulk of the girls at the dances were my Wrens.'

There were even some who would have liked to see contraceptives made available for the Wrens. An Admiral in a very high place, with daughters serving, actually tackled Dr Rewcastle on the subject, adding: 'I am not approaching the Director as I know she would not agree with it.' I had my compliments. Dr Rewcastle, without entering into the question of ethics, quietly answered that there was no indication that such a policy was necessary and then with her usual loyalty came straight to me.

FREYA STARK
The Generous Heart

It is, I think, an ungenerous heart that does not give itself in wartime, when men's mere physical hunger for women is so great. (This incidentally, may be the chief virtue for the semi-military female services, though obviously not one for publication.)

VERILY ANDERSON
A FANY Gets a Proposal

The ten, or so, occupants of the carriage drew together and sought comfort in conversation. Encouraged by a lively young Marine major, we shared sandwiches and played rummy with a pack of cards produced by an elderly naval rating. The major spread newspapers over our knees and, when that failed to warm us, passed round his flask of brandy. Only a sedate girl in civilian clothes refused to join in; but soon the cold and the long waits drove her to accept a warming sip. When at last we reached London, we felt we had been through so much together that it was almost painful to part. The Marine major and I were the last out onto the platform.

'Come on, Fanny,' he said, 'let's go into the hotel and have a civilized sandwich.' He picked up my bag and carried it with his into the station hotel.

'First I must telephone some friends to see if I can spend the night with them,' I said. 'It's too late to get a train down to Sussex.'

I telephoned Elizabeth's parents, who told me they could give me a bed for the night.

When I joined the major in the cocktail bar he seemed quite different from the life-and-soul of the railway carriage.

He looked younger and quieter. We sat down with sandwiches and drinks and exchanged life stories. He was twenty-five and the youngest of four brothers. He, too, was the child of a parson.

'I say, Fanny,' he said suddenly, 'I like you awfully. Will you marry me?'
I laughed.

'Honestly. I want to marry a nice girl like you that I can let my hair down with, and yet who looks all right in public. I expect I can get some sort of a job after the war – trying shoes on people or something.'

'How nice of you,' I said, 'but –'

'Then will you come and dance with me at the Four Hundred tonight?'

'I'd love to, but I've already made a plan to go straight to some friends where I'm staying the night.'

'Pity,' said the major. He got me a taxi. 'I'll be at my club. The Junior Carlton. Ring me in the morning. I'll want to know how you are. You seem to have forgotten you only came out of hospital [with German measles] today.'

I had. The taxi crawled along the icy streets in the black-out, and I realized that neither of us knew what the other's real name was.

FLORENCE SHARP
A Street Sweeper's Proposals

You'd be surprised how many proposals I've had since I've been sweeping. Norwegians, Dutch, and all sorts. I could have been married hundreds of times. Of course, I don't entertain them. I just have a drink and say, 'Yes', and all that kind of thing. 'I'll see you tomorrow'. As a matter of fact, only today I had a proposal from an American sailor. He said: 'I'll marry you', he said, 'and you can come out to America with me'. He meant it. 'Well', I said, 'I'll think it over'. That boy liked me because I was a worker. You know, it's very funny. You go in anywhere, and you'll always find people will fall for a worker. I don't want to get married again: I've got no interest in men. I don't know why. I just don't bother about them. They're very nice to me. Most men treat me with respect. They treat me like a boy, as a matter of fact. Even before I had my uniform it was just the same. But nowadays, you go in anywhere with your uniform on and the men will say, 'Will you have a drink, Florence?' It's just the thought that you're doing something for your country. They think something of you.

I remember there was one nice Norwegian who gave me a watch. He was a very very nice man, if anybody wanted to settle down, but I couldn't be bothered to marry him. I really couldn't be bothered with a man round me. Then there was a Dutch cook once. He was a merchant seaman. After every trip he used to bring me a beautiful long loaf, the kind that mother makes, with currants and things. He used to bring me one every month all through the winter. He made it on his ship, and he used to say: 'I've put three eggs in it'. He wanted to marry me too, but I can cook and all, you know, so I didn't want to marry him.

DIANA HOPKINSON
A Letter to a Husband in North Africa
1943

You speak truthfully when you write to comfort me for our separation by saying that we have been lucky compared to many lovers. I know that. Also that we have learnt to value each other even more through separation and have reached greater unity that way as men do in battle. Those are comforting weapons when the battle against the depression and hopelessness of our separation gets me down. No – I know it is *not* hopelessness and agree with you that we can see some pattern for the future, though when you mention some small part in our future, like reading *Finnegans Wake* together, my heart leaps both with excitement at the prospect of once more spending winter evenings with you and hesitates because it is tempting the fates even to mention the possibility.

MAVIS BUNYAN
Letters to a Husband

No.1
Blackpool 25 October 1943
My beloved,
I do not really want to write this now because it will bring to me all I am
trying so hard to block out. Maybe though you will receive it before you
leave England if I post it right away. Somehow I cannot believe you will
not be in to tea with me and we are not going out together this evening. I
was so afraid I would not see you before the train went when it got so late,
but I prayed so awfully hard to see you and I did. How I wish the next
week were over. I shall not mind so much when I get amongst the family
again but the next week is going to be so full of loneliness without you. I
never thought anyone would ever mean my whole life's happiness, like you
do. You seem to have grown right into me, I am incomplete without you
by my side. Now I am crying again, just what I am afraid of. Letter No.
1., I wonder where you will be when you receive it, and how many I shall
have written by the time I see you again? It was awful, seeing you as just
a number amongst all those boys, knowing you had to go, and there was
nothing we could do about it. To them just a number, but to me my whole
life and happiness. I just feel right now that I can't face it, I feel I'll just go
silly with wanting to see you. I know I will get by though. It is awful to
think of the months without you. I would not mind so much if I could hear
from you every day like I used to, but maybe having to wait months for
letters makes it seem worse. To say 'I love you' seems rather superfluous
doesn't it my beloved because you know the depths of my feeling for you.
I do love you beyond all doubt, you mean so much to me. Every evening
when the pips go for the news I will be thinking of you, sending an 'I love
you' and a 'God bless'. It is two hours and a half since I had your last kiss
and 'I love you'. It seems so long. Last night seems ages away. I cannot
begin to say how much I am wanting you, my whole body seems so empty.
I am now only existing until you come back to me. God bless you and take
care of you my precious boy, I love you beyond everything. I am praying
so hard for you – and courage too.

Your ever-loving wife,
Mavis

No.5
Wimbledon 28 October 1943
My always beloved,
It is nine o'clock and here is my 'I love you'. Darling I do love you so terribly much, I have been feeling so ill these last days. It is only the effect of my mind on my body, I don't think I shall be the same until you come back to me. It is only your presence that can bring that sparkle to my eyes and give that air of 'joie de vivre' to my body. I shall not be my real self until you are once again part of me in body as well as spirit. I must have your presence to give me happiness and a will to enjoy living. Today I brought back from Southfields all your letters. They will help me over the time until I start receiving mail from you again. I have read a few this evening. A couple written before we were married and a few whilst we were waiting for 'Sunny Jim'. I wish the bell would ring now and you would be there when I opened the door, I am almost willing it. It is funny, but I cannot give up hope of you coming again, I want you so much. I never dreamt that anyone could grow to be the difference between having the world and losing it. I am so glad I have baby, the little tinker. She has been dropping things from her pram, so I said 'naughty' in what was meant to be in a fierce tone. The little scamp promptly crinkled her face in a huge grin and I had to laugh. Looking at her now it seems difficult to connect her with the funny little bundle in the nursing home.

I am terribly tired even though it is only 9.35. The fire is getting low too and Lesley is shouting for her supper. I have lots to do to get ready for Torquay but I have been lazy all evening. This morning when I looked out of the window I had a shock. In the fortnight since I left here, winter has come. The sunflowers and daisies are all dead and the trees are bare. I really must go now. I love you beloved for always, and ever and a day after that.

Yours for always, and God bless,
Woodenhead

No.176
Torquay 25 June 1944
My beloved boy,
Today it is eight months since I saw your dearly beloved face and in that time my love and longing for you has increased to such a desperate need. It is becoming so overpowering that I have no will or wish to do anything. Today has been so miserable, I am glad I had to work this Sunday. It looks as though the rain has come to stay for a few days.

26.6.44

Lesley woke up darling so I had to stop and am finishing this before I get up. Your 130 letter has just come and I do love you so very dearly. You are a wicked boy to say I would soon be in my birthday suit if you were here.

Do you know darling, the more I live with me the more I puzzle me. I just do not make sense ... When I say I want all the 'loving' things that we did, it is not my body that is doing the wanting but my mind. I wonder if you will understand. The one thing I want physically is just to be held tight to you and to know that my arms are around your neck, never to let you go from me again. When I say that I want your caresses and to have you close to me it is because I know that I loved all those things when you were here and if I were having them again it would mean that you were here with me. I could never let anyone else share our glorious oneness. All I feel physically is a great emptiness and a longing that sometimes verges on a physical pain. This is what puzzles me though. I love to read of you wanting me because with us physical loving springs from our love of each other. I love it too because it is a memory of all we have been to each other and makes me feel as well as know, that I am your wife and we belong to each other for always unless God decrees otherwise. I am even thinking often of nice clothes, especially pretty nightgowns, so that I can 'lure' you and make you want me and love me lots. This is what is so silly though. Sometimes, something akin to terror comes over me in a wave. I know in my heart that directly I have your first kiss I shall want you never to stop kissing me, but I shall be so terribly shy darling you will have to be patient with me if I am silly. No wonder you once called me a dutch girl. I guess when you come back to me everything will take care of itself, and I will not even think of being shy because my longing for you is so passionate. I do love you so my most precious boy. Lesley has just come up, she looks so sweet. Heavens, she has my handbag. I do so wish I could see you with our baby, 'cos then I would be seeing you too. I do wish you could see her though, as she toddles around the house. You should see the mess this room is in, everything on the floor. My clothes, a pile of nappies, and everything from my handbag. Golly what a mess, but she seems to be having fun. I love you dearly beloved for always.

Just yours always, Mavis

Chapter twelve

CONSOLATIONS

Awoman provided the words for one of the war's first messages of consolation. Minnie Haskins, a retired lecturer from the London School of Economics, wrote the poem quoted by the King in his Christmas Broadcast to the Empire at the end of 1939:

> And I said to the man who stood at
> the gate of the year: 'Give me a light
> that I may tread safely into the unknown.'
> And he replied:
> 'Go out into the darkness and put
> your hand into the Hand of God. That
> shall be to you better than light and
> safer than a known way.'

These lines, with their image of the comforting presence, consoled many women. They quoted the poem to themselves and others, in diaries and letters. The King's choice, suggested to him by the Queen, was a happy one: the Royal Family seemed to fill the role of the comforting presence naturally. 'Bess is really a tip-topper', wrote Margaret Kennedy. 'The woman can't help doing the right thing: smiles and makes little jokes when little jokes are wanted, and bursts into floods of tears when tears are the only comment.'

Making do and improvising, the new skills enforced by dreary austerity as well as sudden catastrophe, were embraced by women willing to turn necessary evil into challenge and virtue. Having to improvise could provide a spur to fresh energy and invention, and this could be a powerful source of satisfaction. Constance Goddard, a farmer in the Dales, was touched by one particular demonstration at her village Make Do and Mend lectures:

> A Make Do that aroused a good deal of interest was the conversion of a clothes-basket into a cradle. All the women inspected that and purred over the tiny mattress made out of chaff that could be so easily renewed, and the tiny blankets cut from shrunken vests. There was a little down quilt too, filled with feathers from someone's ducks. This was quilted in a daisy pattern and the material was cut from a wedding dress. I thought the baby that slept in that little cradle would be happy, so much love had gone to the making and lining of that little nest.

Consolation itself often had to be an improvised affair. The solace and pleasures which women found for themselves and others were a wonderfully diverse mixture of formal and informal, new and traditional, material and spiritual. As this chapter shows, ghosts, Dorchester teas, riding in the lifts of shops and dancing on the tops of tables all played their part in getting women through the war.

Finding and making forms of consolation out of the war itself became an important strand of women's wartime writing. Some got satisfaction in looking at the war as a glorious and heroic enterprise. Many more preferred to see it as an unpleasant obligation, but even before the war ended there was a fond nostalgia for the spirit of Dunkirk and the Battle of Britain. Looking wearily back over the last 'five gruelling years' in 1945, Freda Bruce Lockhart cheered herself with memories of the 'morning glory' and 'deep patriotic pride' of 1940. One of the most frequently repeated commonplaces of the war was the consolation that, in Stella Bowen's words, 'we are getting nicer all the time'.

F. TENNYSON JESSE
The Ecstasy of the Fighter Pilot,
October 1939

Jim Hodge has, in his Spitfire, brought down one of the German raiders over the Firth of Forth, which has made us all feel very elated. I can imagine what *his* elation must have been – he is a quite fearless person – on a brilliantly sunny day, flying and fighting over that glorious stretch of water and shooting down his enemy. I think it will be a bad day for humanity when something as primitive as the emotion he must have felt ceases to spring to life in a man's heart because of over-civilisation. I know that this is difficult to square with one's horror of war, and one's wish that there may be no more wars, but there is always a danger of losing certain high qualities in getting rid of certain fundamental ones. Man is not simple, and only the very simple-minded think he is. There are those who distinguish between love and lust – and, indeed, at the extremes of both it is possible to do so. But love is the more beautiful for the lust that is inextricably mingled with it, and the same thing, I think, applies to the high qualities of a fighting man in relation to the ecstasy of the hunt and the kill, even when the quarry is another human being.

E.M. DELAFIELD
The British Sense of Humour
13 July 1940

It is very important that people in England should notice, and remember, the value of laughter just now, and in the utterly horrible days and nights that probably lie ahead of us. There are – and we all know it – things waiting round the corner for us and – how much harder to bear! – for those whom we love, that can, in essence, be nothing but unspeakably dreadful. But there are also – and there always will be – aspects of anything and everything at which it will be possible to laugh, if we have the high courage and unselfishness to do so.

Most of us have said, on one occasion or another – 'if it hadn't been so awful, one could almost have laughed.'

It is most likely going to be very awful indeed – but if there is anything at which 'one' can almost laugh – *and there will be* – 'one' must do so – and not 'almost' either. [. . .]

It has never been easy to make a good job of everyday life, and it is immeasurably harder now. Men and their wives are being separated; all, in varying degrees, are exposed to danger and suffering, children are either in peril or else being sent away half across the world – and without return tickets either – homes are menaced with possible invasion and all-too-certain taxation – and some hundreds of minor complications of house-keeping have descended, like a plague of small but omnipresent locusts, to play hourly upon the already exasperated nerves of women.

Each single one of us must evolve an inner scheme of defence to hold on to and use, if necessary, ten thousand times a day, to ensure that neither a part nor the whole of this, is to get us down.

I am absolutely certain that one of the main bulwarks in that scheme of defence is the cultivation of a sense of humour. Never, never, let us say or feel that 'this is getting beyond a joke.'

A journalist recently, giving an eye-witness account of the last stand of a British Regiment at St Valéry, wrote:

'We saw one Sergeant taking his men to cover against the shelling in front of the barricades. He was leading them in song, and making them laugh. . . . The minute the shelling stopped, they were at the barricades again.'

He was leading them in song, *and making them laugh* – and next minute, they were at the barricades again.

Good enough, isn't it?

PRINCESS ELIZABETH
Broadcast to the Children of the Empire
October 1940

The following message to the children of the Empire at home and overseas was broadcast in the Children's Hour on October 13 by HRH Princess Elizabeth. This broadcast inaugurated the B.B.C.'s North American service for children evacuated to Canada and the United States.

In wishing you all 'good evening' I feel that I am speaking to friends and companions who have shared with my sister and myself many a happy Children's Hour.

Thousands of you in this country have had to leave your homes and be separated from your fathers and mothers. My sister, Margaret Rose, and I feel so much for you as we know from experience what it means to be away from those we love most of all. To you, living in new surroundings, we send a message of true sympathy and at the same time we should like to thank the kind people who have welcomed you to their homes in the country.

All of us children who are still at home think continually of our friends and relations who have gone overseas – who have travelled thousands of miles to find a war-time home and a kindly welcome in Canada, Australia, New Zealand, South Africa and the United States of America. My sister and I feel we know quite a lot about these countries. Our father and mother have so often talked to us of their visits to different parts of the world, so it is not difficult for us to picture the sort of life you are all leading, and to think of all the new sights you must be seeing, and the adventures you must be having. But I am sure that you too are often thinking of the Old Country. I know you won't forget us: it is just because we are not forgetting you that I want, on behalf of all the children at home, to send you our love and best wishes – to you, and to your kind hosts as well.

Before I finish I can truthfully say to you all that we children at home are full of cheerfulness and courage. We are trying to do all we can to help our gallant sailors, soldiers and airmen, and we are trying, too, to bear our own share of the danger and sadness of war. We know, every one of us, that in the end all will be well; for God will care for us and give us victory and peace. And when peace comes, remember it will be for us, the children of today, to make the world of tomorrow a better and happier place.

My sister is by my side and we are both going to say good-night to you. Come on, Margaret. (*Princess Margaret Rose then said*: 'Good night, children'.) Good night, and good luck to you all.

MARGERY PERHAM
Christmas in Dockland
January 1941

Christmas morning, 3 a.m. in the shelter under the Church. It's a shelter-de-luxe, this, compared with most, but even here, as night goes on, the air becomes thick with the sickly smell of unwashed bodies and bedding. Three hundred pairs of lungs use and use again their small ration of air. The lights are on, and fall upon the stacked humanity in the bunks and the garish decorations looped over them. Many sleepers snore with great power: sometimes there is a word or a groan. In the babies' corner little pink forms lie in the dainty cribs they owe to American kindness. Above them presides a lighted Christmas tree.

Christmas Day, and dinner-time. The shelterers have come up from their refuge into the hall above, and sit at the long decorated tables. Turkey, sausage and Christmas pudding are served to them, the solid realisation of an idea conceived in Hollywood. Undergraduates, male and female, pacifists, responsible matrons from among the shelterers, social workers, permanent and migratory, wait on them with the scrambling eagerness of beginners. The feasters do their part stolidly amidst the altruistic bustle; dockers, labourers, city office-boys and charwomen, factory-hands. They pull their crackers and wear their caps and accept their cigarettes. Of what are they thinking? Of the donors in Hollywood? Of their broken houses? Of their evacuated children? Difficult to say. They seem only half aware of what 'they' are trying to do for them. Most of them seem to accept 'their' services as fatalistically as the bombs.

Christmas evening. There is a pantomime in the shelter. *Cinderella*. It is a home product. One of the clergy has written it – perhaps not up to the highest Hollywood, but admirable for its purpose, none the less; another plays the buffoon most excellently. The pantomime is true to tradition with its topical jokes and its knock-about fun. The ugly sisters, with the properly improper display of underwear, monopolize the cellar in an air-raid, and Cinderella is sent to sit, not in the cinders, but on the roof as spotter. At the royal ball it is not her slipper but her gas-mask that she leaves behind. Hitler is requisitioned to take the part of the bad fairy and appears at intervals in a flash of green spot-light to the music of the sirens, only to be worsted by two clowns with more than professional vigour. Ministers and officials who make wonderful promises about shelter reform get their share of caricature. 'Where's Mrs Brown? I want to see her at once.' 'She's just gone off on the Government evacuation scheme.' 'Oh, that's all right. She'll be back tomorrow.' The audience, perched thickly on its bunks,

221

screams with delight. It catches up other jests too personal and local for the stranger. It joins with strength in the chorus of the dominant song:

There'll always be a Christmas
Whate'er the year may be,
So let old Nasty try his tricks,
He won't stop you and me!

ROSE MACAULAY
Consolations of the War
January 1941

In this horrid business of war, the brightest spots can only be rather melancholy consolations. It is, of course, an extremely horrid business; a grotesquely barbarous, uncivilized, inhumane and crazy way of life to have had forced on us by a set of gangsters who are making us use their own weapons and practise their own horrid incivilities – as if we were jungle savages like themselves instead of twentieth-century men and women who had hoped war to be for ever outlawed. That is the worst outrage that the gangsters have perpetrated on us – forcing us to adopt their own shockingly bad manners. For war, of course, is as revolting an example of bad manners as can well be imagined. We do not think it is a grand life; as a member of the House of Commons remarked lately, we think it is a perfectly beastly life, only to be endured because the things we are fighting against are still more beastly. So its consolations are rather small stars in a pretty murky night.

Well, then, as to these consolations. You begin each day by waking up alive (so far) and a little surprised sometimes to be so. Each extra day, I mean, is not a matter of course, but a gift we had not necessarily counted on having. Your windows and crockery may have got smashed in the night, bits of your walls and ceilings may have fallen down, your house or apartment may be in varying stages of dilapidation or even ruin, but you are indubitably alive.

If you do wake alive, you may enjoy – when you go out – observing the fresh ruins, if any, and if ruins are to your taste. Of course no one wants ruins, but it is no use pretendings that those made last night are not interesting next day. I sometimes think how greatly our eighteenth-century ancestors would have enjoyed them. They paid architects to build picturesque ruins in their parks and gardens; we have hordes of ruin-makers who nightly do it free. We stroll out, then, and see the sights; here is a jumbled pile which was a house, and dangling poised at its very top, high above the street, is a large bath and broken lavatory basin and seat. There – round the next corner, not so far away from my own flat – is the ruin of a house with a little Austin car poised on its summit, blown up there from its garage by blast. The demolition workers fetch it down and stand it in the street, a little battered and thick in grey dust, in which someone inscribes the legend: 'For Sale, Good Condition. One Owner Only.' I've been told that there is to be seen somewhere a trolley-bus which has climbed on to the top of a house, but I cannot find anyone who has actually seen this.

From such bizarre spectacles one must get what interest one can, among the tragedies of smashed homes and broken glories of architecture. Some hopeful souls imagine to themselves the nobler, seemlier buildings which will one day, so they hope, take the place of the destroyed. This cannot always be done, of course; not when we lose our medieval Guildhall, our Wren churches, and (worse) those all too few churches which survived a much earlier fire in 1666 – churches such as St. Giles', Cripplegate, where Milton is commemorated, and the lovely All Hallows by the Tower. There is no pleasure to be derived from the destruction of All Hallows, unless you are so malicious as to feel a little relief that the corner of its interior which was modernised and sentimentalised to commemorate the last war has perished with the rest. Ruin is indiscriminate and stupid; it falls on beautiful and ugly, noble and mean, with the most impartial injustice. On the whole, these ruins depress; you have to look a long time and with great determination for their brighter spots.

For aesthetic pleasure, you must wait until dark. London nights, once garish, have become beautiful: black, with tiny lights like glow-worms faintly piercing the blackness – and on a clear night the stars. Or, on a moony night, magically black and silver, an ivory city sharp with shadows and deep lanes of night. And always the long lances of light that sweep the skies, crossing, seeking, probing. Suddenly the quiet is shattered by a long howling as of wolves on the trail; again and again the uncanny wail rises and drops; it ceases, and after a minute or two comes that deep drone of bombing planes: flashes begin, and crashes; the sky is aflare with golden fruits that burst and are lost in the stars. Sometimes the heavens blaze red, in east, west, or centre – or everywhere at once. Buildings are outlined against fire. Here a water-main has burst, and a great lake floods a street below a mountain of ruins; a gas-main, too, has burst, and flames leap roaring to the sky, mirrored in the water. Oh, what a scene! as Horace

223

Walpole said of the fall of the Bastille. Above it, the enemy zooms malevolently, pitching them down with loud whistling whooshes and thundering crashes, while the guns bark like great dogs at his heels. And I say nothing for this horrid scene, except that, aesthetically, it has a kind of lurid and infernal beauty. And that, if your job calls you out to it, as mine sometimes does, you do at least get an eyeful, and see something you don't see as a rule in the London streets.

Another thing you get is a sense of friendly companionship. The men and women working together among fire and bombs – firemen, ambulance drivers, rescue squads, wardens – they have a new comradeship, which overrides class and sex. The words 'mate' and 'chum' are grown commnon forms of address. That is pleasant; we don't in normal times, in this rather stiff and shy country, get enough of it; it's more like the western states of America, with their companionable 'brother' and 'sister'. This greater friendliness extends beyond the air-raid workers to people in general; you meet it in the streets, in trains, 'buses, and shops; and (I am told by those who frequent them) you meet it in shelters, too. Perhaps especially there.

Shelters we must count among the major consolations of war. They are quite a new pleasure, and are among the town amenities most missed by evacuees to the country. They have taken the place of the cinema as an essential of the good life. I know of one woman – by profession she is a charwoman – who goes to her favourite shelter (I'm told that they differ as greatly as cinemas do) every evening at seven o'clock. She stays there until eleven, when, bombs or no bombs, she goes home to bed. Evening travellers by the underground trains may see the shelterers in the subway stations, dossing down for the night on rugs and pillows and wooden bunks, with canteen workers selling tea and chocolate. Often they have concerts and other entertainments, and sometimes distinguished persons to visit them . . . but I don't think this can be very wholesome, for it seems to start them being a little smug, and shouting 'We can take it!' – which is an irritating cry, since it is hard to see what else any of us can do but take it, whether above ground or below. Still, if it cheers them up . . . Anyhow, shelter life has, I think, come to stay; even in the peace (if any), this odd, communal, troglodyte life led nightly by so many Londoners will, I prophesy, go on; it must save so much trouble.

Being saved trouble is always a major pleasure, of course; and wartime saves us trouble in more than one way. Clothes, for example. It doesn't matter now much what anyone wears; women can go about London in slacks; silk stockings are definitely off, and to wear warm woollen ones and thick brogues or boots in town as well as country is a pleasure that formerly only the strong-minded allowed themselves, but that now even the shy may safely adopt. Evening clothes, too, are seldom seen. The typical Englishman is said to derive pleasure from dressing in a stiff shirt for his dinner each night when living alone in a jungle; he may enjoy this piquant contrast between his surroundings and his clothes, but you can take it from me that he and his sisters enjoy more never dressing for dinner in wartime London. It saves trouble, money, time, and gives us a lazy, go-as-you-please feeling that I find most agreeable. I only wish I could think that the fashion would outlast the war, and not give place to some terrific reaction into formal smartness.

Then, coming back to aesthetic pleasures, the pageant of life is enormously enriched by the presence of so many foreigners in our midst. So far as civilian foreigners go, many of them were promptly interned last summer, as you know, some quite unjustly. But slowly – far too slowly – that injustice is being put right. In any case, the uniforms of Polish soldiers mingle with those of Czechs, Norwegians, Dutch and Free French; women from the Central European countries with handkerchiefs tied about their heads embellish the streets. And not only foreigners. Driving in the country, you are continually hailed by the rich accents of young men in battle-dress from Alberta or Montreal, who seldom know where they are and always want to go somewhere else. They are, as a rule, enormously charming.

I will end with a consolation not aesthetic but psychological; the gratifying feeling that we have the sympathy of the best people: that is to say, the best nations, and the better people of the temporarily less good nations. We haven't had it in all our wars, and rightly. We have by no means always had the sympathy and goodwill of the American people; and the fact that we have it now gives us an enormous amount of support and satisfaction. Sympathy and mutual trust have been cemented by a common hatred of this horrid business of Nazism. We have grown into a relationship of which President Roosevelt can say: 'There was no treaty, no written agreement – but there was a feeling, which has proved correct, that as neighbours we could settle our disputes peacefully. There will be no bottleneck in our determination to aid Britain'.

When I cast my mind back to the earlier history of our relationship, and its stormy beginning, I cannot help recalling Patrick Henry's words of defiance flung at us across the Atlantic in 1775: . . . 'Is life so dear or peace so sweet as to be purchased at the price of chains and slavery? Forbid it, Almighty God. Give me liberty or give me death'.

I think Patrick Henry would now be on our side, and would use those words with a different reference. Among the consolations of war, this community of purpose and ideals with the kind of people with whom community is worth having, ranks high. I think really I should have mentioned it first.

BERTA GEISSMAR
At an English Concert

During the Christmas of 1942 I had an experience which symbolized for me the difference between life in Germany as I had witnessed it since 1933, and life in England. The traditional 'Carol-concert' of the Royal Choral Society under the direction of Dr Malcolm Sargent was sold out. I asked Dr Sargent whether he could get me in, as I wished my mother to hear for once the full Albert Hall singing the lovely age-old Christmas carols. He sent me two seats in his box and I sat down with my mother. Suddenly the door opened, and a lady in grey asked whether this was Dr Sargent's box. We immediately recognized Mrs Churchill. She was with her daughter, who was in the uniform of the ATS, and smilingly tried to prevent us from giving her the front seats in the box.

With what a tremendous panoply and show Frau Goebbels or Frau Emmy Goering would have surrounded themselves on a similar occasion! But here was the wife of the British Prime Minister, bearing a proud and historic name, quietly slipping in to share a box with two refugees. This was democracy: this was England.

C.A. LEJEUNE
The Career of *Gone With the Wind*

After two and a half years in London, *Gone With the Wind* was generally released. It would be graceless and irresponsible to let the occasion pass without remark. The career of *Gone With the Wind* is the current counterpart of the success of 'Chu Chin Chow' during the last war. Novelists and social commentators are noting it down conscientiously, I trust, in their little books. It is as much a part of the issue of London life in wartime as the foreign uniforms in the streets, the altered skyline, and the friendly square gardens now open to the casual strollers.

Gone With the Wind arrived in London one April afternoon in 1940, when Narvik seemed the hub of the world, and errand boys were whistling 'Over the Rainbow.' Messrs Metro-Goldwyn-Mayer, who owned the piece, suggested, with incredible daring, that it might run until Christmas, unless, of course, the air-war should come to England and bombs fall in Piccadilly. That was roughly eight hundred and forty days – I had almost written years – two thousand five hundred performances ago, and when I passed through Leicester Square last week the 'house full' boards were out, the queue was still waiting patiently round the block.

Gone With the Wind has survived, and in its own way helped to lighten, the burden of the worst succession of news this country has had to bear since the Napoleonic wars. Through the Norway campaign, the invasion of the Low Countries, and the fall of France, through Dunkirk and the Battle of Britain, through an autumn, winter, and spring of savage air-attack, through the Greek campaign, the Libyan campaigns, and the assault on Russia, through Pearl Harbour and Hongkong and Singapore, through the Battle of the Atlantic and the Battle of the Pacific, through Rommel's drive to Egypt and von Bock's drive to the Caucasus, the sturdy British citizen has taken his place in line to find out what happened to Scarlett O'Hara in a war that is as remote as Agamemnon's brush with Troy.

What is the secret of *Gone With the Wind's* success? It does not seem to me the greatest film ever made. It has not, to my mind, the sharp, emotional appeal of *Mrs Miniver*, the magic of *Snow White* and *Bambi*, the fertile invention of *Citizen Kane*, the brilliance of *Kermesse Heroique*, the elemental force of *The Grapes of Wrath*. It is not even the longest film ever made: I am told it would seem a mere trailer to the shows one might see in China. It provides a tremendous experience, but one which its title significantly describes. It passes. The very dispassion with which it can be examined indicates its weakness – that it lacks – shall we say? – heart, the high, noble, memorable emotion one associates with great drama.

Few people who have seen it admit – or have admitted to me – that it is their favourite film, and yet few would appear to feel defrauded in any way, few would seem to wish to have foregone the experience. I have no doubt that when it opens outside London the queues will equal those in Leicester Square. Why? Millions of people, I know, have read the book, but you cannot persuade me that the queues are preponderantly made up of Margaret Mitchell lovers.

It is my own fancy that the very characteristics which limit *Gone With the Wind* as a work of art, the qualities in which it falls short of lasting worth, make it a proper and comfortable recreation for the times. There is a closer relation between pastime and the time in which it is passed than most people realize. 'The larger music, the more majestic length of verse called epics, the exact in sculpture, the classic drama, the most absolute kinds of wine, require a perfect harmony of circumstance for their appreciation' as Hilaire Belloc wrote in 'The Path to Rome.' In such days as these, when there is but little harmony and content in our own souls, the need is for something simpler, more varied, more immediate in its effects. A mind that is heavy and disturbed does not want to reach very high or delve very deep. It wants to be carried along, distracted by many and even little things. Great emotion at such a time is painful and dangerous.

For this reason, I think, *Gone With the Wind* just suits our war-time mood. It is a prodigal film, generous to overflowing with facile events. It has, alike with the book from which it is so faithfully drawn, an impersonal narrative style which evokes violence without pain. There is enough catastrophe in *Gone With the Wind* to make the last act of 'Hamlet' seem a jest. But catastrophe without contemplation is no tragedy, and even amongst all these dead and dying, our emotions are seldom overtried.

What audiences will find in *Gone With the Wind* is a graphic account of personal doings and relationships, intimate details of this meeting and that quarrel, the gossip of a dozen homes, and the confidences of a host of interesting people. The film has a hundred different stories, each in its different way absorbing. Each receives and exacts the same engrossed attention, whether it be the Civil War or a domestic tiff, the birth of a nation or the birth of a baby. *Gone With the Wind* runs for three hours and forty minutes, or twice as long as many finer pictures. But few people, anxious to hear what happens to Scarlett O'Hara and Rhett and Melanie, carried along on a wave of sound and colour, and conscious only of the blessed distraction it gives them, will find this enormous picture overlong.

ANNA NEAGLE
The Yellow Canary

My part [in *The Yellow Canary*] was a great change for me. The daughter of parents prominent in the War Office and WVS, I appeared to be spying for the Nazis. It was not until the last few moments of the film that it became clear that I was, in fact, doing secret intelligence work for the WRNS. Richard Greene was released from the Army to play in it with me. I was so busy that I did not see the finished film for nearly a year. Then I caught up with a matinee performance in Newcastle.

Sitting in front of me were two ladies, one very elderly and rather deaf, so that her companion was constantly explaining what the film was about, to the accompaniment of low moans from her elderly friend. 'Oh no. Tch-tch,' she muttered. 'Oh dear me *no*, Anna Neagle would never do that.'

When I finally appeared in my WRNS uniform, and all was made clear, she gave a very relieved sigh. 'There,' she said, turning in triumph to her patient neighbour, 'I *told* you Anna Neagle wouldn't do things like that.'

RACHEL KNAPPETT
The Landolettes

We were running at that time, a concert party known as The Landolettes. The performers were all landgirls working on surrounding farms. They thought the best way of ending an eight-hour day pottering about the wet winter fields, was to cycle through the long dark evenings and meet together to learn tap dancing. Marjorie taught us, and when we were good enough, the girls thought it great fun to undertake engagements in out-of-the-way spots, reachable only by bicycle, with their costumes packed in suitcases on the carriers. In extraordinary dressing-rooms piled high with cups and saucers and tea urns, where worthy local ladies were preparing suppers for the audience, we would throw off our heavy boots, don skimpy cabaret costumes and perform on remarkable stages made of tables which bent and groaned under the appalling weight of fourteen hefty landolettes.

BARBARA CARTLAND
A Reassuring Ghost

A friend of mine in the ATS who was billeted in Dunstable in an old house had a strange experience. She dreamt that she awoke and saw standing at the foot of her bed a middle-aged man wearing the knee-breeches and brocade coat of Nelson's time.

For a moment she was frightened, then the man said to her peremptorily as if she were the intruder:

'Why are you here?'

'Because I am a soldier.'

As she said the words my friend was conscious that she used them deliberately so that the man should understand.

'A woman . . . a soldier?' came the exclamation in astonishment.

'Yes.'

'Then England must be in danger again!'

'Yes, terrible danger.'

The man smiled.

'Do not be afraid,' he said reassuringly; 'if England needs help it is always there.'

'Where?' my friend asked, and knew as she put the question that it was important.

The man turned towards the window as if he were listening, and there came the tramp, tramp of marching feet.

'In the hearts of her people lies England's strength,' he said quietly, and the dream faded.

JANE GORDON
The Church and the Ritz

On my way home I stopped at St Mary's Church. Ever since the Dunkirk days I had acquired the habit of going in for a few minutes on my way to and from the hospital. Today when I slipped into the pew and knelt, I could think of nothing to say. The steel hat and gas-bag slung at my back felt heavy and awkward as they clumped against the woodwork of the pew. My stiff uniform belt dug into me; and before I knew what I was doing my face was clammy with tears and I could feel my nose getting red. The very plain figure of Christ in the centre of the ugly stained-glass windows, high up at the back of the altar, gazed down on me in a friendly way, but after a few moments I stood up feeling too discouraged to bother about anything, even a small prayer. So I went home, changed into my best suit, took extra trouble with my make-up, and joined Charles for luncheon at the Ritz.

VERE HODGSON

Tea at the Dorchester

15 October 1944

I have felt for some time that after three months and more of Fly Bombs, I wanted some new experience of an exciting nature. So I fixed with a friend, who seems to know every hotel there is, to go to the Dorchester for tea. We knew we could not afford a dinner. I have so often longed to enter the best hotel in London. So garbed in my best, I stepped forth. We turned first into the Grosvenor, but it said 6/6d, which we thought beyond us a bit. And we did not want to dance. So we entered a great soft carpeted lounge in the Dorchester, and sank down into some nice armchairs in an alcove. A distinguished looking waiter asked us if we wanted tea – in which case we must wait until 4 p.m.

We smoked and looked round. A few people drifted in. A naval officer had drink after drink, and seemed worried. The little page boy in buttons came hurrying in with a message. Perhaps he had been let down.

At 4 p.m. a very inferior tea was served to us. Sandwiches, thin and beautifully cut, but the insides had no flavour of any kind at all. I think it was just soya bean. Waiter then appeared with a tray full of cakes and pastry – we were allowed two. They were awful. The cups were plain white – I expect all their own were broken. The lounge filled. Several officers. One private. Finally a society beauty swept in. She was in black, with feathers in her hat. Seeing no corner seat she flowed back to the centre of the room, nearly knocking a man over. They sat down and soon were both absorbed in newspapers. Obviously a husband and wife.

At a quarter to five we asked for our bill, and felt lucky to get out at 4/6d each, for a tea the like of which I should have been ashamed to serve in my flat. But I had had tea at the Dorchester, and that is another ambition satisfied.

Had a lovely stroll back through the Park, as I considered we could not afford the bus. I prepared a very nice dinner ... chops, potatoes and tomatoes. For cocktails – Auntie's own ginger wine. For sherry – Government lemon squash, and for port – more ginger wine. All much better than the Dorchester would have provided!

HILARY WAYNE
The Solace of Shops

Floating day after day from basement to ground floor, from ground floor to first floor, second floor, third floor, on the escalator, I look down on the departments and begin to appreciate their subtle methods of enticement. I realize how stimulating colour is: a cascade of scarlet silk here, a blaze of artificial flowers there, clusters of gay scarves and glittering bottles of creams and cosmetics, catch the tired eye and light up the tired mind. Movement, too, is exciting. The escalator is too sluggish, but the flash of the lift registering the progress of its journey in rapidly changing lighted figures brings life to that end of the shop. The short swift flight in the lift releases energy and sends the customer out more reckless for the adventure of spending. I begin to see that the shop is more than a place in which to buy things. Long ago, before the days of coupons and war work, its allurements used to be the main temptation of idle women. Now the choosing of a coat or dress seems to be a family affair, and in a world where there is little free entertainment even the escalator is an event in the life of a child.

ELIZABETH BOWEN
Calico Windows
1944

Calico windows are something new – in a summer bare of fashions, 'crazes' or toys. They pitch home life in a hitherto unknown mood. In the theatrical sense, they rank as 'effects' of the first order. They cast on your ceiling, if you have a ceiling left, a blind white light, at once dull and dazzling, so that your waking thought every morning continues to be, 'Why, it must have snowed!' They lighten and darken slowly: inside calico windows it might be any time of year, any time of day. Through their panes you hear, with unexpected distinctness, steps, voices and the orchestration of traffic from the unseen outside world. (Talkers outside a calico window should be discreet.) Glass lets in light and keeps out sound; calico keeps out (most) light and lets sound in. The inside of your house, stripped of rugs, cushions and curtains, reverberates.

232

Few of these new-fashion windows are made to open: you cannot have everything. However, the sashes of those that do fly up with ghostly lightness, almost before you touch, showing you summer still outside.

This cotton and cardboard 1944 summer home, inside the shell of the old home, is fascinating. With what magic rapidity was it improvised and tacked together by the kind workman. The blast of the buzz bomb marked the end of the former phase. The dreamlike next phase began with the arrival of workmen. As though just hatched, or dropped from the skies, these swarmed in their dozens in your street. Soon they had disappeared, without trouble, inside the blasted-open front doors – yours having its share. So many and so alike were the workmen that, still dazed, you failed to distinguish one from the other, and only attempted to guess their number when it came to finding cups for their tea. They were at it almost before you knew they were there – smashing out what was left of glass, smashing down what was left of plaster, wrenching out sagging frames and disjointed doors. The noise they made at their beginning, if just less, was more protracted than that of the explosion. But nothing makes you feel calmer than being taken in hand.

Coughing in the fog of dust they had raised, scrunching over chips of glass on the floors, the workmen, godlike, proceeded towards their next stage, that of sweeping, hauling, measuring, hammering. Only just pausing, they listened patronizingly to other buzz bombs passing across the sky: you knew nothing more could happen while they were with you. To watch them filled your post-blast blankness; to watch them made you feel you were doing something yourself; and to know that *you* were not paying them was most heartening.

The calico for the windows arrived in bales, along with the felt and boarding. Workmen carrying these in wove their way between workmen carrying rubble out. The rubble was tipped from baskets on to a mounting mountain outside your doors; and the mountain was by-passed by still more workmen with tarpaulins with which to drape your roof – these last disappeared upstairs and, for all you knew, never came down again.

The whole scene was one of rhythm and, soon, of order. Watching the bold creation shape itself, you exclaimed, 'Of course, of course!' The light new window-frames, primitive as a child's drawing, which have been constructed out on the pavement, are now fitted into the old windows. The outside world disappears. The workmen's are the first faces you see in this to-be-familiar calico light. You have now been tied up, sealed up, inside a tense white parcel. The workmen see it is good. They go.

You are left alone with your new sensations. The extraordinary is only at the beginning of its long reign. So many footprints are in the dust that you lose track of your own; you lose track of yourself, and you do not care. The peace of absolute dislocation from everything you have been and done

233

settles down. The old plan for living has been erased, and you do not miss it. Solicitous for the safety of your belongings, the considerate workmen have hidden everything: the lamps are in the hat-cupboard; the telephone has been rolled up inside a mattress; your place in the book you were reading when the bomb went off has been religiously marked with a leg that blew off the sofa; more books are in the bath. And everything seems very well where it is. Especially does it seem good that the position of the telephone makes it impossible for you to tell anyone what has happened, or to reply if anyone asks you. Already you feel secretive about your pleasure at the dawn of this new, timeless era of calico.

And next door? For you are not the only one. You run in to ask how the next-doors sustained the blast, but how they feel inside their white box is a more intimate question. Next door – now that you come to listen – sounds remarkably silent: can they have gone to the country? If so, have they any notion how much they miss? Next-door-but-one, and next door to that, add their quota to the deserted silence.

No doubt, however, everyone else, like you, is standing still, taking stock, looking round. Now you think, you find you are making no noise yourself – they probably think you have gone away.

But perhaps as that first dusk falls your curiosity heightens, till you go out to make a reconnaissance. Your street, chequered over with black and white, looks somehow coquettish and self-conscious. Going farther, you are perhaps diminished by finding your entire neighbourhood endowed with this striking new thing in panes. Seen from the outside, all the way down a street, calico windows lose tone. You begin to wonder, inimically, how long these good people's windows will stay clean, and what they will look like when they no longer are. Now, in this hour before black-out, lights flower behind the criss-crossed frames. Do that young couple realize, or should you tell them, that they perform a shadow-play on a screen? No polite person stares in at a lighted window, but what is to stop you staring at calico?

Back home, you remember you have no black-out. You grope to bed in the calico-muffled dark.

Those first twenty-four hours are only the sharp-edged beginning of the mood. You must live, of course; you must pick up at least some of the pattern; you must at least play house. You discover that what turned on, turns on still – hot water, wireless, electric light. Whether willing or not, you disinter the telephone from the mattress, to explain you are quite safe, perfectly all right, happy; and to learn, from the pause on the wire, that you are disbelieved.

But everything comes from a distance; nothing disturbs you. Each time you return home, shutting the door behind you, you re-enter the mood. The hush of light, the transit of outdoor sounds, the bareness in here become familiar without losing their spell. Life here – life in a blasted, patched-up house – is *not* life, you have been indignantly told. What is it, then – a dream? We are, whatever else we may be, creatures of our senses, varying with their food. Is this different food for our senses making us different creatures?

This tense, mild, soporific indoor whiteness, with, outside, the thunder of world events, sets the note of the summer for Southern England. I say to myself, all my life when I see a calico window, I shall be back in summer 1944. Then I remember – when war is over, there will be no more of this nonsense; we shall look out through glass. May the world be fair!

Chapter thirteen

SPEAKING OUT

Women were in the vanguard of European writers who protested against Hitler. Books from Germany and Poland were widely reviewed and discussed, in particular Irmgard Litten's highly praised *A Mother Fights Hitler* (1940), a dispassionate report of her five year struggle and failure to save her lawyer son from Nazi persecution.

More openly emotional were the messages going to and from America. A stream of British books with uplifting titles bombarded America before her entry into the war at the end of 1941: F. Tennyson Jesse's *London Front*, Margaret Kennedy's *Where Stands a Wingèd Sentry*, Vera Brittain's *England's Hour*. These writers were among many who saw that they had an important function in cementing the special Anglo-American relations that held throughout the war. Americans had to be thanked for the massive aid they were sending across the Atlantic, and to be encouraged in pro-British sentiments. The mothers, wives and girlfriends of American GIs stationed in Britain needed reassurance that they were being well looked after.

American women journalists toured Britain and reported on their findings, as did the wives of visiting politicians, notably Eleanor Roosevelt. Sometimes it seemed as if rumours were being countered. 'People look healthy ... thinnish, firm and fit', wrote one American woman to her daughter in 1942. Her eagle eye spotted 'a good deal of handholding between soldiers and their girls, but nothing more'. The fervent anti-Nazi journalist Dorothy Thompson wrote and broadcast frequently to both English and American women. Her 'tributes' to the women of Britain were an explicit attempt to bring the war closer to Americans, to 'make the women of America *imagine* the women of Britain'.

A group of Scottish women were so moved by the plight of their sisters in Leningrad (now St Petersburg) that they compiled an album of messages of support. This album, with its letters, postcards of Scottish towns and six thousand signatures, was sent to Russia in December 1941. In 1943, when the siege of Leningrad was in its third year, the Leningrad Album arrived in Scotland, a beautifully illustrated reply from the Russian women.

Throughout the war women continued to speak and write about the sufferings in Europe. They wrote on behalf of the Jews, and on behalf of starving children. They also spoke out against the mass bombing of civilian targets and in favour of peace, and not always to deaf ears. Although Vera Brittain had some of her *Letters to Peace-Lovers* returned to her (once with the message 'We're all too busy doing our bit to bother with such nonsense'), her 1942 pacifist pamphlet 'Humiliation with Honour' sold ten thousand copies by February 1943.

QUEEN ELIZABETH
The Mark of the Good Neighbour

*The Queen's Message to the Women
of America* August 1941

It is just over two years since I spoke to the American people, and my purpose then was to thank countless friends for much kindness. It is to those same friends and of even greater kindness that I want to speak today. We, like yourselves, love peace and have not devoted the years behind us to the planning of death and destruction. As yet, save in the valour of our people, we have not matched our enemies, and it is only now that we are beginning to marshal around us in their full strength the devotion and resources of our great British family of nations which will, in the end, please God, assuredly prevail.

Through these waiting months, a heavy burden is being borne by our people. As I go amongst them, I marvel at their unshakable constancy. In many cities, their homes lie in ruins, as do many of those ancient buildings which you know and love hardly less than we do ourselves. Women and children have been killed, and even the sufferers in hospitals have not been spared. Yet hardship has only steeled our hearts and strengthened our resolution. Wherever I go I see bright eyes and smiling faces, for though our road is stony and hard, it is straight, and we know that we fight in a great cause.

It is not our way in dark days to turn for support to others, but even had we been minded so to do your instant help would have forestalled us. The warmth and sympathy of American generosity have touched beyond measure the hearts of all of us living and fighting in these islands. We can, and shall, never forget that in the hour of our greatest need you came forward with clothing for the homeless, food for the hungry, comfort for those who were sorely afflicted. Canteens, ambulances and medical supplies have come in an unceasing flow from the United States. I find it hard to tell you of our gratitude in adequate terms, though I ask you to believe that it is deep and sincere beyond expression. Unless you have seen, as I have seen, just how your gifts have been put to use, you cannot know, perhaps, the solace which you have brought to the men and women of Britain, who are suffering and toiling in the cause of freedom.

Here in Britain our women are working in factory and field, turning the lathes and gathering the harvest, for we must have food as well as munitions. Their courage is magnificent; their endurance amazing. I have seen them in many different activities. They are serving in their thousands with the Navy, Army and Air Force, driving heavy lorries, cooking, ciphering,

238

typing, and every one of them working cheerfully and bravely under all conditions. Many are on the land, our precious soil, driving the plough and making a grand job of it. Others are air-raid wardens or ambulance drivers, thousands of undaunted women who quietly and calmly face the terrors of the night bombings, bringing strength and courage to the people they protect and help.

I must say a special word for the nurses, those wonderful women whose devotion, whose heroism will never be forgotten. In the black horror of a bombed hospital they never falter, and though often wounded think always of their patients and never of themselves. And I need not remind you, who set as much store by your home life as we do, how great are the difficulties which our housewives have to face nowadays and how gallantly they are tackling them.

I could continue the list almost indefinitely, so manifold is the service which our women in Britain are giving, but I want to tell you that whatever the nature of their daily, or nightly, tasks, they are cheered by the evidence of your help for them. We like to picture you knitting on your porches, serving in your committee rooms, and helping in a hundred ways to bring relief to our civilian garrison here. So I speak for us all in Britain in thanking all of you in America. I feel I should like to send a special message of thanks to American women. It gives us strength to know that you have not been content to pass us by on the other side. To us, in the time of our tribulation, you have surely shown that compassion which has been for two thousand years the mark of the Good Neighbour. Believe me – and I'm speaking for millions of us who know the bitter, but also proud sorrow of war – we are grateful. We shall not forget your sacrifice. The sympathy which inspired it springs not only from our common speech and the traditions which we share with you, but even more from our common ideals. To you tyranny is as hateful as it is to us. To you, the things for which we will fight to the death are no less sacred, and, to my mind at any rate, your generosity is born of your conviction that we fight to save a cause which is yours no less than ours, of your high resolve that, however great the cost and however long the struggle, justice and freedom, human dignity and kindness shall not perish from the earth. I look to the day when we shall go forward hand in hand to build a better, kinder and a happier world for our children.

May God bless you all.

THE GREENHILL KNITTING CIRCLE

A Message to the Women of Leningrad

Dear Women of Leningrad,

We are glad of this opportunity of expressing our gratitude to your country and our admiration of the terrific battle you are waging against our common foe, the enemy of all progress and humanity.

We are horrified at the suffering brought on the people of Europe by fascism but we know that Britain and Russia and America together will eventually defeat this fascist horror. Fighting together we can do it.

The women here will 'do our own bit' to the best of our ability and we look forward with you to the time when we shall build a new world of peace and goodwill amongst men and women the world over.

With our best wishes to our splendid ally.

From the women of Greenhill Knitting Circle, Coatbridge.

LUCY OLBROMSKA

Poland's Women Appeal to the Conscience of the World
July 1941

The other day I read a letter from a Polish mother to her son in England. Here is a literal translation of what this Polish mother, veteran of one Polish war, robbed in another of her husband and her children, enduring the bitterest hardships, looking on at the transformation of her country and home into one vast concentration camp, writes:

'My little son, far from me, irreplaceable. We are scattered through the world like leaves from a tree. It is autumn again. I too am like the bare tree that has lost all its green leaves. My branches are empty. Oh my children! My littlest one, how glad I am that you are with your brother. How glad I am! Grow up strong and learn your lessons. How I live you probably both know. I have sold the piano and with that I bought a little coal. Your

240

father's high boots I traded for potatoes and flour. The money I got for the cupboard with the mirror was enough for me for a month. There is very little left for sale. I work how I can. I get some food from the Polish Red Cross. I live by faith and longing. My dearest ones, may God keep you. My longing for you accompanies you throughout the world.'

But victory will come. And a day will also come, when there will be another International Congress of Women and before that Congress they, the women of Poland, are going to stand. They are going to say: 'We stood first in the fight for freedom. We stood, and endured, alone. How have privileged women of freer continents stood behind us? What protests, what efforts, have other women made before the spectacle of our long agony and humiliation? Yes, and before the spectacle of our magnificent and prolonged and never-to-be-abandoned resistance?'

What answer will they get?

BLANCHE E.C. DUGDALE
All Ye that Pass By
December 1942

In March 1942, Himmler visited Poland, and decreed that by the end of this year 50 per cent of the Jewish population should be 'exterminated' – in plain English, put to death – and the pace seems to have been hastened since. Now the German programme demands the disappearance of all Jews, men, women and children, natives of occupied Poland or deportees from Western or Central Europe. Mass-murders on a scale unheard-of since the dawn of civilization began immediately after the order was issued. At first the details of these were hardly believed, even in quarters capable of judging the reliability of the news that percolated from behind the dreadful barriers of the 'sealed ghettos' all over the country. But the accounts were confirmed again and again, and it became evident to those who received them that the German genius for organization was being applied methodically to the slaughter of Jews. Nevertheless, it was not until the Gestapo Chief reviewed the results in person this summer that Nazi efficiency reached its peak. The exact date of highest achievement, in the Warsaw ghetto, the biggest of all, was July 24th, 1942, when ten thousand Jews were assembled for so-called deportation. The curve then declined for some time to seven thousand a day. By September 1st some 250,000 people had disappeared. For that month 120,000 Jewish ration-cards were distributed in the Warsaw ghetto (entitling the possessor to a pound of bread per week and very little else). For October only 40,000 such cards were deemed necessary. Now the Warsaw 'deportations' sink as low as three thousand persons in a day. Before I go on to give an idea of what happens to them, the origins of these appalling reports must be named. There is a sponta-neous reaction against 'atrocity-stories' and a desire to believe them exag-gerated, which is rooted as much in the healthier forms of incredulity as in the instinct to spare oneself pain. But my facts and figures are quoted primarily from documents issued by the Polish Ministry of Information in London dated December 1st.

If support were needed it could be found in a speech delivered recently in New York by Dr Stephen Wise, the well-known Jewish leader, based on information given him by the State Department in Washington. No room seems to be left for doubting the reports, tallying as they do with things known to responsible Jewish bodies in the Allied countries. The facts do indeed surpass imagination. Here is one sample from the Polish Government Report. It describes what happens after the daily quota of victims has been assembled at the clearing-stations. They are carried off to death with the 'maximum of suffering'. A hundred people of both sexes and all ages are packed into trucks that would hold forty and the floors covered with unslaked lime. To enhance the effect of this, the deportees may be ordered to take off their boots. The trucks are sealed before they are started on their journey to the camps of execution at Belzec, Sobibor and Treblinka, places east of Warsaw. There the Polish peasantry can hardly endure the continual stench of putrefying flesh, for when the trucks are opened they reveal a mass of the dead and dying, standing upright for lack of room to fall down. Those who still breathe are shot, electrocuted or gassed. [. . .]

These things have been happening all through this November of cheerful memory. They are happening now. Scepticism cannot much longer serve as excuse for inaction, as the burden of providing proof shifts from those who believe that such crimes are being committed to those who refuse credence. So the question arises of what to do, or rather of whether there is anything that can be done while the war lasts. Certain it seems that Polish Jewry will be beyond help if the murder-campaign cannot be stopped before the war ends. But the spectre of defeat may already be lying in wait for the German people. Now is the time to enlist its help, for the argument of fear is one which Germans understand more than most.

The United Nations have sworn to exact full retribution for war crimes. Let them now repeat the pledge with specific reference to the Jews in occu-pied countries, and so remove any possible idea that atrocities against Jews will be punished less severely than those against peoples who are not in a minority everywhere. [. . .] It would be a shameful thing if the British

Government, Parliament and nation were to remain supine or mere critics of what others try to do on behalf of tortured people. [. . .] The jaws of the trap are not closed everywhere – at any rate not yet. Palestine is not the only place within the British Empire where safety awaits those who succeed in escaping. Men who do not open doors to those who are hunted by murderers participate in the crime.

ANNA NEY

Anti-Semitism
April 1943

Anti-semitism, unfortunately, has lately become a popular feature, and every now and then we find in the press an attempt to explain the growth of this evil by one or another fault of the Jews, or even more often, by the faults of 'the foreign Jews' . . .

A whole nation is being exterminated amidst so-called civilized peoples. There is nothing and nobody to stop or at least to try to stop it. (I should like at this point to pay high tribute to the leaders of the Churches together with the few other personalities who try to stir up public opinion in favour of the persecuted and advocate before the Government an effective help for the Jewish victims.) The Jews have no country, no government, no representative. If they had had, this country, this government, this representative of theirs would have saved them in time before hell was reached. There was no such preventive action. The early Christians had no backing either and were therefore attacked and made responsible for all the evil like the Jews are to-day. But is there really no prospect of destroying anti-semitism? I think anti-semitism is a mental disease like many others not yet recognized by us as such and it would lead me to a study of psycho-pathology to discuss the possible prospects of its curing. But let me tell you one thing which I know for certain about the average anti-semite, the man in the street or, more precisely, the woman in the home; the worried, the tired, the cross and envious housewife. If she were shown reality, if she could witness a farewell scene between Jewish parents and children sent apart to death; if she could hear the voices of the massacred, if she could see the eyes of children in agony, eyes and voices which God, not men, will account for: if the housewife of Hampstead or Vienna, Chicago or Melbourne would have been confronted with them: do you think she still would envy chickens and fur coats? Her heart would be filled with terror and her only wish would be – to help the victims. But as long as she does not see, she does not think. And her imagination does not go beyond the narrow horizon of the jealousies of her street.

MARGERY WITHERS
Children Under Hitler
February 1943

The story of children inside Europe to-day is not for the squeamish. A Greek officer said in a broadcast recently: 'In Athens one morning last winter I was standing in a street near Omonia Square. I had noticed one of the German bread lorries, for Germans only, parked by the pavement. It was the same with all their food lorries. They used to leave them about in the street while the population was starving. The grown-ups stood it very well, but it was heart-breaking to see the children staring at the good things they could not have. This particular morning I suddenly heard firing. I ran back to see what was happening. What I saw was a little child – he might have been seven or ten – lying face downwards in the road. In front of him he had been holding a loaf which he had managed to take from the lorry when he thought no one was looking. The loaf stuck out a little way from under his body. He had three shots in his back.'

The docks in Greek ports are crowded with children begging for food. You can see them near restaurants and canteens, searching in dustbins and gutters for anything they can possibly eat. Many of them are so swollen and weak from hunger that they can only drag themselves miserably along the pavement or lie whimpering in some corner. Sometimes they stop whimpering and lie quietly for hours as if they were asleep, until someone realizes that it is not sleep this time, but death. A report from the Athens Child Welfare Service said that nine out of ten babies in the city died before they were six months old because their mothers were too starved to feed them. A young Greek mother writes: 'My baby died. I couldn't get any proper food for her. What can you give to a tiny baby – grass or cabbage?'

VERA BRITTAIN

from *Seed of Chaos: What Mass Bombing Really Means*

April 1944

The purpose of this book is to inquire how far the British people understand and approve of the policy of 'obliteration bombing' now being inflicted upon the civilians of enemy and enemy-occupied countries (including numbers of young children born since the outbreak of war) by ourselves and the United States. The propagandist press descriptions of this bombing and its results skilfully conceal their real meaning from the normally unimaginative reader by such carefully chosen phrases as 'softening-up' an area, 'neutralising the target', 'area bombing', 'saturating the defences,' and 'blanketing an industrial district'.* [. . .]

'I wouldn't wish this trouble on any other woman!' cries the young mother in A. Burton Cooper's Lancashire play, *We Are the People*, after her small boy has been blown to pieces by a daytime bomb on a local playground. And that, I believe, is the normal reaction of every decent person, once real knowledge has come to him or her through individual suffering.

It is because I want you, the readers of this book, to have such knowledge, so far as facts ascertained from sources available under wartime conditions can give it to you, that I am going to describe, with references to my sources of information, what our bombing policy means to those who have to endure its results. I shall have to quote some horrible details, but these are not included from sensational motives. They are given in order that you who read may realize exactly what the citizens of one Christian country are doing to the men, women and children of another. Only when you know these facts are you in a position to say whether or not you approve. If you do not approve, it is for you to make known your objection – *remembering always that it is the infliction of suffering, far more than its endurance, which morally damages the soul of a nation.* [. . .]

Apart from all that we have done to Italy and to German occupied countries, our reprisals mean that on Germany alone, up to the end of October, 1943, we had already inflicted more than twenty-four times the amount of suffering that we had endured. No doubt there are many non-adult minds

---

*The use of soporific words to soothe or divert the natural human emotions of horror and pity is a characteristic and disturbing feature of this war.

which find reason for satisfaction in the anguish that we have caused to the enemy. But others will reflect more responsibly that each one of those million dead (to say nothing of the injured and seven million homeless) have relatives and friends who will remember.

Chapter fourteen

RECORDING THE WAR

Women recorded the war for public as well as private purposes. British women war correspondents were not allowed near the front; the rules were stricter for them than for American newspaper-women. The communist Charlotte Haldane was one of the few exceptions, and her account here is a striking example of how the experience of recording the war could force writers to revise their preconceptions.

The war split up families in unprecedented ways, as people were mobilised for war work and service overseas. Between 1939 and 1945 nearly thirty-five million changes of address were recorded, in a civilian population of about thirty-eight million. As leave and telephone calls were expensive and difficult, it was primarily through their letters that women hoped to keep their families together in this last golden age of letter writing. If recording the war was the duty of the historian, it could also be a conversation with a friend, an act of love.

Magazines and radio broadcasts urged women to send daily and weekly letters to servicemen away from home. For these women writing to their men, Daphne du Maurier had some firm advice in her *Good Housekeeping* article of September 1940: 'There must be no weakness in these letters of ours, no poor and pitiful hinting at despair. We must be strong and confident, and full of faith.' In 1941 the Post Office introduced the airgraph for overseas letters, which would be photographed on to microfilm, and enlarged and printed on arrival. Between 1941 and 1945 the Post Office transmitted over three hundred and fifty million of these airgraphs.

As well as the internalised censor urging strength and confidence, the figure of the official Censor also had to be considered. Letters coming from and going abroad passed through the Censor's Office, and would probably be read by women who made up the majority of the Censorship staff. 'I find the work very interesting,' wrote Barbara Pym in 1942 about the Censor's Office in Bristol, 'though the secrecy is rather annoying as I can't talk about it or share jokes with any except my colleagues.' Internees were

247

further constrained in what they might say, according to Livia Laurent: 'An internee is permitted only twenty-four lines in a letter, and we had to use prisoner of war paper, on which the pen stuck every time we became intense.'

CHARLOTTE HALDANE
Russian War Correspondent

I was living in the Swiss Cottage flat in June, 1941, when, without any declaration of war, Hitler launched his attack against the Soviet Union. I immediately felt an ardent desire to go there as a war correspondent, partly to round off my experiences in Spain and China, but chiefly because I was filled with a passionate urge to help the Russian comrades in their great and glorious resistance. [. . .]

My unshakeable enthusiasm and utterly uncritical attitude during this trip did nothing to allay the annoyance of my colleagues. On one occasion two of them with whom, much to their dissatisfaction, I shared a car, attacked me with such verbal violence that it amounted to a blunt accusation of being a traitor to my own country. They were in a particularly black mood on account of a small incident that had occurred during the morning. We had been taken to view a dump of allegedly captured German war material; gun carriages, and other small transport stuff. When we had examined it, one of my companions re-entered the car, livid with anger. On my asking the reason for his annoyance, he replied: 'Next time they show us "captured" German war material they might have the elementary intelligence to remove the stamp of the Stalin motor factory from the hub of the wheels!'

This incident made a bad impression on me, too, from a different point of view. I thought it stupid and careless of the Russians to allow themselves to be found out in so blatant and simple a trick. Either they did not realize that if they put on a show for the correspondents it should be sufficiently convincing to impress them, or they were gratuitously insulting the intelligence of men who prided themselves on their professional sharpness of observation, and who would not easily forgive such clumsy deception.

However, a far greater shock was in store for me.

During the tour we spent a night in a military camp near a little town called Dorogobuzh. This had been very badly blitzed by the Luftwaffe in the German advance a few weeks previously. The place was practically in ruins. The Russians made a great show of it, as an example of ruthless German bombing. To the British visitors, it was no novelty. We had seen devastation on an equal scale in our own home towns, on our own doorsteps. But to the Americans, in the autumn of 1941, it was an impressive sight. Most of them, before coming to Russia, had not been in England, and at that time had no conception of the punishment Britain was taking, night after night. Among the American party were Erskine Caldwell, author of *Tobacco Road*, and his wife, the photographer, Margaret Bourke-White, who enjoyed particular favour with the Soviet authorities. She had been given permission to take all the photographs she wanted, and special facilities were put at her disposal. She was anxious to obtain some good shots of devastated Dorogobuzh, and its suffering inhabitants. She was going to get them one morning at dawn. She allowed me to accompany her, as I, too, wanted to see the ruins, for comparison's sake. We set off in a car, accompanied by a uniformed NKVD man. A needle-sharp wind was blowing, and a fine drizzle was falling. We stopped the car in the main street and waited for sufficient daylight, as visibility was extremely bad. It was about six o'clock in the morning. The place was completely deserted, except for an old peasant woman, in a dark shawl, hurrying along, bent against the wind and rain. Miss Bourke-White wanted a shot of this pathetic picture, and asked the NKVD man to stop the woman. This he vigorously refused to do. He pointed out, politely but firmly, that it was forbidden to photograph citizens of the Soviet Union, except in Moscow. But he obligingly volunteered to pose for the photograph himself, and did so, standing patiently against one of the ruined buildings until it had been taken. As we sat in the car, waiting for the light, the sad silence was suddenly broken by the distant tramp of many feet; it was more like a shuffle than a tramp. As it came closer, we peered out to see the cause of it. Along the straight cobbled road came an amazing procession. There were about two hundred men, peasants. They carried primitive agricultural implements. They were in rags. Their long, fair, unkempt hair fell to their shoulders. Their legs and feet were encased in ragged puttees and straw sandals. Each man had a string around his neck, from which hung, at the back, a small sack, containing a hunk of bread. At first I thought they must be prisoners, but no guards were visible, either at the head or the tail of the procession. The men, roughly between the ages of sixty and sixteen, trudged along in absolute silence, their faces pinched, pale, and wan, their eyes on the ground, not even lifted to gaze at the large opulent car, with the two foreign women and the NKVD man. When we asked him who or what they were, he merely answered: 'I don't know,' and said no more. Never, on any of my travels, had I seen such a forlornly tragic sight, human beings registering such complete and final hopelessness. So they passed, in silence and mystery. After about ten minutes, another procession, a smaller one, followed them. It consisted exclusively of women, also carrying agricultural implements, with the sacks of bread hanging down their backs, their heads and faces bent against the wind, also completely silent. The whole picture might have been a nightmare. It was certainly not the kind that is transmitted abroad by VOKS for foreign propaganda purposes.

My first reaction to the scene was one of the deepest pity and sorrow for these utterly disconsolate unfortunates. But it was followed by a fierce sense of guilt and shame. I saw myself at home, on CP platforms, making impassioned speeches, from a sincere conviction, to the British people,

exalting the great and glorious Soviet Union, home of every toiler, the hope
of the workers of the world. The scene I had just witnessed, more tragic
and powerful than any engraving to Dante's Inferno by Doré or Blake,
seemed to mock my facile and naive optimism, my wishful dreaming, and
to accuse me of bearing false witness to my own people.

F. TENNYSON JESSE
The Right to Speak

27 April 1941 [after a heavy blitz on London]
There is one great advantage for civilians, particularly for women, in this
war, we have a right to speak because we are all in danger, we can speak
without laying ourselves open to the accusation of being armchair critics
or of having no right to speak because it is only the young men who go out
and fight who are taking risks.

BARBARA NIXON
Biased Reporting

On one of the March [1941] raids the Café de Paris was hit. The melodramatic nature of the incident caught the fancy of the reporters, and for
three days the papers were full of the gallantries of expensive girls who had
torn their expensive dance frocks into strips to make bandages. The
reporters seemed surprised; but the most light-headed society girl would
not refuse a strip of her skirt in such circumstances. Even 40 guineas cannot
weigh against another's life-blood. It was a gory incident, but the same
week another dance-hall a mile to the east of us was hit and there were
nearly 200 casualties. This time there were only 10/6 frocks and a few lines
in the paper followed by 'It is feared there were several casualties'. Local

feeling was rather bitter. At the end of the week one or two papers which had actually implied that it was a commendable thing to go to the Café de Paris, for instance, and thereby show that the air-blitz was not affecting West End morale, now said that to go to a local 'hop' was irresponsible and flippant.

CLARA MILBURN
Writing to a Prisoner-of-War Son

Wednesday 24th July [1940]
A letter from the War Office Casualty Branch giving us Alan's address: 'Stalag XXA', Germany. That cheered us a bit, for now we can write to him. And, of course, it was not long before I wrote him a stilted little letter on a single sheet of notepaper, which is all one may do at a time. One can write as often as one likes – but how little one can really say! For one thing, news is scarce when one cuts out the war, and one may not say anything to give any information to the enemy. So things have to be carefully sifted till there is very little said. However one can send love and give facts in a veiled way, as I did today when I wrote: 'Little Bert Austin takes your father to his daily work', which meant 'Father has an Austin 7 to drive into Coventry, where he has taken a job at the Labour Exchange'. And then continued: 'and Maria stays with me at Burleigh. She is as good a girl as ever and behaves nicely, so I am glad to have her with me'. That meant: 'I have the Rover car for my use', because we call the Rover 'Maria'. He knows that and will put two and two together.

NELLA LAST
Where Do the Letters Go?

Tuesday, 25 August 1942

It will be six weeks on Monday since Cliff sailed. I wonder if he has reached his journey's end. A letter and an air mail card gave me a sadness, for he has not had any of my letters for a while. Where do they all go, I wonder? I send an airgraph nearly every week, and a long letter every three or four weeks – a 'diary' letter. I write the ones to Cliff and Arthur in that way now, so as not to forget any little incident that may interest them. I've four pads going at once, in an old stiff book-back to write on: always writing, always trying to interest or amuse my boys, and where do they go? And all the letters I hear of that go missing – surely all of them cannot be destroyed by 'enemy action'? A little sad-hearted wife said to me one day, 'It makes me wonder if they bother to take any letters out of the country. I write twice a week and rarely hear from Bert, who I know does the same. But when he does write, he always says the same – "Still no letter from home." '

VERE HODGSON
A Diary is Passed Round

21 August 1942

Excitement over the mulberry tree in the next garden – house unoccupied. Along with various others our caretaker raided the fruit. A policeman came to know if we were allowing our Printing Works boys over the wall. The Manager swept him off the premises. We suspected he wanted a mulberry pie for himself. Our lady gardener, also, is a formidable person, and would rout Scotland Yard, if they interfered with her. The net result was a Mulberry Pie for all. Excellent – something between a raspberry and blackberry, only sharper. The moral side appealed to me. If I had been caught I should have appealed to Lord Woolton himself, saying it was against the national interest to let fruit rot on the trees. Our conscience is clear, for we have tried to get in touch with the owner. [. . .]

5th March 1944

Gratifying letter from John Fossett: 'Very many thanks for two instalments of diary. Joan and I derived hours of pleasure from reading it aloud to each other. How we laughed about the Mulberry Tree. We passed it over to the RAF and how they enjoyed it. It seemed like being at home again as we lived through your experiences.' He was in South Africa.

SYLVIA TOWNSEND WARNER
The Censor
November 1940

Do you ever think of the Censor? I don't mean from the point of view of muttonising your language, for it's obvious you don't do that. But do you ever think of him as roomfulls of ladies and gentlemen, all engaged in the embarrassing occupation of reading other people's letters? What will they do when they can't be censors any longer (for they can't all become village postmistresses or go into the CID)? Will they pine and languish, and feel themselves suddenly cut off from humanity? Or will they spend the evening of their days reading Madame de Sévigné and the Reverend Leman White (I think he was called that; anyway, he loads the shelves of every second-hand bookshop, letters to ladies about their souls)? Or will they demonstrate their freedom by never opening another envelope, not even envelopes addressed to them, whitey brown envelopes marked On His Majesty's Service and containing income tax demands? Valentine had a terrible time when we got back a year ago, yearning to go into the censor's department. She has always been perfectly shameless about reading letters not meant for her, and, as she said, she was ideally suited for the work by never having much inclination to answer letters back.

C.A. LEJEUNE
Cinema and the Prose of War

It seems tolerably clear by now that the best thing the war is likely to draw out of the cinema is not poetry but prose: no masterpiece, but a number of small, candid snapshots of the soul of the people. This is probably as it must be, for war in these days is not a divided thing; they no longer fight battles in one parish and contemplate them in the next; there is no hermitage for the non-combatant in which he can refine, in sound or picture, the thoughts that have come to him from the battle-front; nor is there, indeed, in any real sense a non-combatant. To create or to savour the larger forms of art requires leisure of mind, and *that* is a thing we have not, neither by ten minutes nor by ten hours. But when a man's mood is disturbed, he is quicker to catch the mood of others. Human beings, rather than abstractions, are a necessity to him. He needs people; he sees people more clearly than ever before; if he has the talent he can sketch them with a remarkable fidelity.

The best film to come out of the war yet – for *Citizen Kane* was made when America was technically at peace – is a group-portrait, Noel Coward's *In Which We Serve*. In their more deliberately functional way, too, the documentary directors have made an acute study of men and women at war. Some historian of the future, with more leisure and serenity than we have, will be able to base a superb film drama on the faces and impressions recorded for him in the moment of action.

Now a new film adds to the collection of discerning wartime sketches. *The Gentle Sex* is a story of seven girls in the ATS. It isn't much of a story, if by story you understand excitement, magnitude, crisis, and a nice shiny medal at the end of it. These seven girls, with different backgrounds, different types of schooling, different codes, and different accents, simply go through their common training and do their jobs in company with thousands of others. Just a little emerges of their private lives, not much. Just a hint, but only a hint, is given of their future. The film is straitly concerned with their day-by-day experiences in the ATS – the humours and rigours of training, the physical weariness of night-driving, the easy fellowship, the sudden flare-ups of frayed nerves, the thought of marriage, so rigidly repressed, so irresistibly crowding to the surface.

The Gentle Sex was written by a woman and has a woman's understanding of women. It is acted by Rosamund John, Lilli Palmer, Joyce Howard, Jean Gillie, Joan Gates, Joan Greenwood, and Barbara Waring with a give-and-take that excites one's admiration. Leslie Howard directed, appears as a Back at the opening, and intervenes with a whimsical, speculative

255

commentary. Mere men who turn up here and there are played by John Laurie, Jimmy Hanley, and John Justin, in two out of three cases with a nice sense of their blundering intrusion. A pleasantly ironic touch is provided by a Victorian sampler, bidding women cultivate 'a spirit of modesty, humility, obedience, and submission.' The film's most subtle irony may possibly be an unintended one – a cross-stitch credit to the War Office and the ATS.

Chapter fifteen

THE LAST YEAR

The end of the war was a long time coming. The Allied invasion of France began on D Day, 6 June 1944, but the German surrender didn't come until nearly a year later, on 7 May 1945. The war in the Far East continued until the Japanese surrender on 14 August 1945.

In Britain the last year of the war was made worse by two new German weapons, the VIs – pilotless planes often referred to as doodlebugs – and later the V2 rockets. Freya Stark, who had been abroad working for the Ministry of Information in the Middle East, passed through London and was able to give a traveller's eye view of the new phenomenon of the doodlebug.

The end of the war had been in people's sights from the early days. Women wondered whether their lives would return to prewar patterns of marriage and home, or whether some of the changes had come to stay. Discussions about the shape of postwar society had been fuelled by the publication of the Beveridge Report in December 1942. On the whole optimism prevailed with hopes for the birth of the welfare state, although there were some gloomy predictions of a drop in women's employment once the men were demobbed.

For many of the women who had started their diaries in September 1939, VE Day on 8 May presented itself as the obvious closing entry, an epilogue of relaxed spontaneity. But even as they celebrated, many women felt the need to remember those who suffered or died. As facts emerged from mainland Europe about the concentration camps and the terrible devastation caused by the war, Rebecca West was not the only one to feel that 'their celebrations might be ironical. . . . We sang, we danced until midnight, but we knew that we were on the edge of doom unless the whole of humanity walked carefully.'

ZELMA KATIN
Long Days on the Trams

Summer days. [. . .] Work became harder, hotter and more tiring. My feet swelled, I acquired painful corns, and I took to wearing my son's shoes, because they were so much larger than my own. But there were compensations. There were the compensations not only of the vistas but of a temporary farewell to the blackout, of natural light for punching tickets and giving change, of cool dawns for the early shifts, of lengthened shopping hours which gave me a fairer chance to compete with full-time housewives, and of raw green salads for my meals at home.

My hands were burnt a nut brown. I rolled my sleeves up to the elbows and took my fares. Inspectors opened their eyes a little wider when they saw my bare arms but said nothing. 'Do you want a fight then?' said a passenger. Others said, 'Are you sweating lass?' 'Is the washing nearly done?' 'You do look cool, miss.' But not one conductress or motorman followed suit. [. . .]

I am glad I have done this kind of war work, proud that I still have the moral and physical energy to follow it and I hope that out of this experience I shall have gained a new understanding of life, people and marriage. Like millions of men and women in uniform I cannot pretend I am liking it. Perhaps the sacrifice and hardship are giving us a strength which will enrich us in the future and toughen us for the struggle which lies ahead.

I will confess that I am thinking not only of a future for humanity but a future for myself. I want to lie in bed until eight o'clock, to eat a meal slowly, to sweep the floors when they are dirty, to sit in front of the fire, to walk on the hills, to go shopping of an afternoon, to gossip at odd minutes.

FREYA STARK
The Doodlebug

21 July 1944
Something very curious has happened here with these great robots. One has gone back into those ages when men saw the Inevitable take on a visible shape and recognised their gods, unpersuadable, unreasonable in human

ways, full of fascination and terror. I have a window facing the direction from which they come and spent an hour or so watching them last night – about midnight the sky still green with twilight faint and straight like faded streaks in old silk. Then the little droning things began far off, the houses mauve and dark within their outlines: we looked like an uninhabited city and the drone came nearer, it is quite slow, you hear it from so far. The sky had a few clouds, their high tips touched with light. And at last, the drumming loud now like an orchestra working up to the opening of a ballet, the fireball came skimming above the houses whose chimneys seemed to darken under her feet. (Everyone I ask tells me they think of it as feminine.) She did not give one the feeling of being wicked, but rather as if she were a planet or other creature of the natural forces, which has wilfully left its own cited circuit and gone wandering, and the destruction comes merely as a result of her unsuitability to the general surroundings. When she comes near, you hear the brazen flapping of her garments, you see that she is shod with flames or perhaps 'makes the cold air fire'. Shelley could have described her, and the Greeks would have known her ancestry. She went off, hurrying over the human world that cowered as she came, until she touched it far away across the houses, in a noise of death that seemed to fall like a stone into the stillness. It is a strange life, and a strange feeling of fear which, like a touch of black, sets off all the other colours. I would not be missing it for anything, nor the sight of London now, very gallant.

INEZ HOLDEN
The Flying Bombs

10 July 1944

At the hairdresser the girl who washed my hair said that on Sunday she and her husband had gone round to tidy up her father's flat which had been blasted by bomb damage. They got the place into working order for him and started back home. At the end of the road wardens and firemen were still clearing up the street and from the windows of a big block of flats the people looked down on to the street scene. 'They weren't sightseers, you understand,' she said, 'only ordinary people looking out at the fire engines. There were old women and children, girls and soldiers on leave.' Then suddenly she had seen the pilotless plane descending in an arc curve at great speed. She called out to her husband and flung her arms round a pillar box. Her husband had thrown her down the area steps and fallen after her. They heard the glass come crashing in around the area and when she looked up she saw her father running down the street waving his arms and calling out, 'My children were there.' The girl told me, 'All the time I see those people in my mind, with the plane coming down on to the roof and they not knowing anything about it.' She said several times, 'All those people – all those people. I don't seem able to forget them – all those people.'

VITA SACKVILLE-WEST
The Future of the Landgirl

When the Land Army was disbanded after the last war, many members took advantage of the free passage to the Dominions offered to ex-service women. It is much to be hoped that the same thing may happen again. It seems likely that it will, for young women today are far more enterprising and adventurous than they were even in 1919, and what could be more desirable than that the stock of these fine girls should mix with their consanguineous friends in Canada, Australia, New Zealand? . . . I can visualise a new 'Mayflower', blossoming on every deck with the waving hands of a new sort of pioneer, a sort which would have astonished our Mayflower forefathers whose women were encumbered by huge skirts and tight stomachers, and encumbered even more by the convenient prejudices established by man for the control of his subservient woman. My new Mayflower carries a different muster. It carries gay young creatures, untrammelled by bulky clothes; legs are allowed to appear as legs, breeched and gaitered; the soft loose jersey replaces the whale-boned bodice, the elastic belt replaces the rigidity of the unnatural corset. And above all the liberty of the spirit replaces the rigidity of the conventional mind.

By the way, a strange idea appears to exist among Landgirls, to the effect that they may be *compelled* to 'go abroad' after the war. Let me contradict this idea emphatically and at once. Land Army officials are much puzzled to know how it can have got about. If a girl wants to go either into liberated Europe or into the colonies or Dominions, it will be entirely by her own choice. The idea of compulsion is without any foundation whatsoever, it just waves vaguely about in the air, and has roots only in the minds of those who like to believe in any stray bit of gossip they may have heard or may perhaps have read in some irresponsible newspaper.

VERE HODGSON
VE Day, 8 May 1945

Victory in Europe Day, Tuesday 8th

Today we have been celebrating! Thunderstorm in the night. No one slept much for excitement. But the sun shone warm, and it has been a Glorious Day.

Kit and I reached St Paul's about 11 a.m. One service was in progress, but another was soon due to begin. All through I continued to give thanks for our great deliverance. We had a splendid view of the Lord Mayor of London walking down the aisle, and his Chain of Office seemed to glitter with diamonds. The Choir sang the *Te Deum*. All the little boys were back. We sang all three verses of the National Anthem with great firmness, confounding their politics with tremendous enthusiasm.

Lovely and warm outside. We thought of the wonderful fire-watchers the Cathedral has had. They held their own Service. I remembered that Sunday when I walked past it, smoking ruins around, and a few weary firemen gathering their apparatus together.

We sauntered down to the River, and ate our lunch above the Temple stairs, near the *Discovery*. Carefree after so many years of anxiety. Then along to Westminster and Whitehall. We stood in Parliament St. What a squash! The buses scraped within an inch of us, and the horses of the mounted police rubbed their flanks against us.

Precisely at 3 p.m. Big Ben's chimes told us the moment was about to begin. All traffic stopped. The mounted policeman wiped the sweat from his brow. All was still. How wonderful to be standing in Whitehall, in the shadow of the House of Commons, listening to That Voice which had steered us from our darkest hours to the daylight of deliverance. No words can express what we owe him. He mentioned the Channel Islands to tremendous cheers. Kit was thrilled that they should be specially mentioned on such an occasion. She has not heard from her father for eleven months.

By now we were exhausted with heat and standing. Heaps of people on bicycles. There was a tandem – Mother, Father and Baby. Spectators were horrified at the position of this tiny mite, with a great bus towering above it – but the baby did not worry. We reached Downing St with a great effort. But I could no more. We had heard him speak.

The tube at Trafalgar Square was impossible of entrance, so we walked along Pall Mall. Cars passed us with people riding on the hoods and the bonnets. Everyone was just letting themselves go. We were glad to get to the flat for a cup of tea!

In the evening we had our own party. We were quite a United Nations. A Russian, a Swiss, a Channel Islander, a Scot-cum-Welsh and me, a true-blue English Midlander. We had ersatz champagne. Tinned grapefruit. Salad. Tongue. Tin of crayfish – and a Plum Pudding. All of us had been saving these viands up for a long time. All Beautifully prepared by Miss Cameron. It was in Barishnikov's garden flat, which is bigger than mine. We had lovely coffee, and then he produced his pièce de resistance, some 1898 port . . . or some such date. We drank numerous Toasts . . . Churchill, Stalin, Auntie Nell, Kit's father in Guernsey . . . then the men drank to us.

We listened to the radio, and just tuned in to the moment when Mr Churchill came out in his Siren sunt and conducted *Land of Hope and Glory*. He was wearing a black Homburg Hat. What a lad! He was cheered to the echo. God bless him!

MARGARET CRISP
VE Day in Hospital

VE Day, for which we had all waited so eagerly and which had been made possible by the men who were now in our care, would have passed in a manner no different from any other day, but for the efforts of individual nurses. A dance had been arranged for the nursing and medical staff, and all the patients who were able were allowed to go on four days' leave; but nobody bothered to think of the very lonely bed-patients left behind in a half-empty ward, the lads who had risked their lives, given their young limbs, and sacrificed their health so that others could celebrate this occasion. Sounds of distant laughter, community singing, and a dance band's blare reached the ears of those almost forgotten men in a war now nearly won.

GRACIE FIELDS
The End of the War in the Far East

Piva, Bougainville, 16 August 1945
My Dear All

Here we are on the day of celebration – this morning I sang The Lord's Prayer at thanksgiving service, and it was very impressive.

I've now given five small concerts in five different hospital wards, and tonight we give a big show to about fifteen thousand – about ten thousand American boys will also be there. My pianist's young lady is a Gilbert and Sullivan opera singer and she does her bit, also a squeeze-box hurdy-gurdy boy to play a few tunes, and a man singer, and we do the old servant sketch when and where it's possible.

It's dreadfully sticky hot, it is all jungle and so different to all the other theatres of war I've sung in. You can just imagine what the poor lads have gone through and it's usually raining, something awful sometimes, easily six inches of rain. We are lucky, it's fine for us today, they say it rains every afternoon. The boys are so very happy it's all over, they're all shouting HTM – Home to Mom, boys!

Chapter sixteen

THE END OF THE WAR

Although the Allies won the war, the atom bombs dropped on Hiroshima and Nagasaki, and the evidence of the Holocaust, cast long shadows over their victory. At home, in what Mollie Panter-Downes called 'this island of tired people', many women who had kept going during the six years of war now found themselves suffering from exhaustion. Frances Partridge's friend Julia Strachey wrote to her in May 1945 that 'the dynamic principle has given way and one feels like a printed page, a sheet of newspaper or a pressed dried grass'. More prosaically, Sylvia Townsend Warner wrote at the beginning of 1946, 'No one feels well or happy just now.'

This was a time of return, readjustment, rehabilitation. Nurses and welfare workers worked with survivors from the concentration camps, and helped returning prisoners of war on their journey back home. Women working in factories and forces alike faced the prospect of demobilization, sometimes with relief and sometimes with no enthusiasm at all. For some though, the future offered an exciting new world: seventy thousand GI brides set sail for America.

Women were strongly represented among the journalists, observers and war artists who entered Germany and German-occupied countries at the end of the war. The shock was intense. 'I remember every detail of Dachau,' wrote Martha Gellhorn years later, 'and probably will as long as I live.' Recording what they saw forced a particular sort of attention, a slowing of the narrative to an appalled standstill. At the War Crimes Trials in Nuremberg too, women recognized that they were witnesses to a devastating history.

MOLLIE PANTER-DOWNES
The Power of Photography

29 April 1945

If the San Francisco Conference is the big worry of the moment, the big sensation, which also has to do with the future, because it brings up the subject of our treatment of the conquered, is the revelation of the horrors of the German concentration camps. It has taken the camera to bring home to the slow, good-natured, skeptical British what, as various liberal journals have tartly pointed out, the pens of their correspondents have been unsuccesfully trying to bring home to them since as far back as 1933. Millions of comfortable families, too kind and too lazy in those days to make the effort to believe what they conveniently looked upon as a newspaper propaganda stunt, now believe the horrifying, irrefutable evidence that even blurred printing on poor war-time paper has made all too clear. There are long queues of people waiting silently wherever the photographs are on exhibition. The shock to the public has been enormous, and lots of hitherto moderate people are wondering uncomfortably whether they will agree, after all, with Lord Vansittart's ruthless views on a hard peace. While the violent revulsion has not produced any particularly helpful answers to the question of what is to be done with the Germans, it has suggested one or two things that might not be done with them. Plenty of angry Englishmen would like to know that German prisoners of war here would no longer draw double the rations a civilian gets. After photographs of Buchenwald's walking skeletons, Britons were understandably incensed by the thought of Nazis growing plump in English prison camps. If, as some people think, the sudden piling on of the horrors is an attempt to prepare the British and American publics for the stiff terms Moscow seems determined to impose on Germany, it has certainly succeeded here. Whatever the Russians ask, it will not be enough to wipe Buchenwald and the rest from shocked British minds.

MARTHA GELLHORN
Dachau

May 1945

We came out of Germany in a C-47 carrying American prisoners of war. The planes were lined up on the grass field at Regensburg and the passengers waited, sitting in the shade under the wings. They would not leave the planes; this was a trip no one was going to miss. When the crew chief said all aboard, we got in as if we were escaping from a fire. No one looked out the windows as we flew over Germany. No one ever wanted to see Germany again. They turned away from it, with hatred and sickness. At first they did not talk, but when it became real that Germany was behind forever they began talking of their prisons. We did not comment on the Germans; they are past words, there is nothing to say. 'No one will believe us,' a soldier said. They agreed on that; no one would believe them.

'Where were you captured, miss?' a soldier asked.

'I'm only bumming a ride; I've been down to see Dachau.'

One of the men said suddenly, 'We got to talk about it. We got to talk about it, if anyone believes us or not.'

Behind the barbed wire and the electric fence, the skeletons sat in the sun and searched themselves for lice. They have no age and no faces; they all look alike and like nothing you will ever see if you are lucky. We crossed the wide, crowded, dusty compound between the prison barracks and went to the hospital. In the hall sat more of the skeletons, and from them came the smell of disease and death. They watched us but did not move; no expression shows on a face that is only yellowish, stubbly skin, stretched across bone. What had been a man dragged himself into the doctor's office; he was a Pole and he was about six feet tall and he weighed less than a hundred pounds and he wore a striped prison shirt, a pair of unlaced boots, and a blanket which he tried to hold around his legs. His eyes were large and strange and stood out from his face, and his jawbone seemed to be cutting through his skin. He had come to Dachau from Buchenwald on the last death transport. There were fifty boxcars of his dead travelling companions still on the siding outside the camp, and for the last three days the American Army had forced Dachau civilians to bury these dead. When this transport had arrived, the German guards locked the men, women and children in the boxcars and there they slowly died of hunger and thirst and suffocation. They screamed and they tried to fight their way out; from time to time, the guards fired into the cars to stop the noise.

This man had survived; he was found under a pile of dead. Now he stood on the bones that were his legs and talked and suddenly he wept. 'Everyone is dead,' he said, and the face that was not a face twisted with pain or sorrow or horror. 'No one is left. Everyone is dead. I cannot help myself. Here I am and I am finished and cannot help myself. Everyone is dead.'

The Polish doctor who had been a prisoner here for five years said, 'In four weeks, you will be a young man again. You will be fine.'

Perhaps his body will live and take strength, but one cannot believe that his eyes will ever be like other people's eyes.

The doctor spoke with great detachment about the things he had watched in this hospital. He had watched them and there was nothing he could do to stop them. The prisoners talked in the same way – quietly, with a strange little smile as if they apologized for talking of such loathsome things to someone who lived in a real world and could hardly be expected to understand Dachau.

'The Germans made here some unusual experiments,' the doctor said. 'They wished to see how long an aviator could go without oxygen, how high in the sky he could go. So they had a closed car from which they pumped the oxygen. It is a quick death,' he said. 'It does not take more than fifteen minutes, but it is a hard death. They killed not so many people, only eight hundred in that experiment. It was found that no one can live above thirty-six thousand feet altitude without oxygen.'

'Whom did they choose for this experiment?' I asked.

'Any prisoner,' he said, 'so long as he was healthy. They picked the strongest. The mortality was one hundred per cent, of course.'

'It is very interesting, is it not?' said another Polish doctor.

We did not look at each other. I do not know how to explain it, but aside from the terrible anger you feel, you are ashamed. You are ashamed for mankind.

'There was also the experiment of the water,' said the first doctor. 'This was to see how long pilots could survive when they were shot down over water, like the Channel, let us say. For that, the German doctors put the prisoners in great vats and they stood in water up to their necks. It was found that the human body can resist for two and a half hours in water eight degrees below zero. They killed six hundred people in this experiment. Sometimes a man had to suffer three times, for he fainted early in the experiment, and then he was revived and a few days later the experiment was again undertaken.'

'Didn't they scream, didn't they cry out?'

He smiled at that question. 'There was no use in this place for a man to scream or cry out. It was no use for any man ever.'

A colleague of the Polish doctor came in; he was the one who knew about the malaria experiments. The German doctor, who was chief of the Army's tropical medicine research, used Dachau as an experimental station. He was attempting to find a way to immunize German soldiers against malaria. To that end, he inoculated eleven thousand prisoners with tertiary malaria. The death rate from the malaria was not too heavy; it simply meant that these prisoners, weakened by fever, died more quickly afterward from hunger. However, in one day three men died of overdoses of Pyramidon, with which, for some unknown reason, the Germans were then experimenting. No immunization for malaria was ever found.

Down the hall, in the surgery, the Polish surgeon got out the record book to look up some data on operations performed by the SS doctors. These were castration and sterilization operations. The prisoner was forced to sign a paper beforehand, saying that he willingly undertook this self-destruction. Jews and gypsies were castrated; any foreign slave laborer who had had relations with a German woman was sterilized. The German women were sent to other concentration camps.

The Polish surgeon had only his four front upper teeth left, the others on both sides having been knocked out by a guard one day, because the guard felt like breaking teeth. This act did not seem a matter of surprise to the doctor or to anyone else. No brutality could surprise them any more. They were used to a systematic cruelty that had gone on, in this concentration camp, for twelve years.

The surgeon mentioned another experiment, really a very bad one, he said, and obviously quite useless. The guinea pigs were Polish priests. (Over two thousand priests passed through Dachau; one thousand are alive.) The German doctors injected streptococci germs in the upper leg of the prisoners, between the muscle and the bone. An extensive abscess formed, accompanied by fever and extreme pain. The Polish doctor knew of more than a hundred cases treated this way; there may have been more. He had a record of thirty-one deaths, but it took usually from two to three months of ceaseless pain before the patient died, and all of them died after several operations performed during the last few days of their life. The operations were a further experiment, to see if a dying man could be saved; but the answer was that he could not. Some prisoners recovered entirely, because they were treated with the already known and proved antidote, but there were others who were now moving around the camp, as best they could, crippled for life.

Then, because I could listen to no more, my guide, a German Socialist who had been a prisoner in Dachau for ten and a half years, took me across the compound to the jail. In Dachau, if you want to rest from one horror you go and see another. The jail was a long clean building with small white cells in it. Here lived the people whom the prisoners called the NN. NN stands for *Nacht und Nebel*, which means night and mist. Translated into less romatic terms, this means that the prisoners in these cells never saw a human being, were never allowed to speak to anyone, were never taken out into the sun and the air. They lived in solitary confinement on water soup and a slice of bread, which was the camp diet. There was of course the danger of going mad. But one never knew what happened to them in the years of their silence. And on the Friday before the Sunday when the Americans entered Dachau, eight thousand men were removed by the SS on a final death transport. Among these were all the prisoners from the solitary cells. None of these men has been heard of since. Now in the clean empty building a woman, alone in a cell, screamed for a long time on one terrible note, was silent for a moment, and screamed again. She had gone mad in the last few days; we came too late for her.

In Dachau if a prisoner was found with a cigarette butt in his pocket he received twenty-five to fifty lashes with a bull whip. If he failed to stand at attention with his hat off, six feet away from any SS trooper who happened to pass, he had his hands tied behind his back and he was hung by his bound hands from a hook on the wall for an hour. If he did any other little thing which displeased the jailers he was put in the box. The box is the size of a telephone booth. It is so constructed that being in it alone a man cannot sit down, or kneel down, or of course lie down. It was usual to put four men in it together. Here they stood for three days and nights without food or water or any form of sanitation. Afterward they went back to the sixteen-hour day of labor and the diet of water soup and a slice of bread like soft gray cement.

What had killed most of these people was hunger; starvation was simply routine. A man worked those incredible hours on that diet and lived in such overcrowding as cannot be imagined, the bodies packed into airless barracks, and woke each morning weaker, waiting for his death. It is not known how many people died in this camp in the twelve years of its existence, but at least forty-five thousand are known to have died in the last three years. Last February and March, two thousand were killed in the gas chamber because, though they were too weak to work, they did not have the grace to die; so it was arranged for them.

The gas chamber is part of the crematorium. The crematorium is a brick building outside the camp compound, standing in a grove of pine trees. A Polish priest had attached himself to us and as we walked there he said, 'I started to die twice of starvation but I was very lucky. I got a job as a mason when we were building this crematorium, so I received a little more food, and that way I did not die.' Then he said, 'Have you seen our chapel, madame?' I said I had not, and my guide said I could not; it was within the zone where the two thousand typhus cases were more or less isolated. 'It is a pity,' the priest said. 'We finally got a chapel and we had Holy Mass there almost every Sunday. There are very beautiful murals. The man who painted them died of hunger two months ago.'

Now we were at the crematorium. 'You will put a handkerchief over your nose,' the guide said. There, suddenly, but never to be believed, were the bodies of the dead. They were everywhere. There were piles of them inside the oven room, but the SS had not had time to burn them. They were piled outside the door and alongside the building. They were all naked, and behind the crematorium the ragged clothing of the dead was neatly stacked, shirts, jackets, trousers, shoes, awaiting sterilization and further use. The clothing was handled with order, but the bodies were dumped like garbage, rotting in the sun, yellow and nothing but bones, bones grown huge because there was no flesh to cover them, hideous, terrible, agonizing bones, and the unendurable smell of death.

We have all seen a great deal now; we have seen too many wars and too much violent dying; we have seen hospitals, bloody and messy as butcher shops; we have seen the dead like bundles lying on all the roads of half the earth. But nowhere was there anything like this. Nothing about war was ever as insanely wicked as these starved and outraged, naked, nameless dead. Behind one pile of dead lay the clothed healthy bodies of the German soldiers who had been found in this camp. They were shot at once when the American Army entered. And for the first time anywhere one could look at a dead man with gladness.

Just behind the crematorium stood the fine big modern hothouses. Here the prisoners grew the flowers that the SS officers loved. Next to the hothouses were the vegetable gardens, and very rich ones too, where the starving prisoners cultivated the vitamin foods that kept the SS strong. But if a man, dying of hunger, furtively pulled up and gorged himself on a head of lettuce, he would be beaten until he was unconscious. In front of the crematorium, separated from it by a stretch of garden, stood a long row of well-built, commodious homes. The families of the SS officers lived here; their wives and children lived here quite happily, while the chimneys of the crematorium poured out unending smoke heavy with human ashes.

The American soldier in the plane said, 'We got to talk about it.' You cannot talk about it very well because there is a kind of shock that sets in and makes it almost unbearable to remember what you have seen. I have not talked about the women who were moved to Dachau three weeks ago from their own concentration camps. Their crime was that they were Jewish. There was a lovely girl from Budapest, who somehow was still lovely, and the woman with mad eyes who had watched her sister walk into the gas chamber at Auschwitz and been held back and refused the right to die with her sister, and the Austrian woman who pointed out calmly that they all had only the sleazy dresses they wore on their backs, they had never had anything more, and that they worked outdoors sixteen hours a day too in the long winters, and that they too were 'corrected,' as the Germans say, for any offense, real or imaginary.

I have not talked about how it was the day the American Army arrived, though the prisoners told me. In their joy to be free, and longing to see their friends who had come at last, many prisoners rushed to the fence and died electrocuted. There were those who died cheering, because that effort of happiness was more than their bodies could endure. There were those who died because now they had food, and they ate before they could be stopped, and it killed them. I do not know words to describe the men who have survived this horror for years, three years, five years, ten years, and whose minds are as clear and unafraid as the day they entered.

I was in Dachau when the German armies surrendered unconditionally to the Allies. The same half-naked skeleton who had been dug out of the death train shuffled back into the doctor's office. He said something in Polish; his voice was no stronger than a whisper. The Polish doctor clapped his hands gently and said, 'Bravo.' I asked what they were talking about.

'The war is over,' the doctor said. 'Germany is defeated.'

We sat in that room, in that accursed cemetery prison, and no one had anything more to say. Still, Dachau seemed to me the most suitable place in Europe to hear the news of victory. For surely this war was made to abolish Dachau, and all the other places like Dachau, and everything that Dachau stood for, and to abolish it forever.

MAVIS TATE MP
More on Buchenwald
May 1945

Millions of people will in the last few days have seen films of the German internment camps at Buchenwald and Belsen. They will think they have gained some impression of the conditions under which thousands of people died who had committed no crime and faced no trial. After having studied every available photograph and been to all the films on what are now known as the 'horror camps', I can say without any hesitation whatever that they give but a very faint impression of the reality. [. . .] Photographs, if they shock one, shock through the eyes; one is not shocked through any other sense. In fact, while it is possible to photograph some of the results of suffering, there are no means by which suffering itself can be photographed. [. . .]

The so-called children in the camp present a tremendous problem. They speak with utter calm of having seen their relations shot or removed to be put into a gas-chamber. They have many of them lived their most formative

271

years knowing only cruelty, squalor and want in its extreme forms, and they give the impression – and none can wonder at it – of callousness and of lack of interest in anything beyond personal preservation. Those who have survived are tough, and will be unlikely to prove a centre of stability or of kindliness wherever they settle. They should be under care and guidance of a high order for a time and not let loose lonely and stateless in a distraught Europe.

Some German civilians from Weimar were visiting the camp when we were there, but one woman only did I see who appeared genuinely upset. When I said to her, 'Well you have behaved in a wonderful way under Hitler, have you not?' she burst into tears and said, 'I am ashamed of being a German.' The citizens of Weimar in the main looked anything but cowed. They have never been bombed – their land has been cultivated to the last inch with the help of slave labour, and they look well-fed, truculent and aggressive. I repeatedly said to my fellow delegates that I was deeply shocked by the faces of many of the German women in Weimar. They were cruel and hard beyond belief, and I had seen none like them anywhere – until I looked at the photographs of the women guards of Belsen camp.

MARY KESSELL
German Diary by a War Artist
August-October 1945

BERLIN

Berlin smells of death. Incredible, like a million-year-old ruin, so silent that crickets sing and one can hear them, with pale figures creeping around cutting trees, hidden in dark. Pools of water, pale in moonlight, and white ruins like great teeth bared. Oh, unforgettable smell of thousands of dead. Burnt-out cars and tanks in the gutters, and mile on mile on mile where no one lives or can ever live again, just smelling, and there the cricket sings.

Across a desert of sand and fossilised trees to the Reichstag. A noble grey-green ruin, splintered by battle, the last stand in Berlin. Ruins so vast surrounding it that it seemed as if it had been there for decades, and such stillness. One American soldier was reading or looking at the Russian names chalked and painted everywhere. Great candelabras strewed the floor of the Banqueting Hall, and things flapped from bits of wire and made fluttering noises. It was as silent as the grave. We walked through miles of beautiful ruins, and I decided that this must be my first painting. At the door as we left was an old woman with a dirty piece of rag. She asked us to let her wipe the dust from our shoes, but somehow we couldn't let her do it.

Then on to the Chancellery. This is in the Russian zone. Russians are racing up and down in looted cars, using hooters all the time, like children. The noise is terrific. There is a notice outside the Chancellery. 'Open on Sundays only, 2–4.' A grimy looking policeman is sitting on an old sofa outside. We just walk past him. He gets off and salutes us and in we go. Dear God, if only all the world could see this. It's vast, endless. Here is where all the plans were made, huge filing cabinets unhinged, papers like snow to walk upon. Chairs with all the stuffing gone tipped up on steps. Paper everywhere. A Russian soldier came out wiping his lips. In a minute a German woman left, and went the other way. The paper serves as a bed: the price, a cigarette or some sugar candy. The Chancellery a brothel, run by nobody, but everybody goes there. I helped myself to notepaper and envelopes from the room upstairs, in which were hundreds of torn mutilated photographs of Hitler.

LAURA KNIGHT
From My Nuremberg Diary

On the 5th January, 1946, I was sent there [to the Nuremberg War Trials] by the War Office to do British Government war records. [. . .]

Several of the defendants have now become aware that I am picturing them; Hess again looked up at me with his mad stare. The blacks of his deep set eyes are so big that they don't show any of the white eye-ball.

Sometimes, for a rest from my own work, I put my drawing materials down and hold the earphones to my ears. In my opinion, Maxwell Fyfe is outstanding in the masterly composition of his matter; few of the other prosecutors possess his clarity. Again and again, the theatre comes to mind: 'good lines', 'bad lines', 'good diction', 'bad diction'.

Aloof as I am, alone at work in my box – not a participant in what is taking place – I need to remind myself that the drama being enacted before me does not belong to the theatrical stage, that the performing cast in the dock do not put all matter aside at the drop of the curtain, go straight to their dressing rooms and take off their make-up. At the close of still another day's session, again I peered through that slit of a window in the steel-bound door and watched the prisoners, each with a US army Snowdrop between him and the next, despairingly mount the wire-netted stairway to their cells.

I have again had an interrupted day's work. I only have the use of my box by the grace of the people who own it, a USA broadcasting company. The US press and photographers often come into focus, and click their cameras at me. Once I was a perfect picture of a German sausage, my fur coat covered with a travelling rug wound round from head to foot with rope. The outer door, leading to an unheated passage-way, had lost its handle and the thermometer was way below zero.

While working this morning I become aware of tension in court; you don't need headphones to know when something damning is taking place. Documentary evidence is produced of Doenitz having given orders to German submarine officers to annihilate ships and crews. He had actually written this in his diary – and the extraordinary thing was that he looks as ordinary as any other man you would meet in the streets.

The clock strikes eleven and, as on any other morning, the prisoners munch biscuits, stand and bend their stiffened joints, discuss points in question with the calm of actors at rehearsal. A Snowdrop, in enmity as frigid as a block of ice, pours out a drink of water for von Papen, who has to lean over the barrier to reach it.

Eleven-fifteen: the judges return, everyone resumes their seats, the Snowdrops line up again behind their prisoners. Today, as the hours pass monotonously by, one of the Snowdrops faints – passes right out, to fall without bending a joint against the wainscoting behind – and, stiff as a log of wood, is carried out.

The smell of peppermint chewing-gum prevails. All is today as it will be tomorrow, and the day after that: Snowdrops on duty everywhere, even under the bare rafters in the passage-way outside my box; icy draughts. [. . .] home-sick? . . . yah! Texas? . . . California? They long for sympathy, for someone to talk to and to look at their snaps of wives, mothers and children, carried in their breast-pockets. I haven't the heart to tell them that I can't concentrate on my work and talk as well.

REBECCA WEST
Nuremberg

The Germans listened to the closing speeches made by Mr Justice Jackson and Sir Hartley Shawcross, and were openly shamed by their new-minted indignation. When Mr Justice Jackson brought his speech to an end by pointing a forefinger at each of the defendants in turn and denounced his specific share in the Nazi crime, all of them winced, except old Streicher, who munched and mumbled away in some private and probably extremely objectionable dream, and Schacht, who became stiffer than ever, stiff as an iron stag in the garden of an old house. It was not surprising that all the rest were abashed, for the speech showed the civilized good sense against which they had conspired, and it was patently admirable, patently a pattern of the material necessary to the salvation of peoples. It is to be regretted that one phrase in it may be read by posterity as falling beneath the level of its context, because it has a particular significance to all those who attended the Nuremberg trial. 'Goering,' said Mr Justice Jackson, 'stuck a pudgy finger in every pie.' The courtroom was not small, but it was full of Goering's fingers. His soft and white and spongy hands were for ever smoothing his curiously abundant brown hair, or covering his wide mouth while his plotting eyes looked facetiously around, or weaving impudent gestures of innocence in the air. The other men in the dock broke into sudden and relieved laughter at the phrase. Goering was plainly angered, though less by the phrase than by their laughter.

But the next day, when Sir Hartley Shawcross closed the British case, there was no laughter at all. His speech was not so shapely and so decorative as Mr Justice Jackson's, for English rhetoric has crossed the Atlantic in this century and is now more at home in the United States than on its native ground, and he spoke at greater length and stopped more legal holes. But his words were full of a living pity, which gave the men in the box their worst hour. The feminine Shirach achieved a gesture that was touching. He listened attentively to what Sir Hartley had to say of his activities as a Youth Leader; and when he heard him go on to speak of his responsibility for the deportation of forty thousand Soviet children he put up his delicate hand and lifted off the circlet of his headphones, laying it down very quietly on the ledge before him. It seemed possible that he had indeed the soul of a governess, that he was indeed Jane Eyre, and had been perverted by a Mr Rochester who, disappearing into self-kindled flames, had left him disenchanted and the prey of a prim but inextinguishable remorse. And when Sir Hartley quoted the deposition of a witness who had described a Jewish father who, standing with his little son in front of a firing squad, 'pointed

275

to the sky, stroked his head, and seemed to explain something to the boy', all the defendants wriggled on their seats, like children rated by a school-master, while their faces grew old.

MARY TREVELYAN
Prisoners of War
Belgium, April 1945

The Canteen has become the central meeting-place for everybody, officers and men alike, which is just as it should be. There are always long queues at the counters for tea, buns, sweets, cigarettes and, greatest luxury of all, chopped-up pieces of chocolate. And, not least in demand, liver salts, which are the quickest way of doing something to recover from eating again. The Canteen is never empty. Most of the green arm-chairs in the far corner, where it is a little quieter, are filled with sleeping men, their heads thrown back in complete exhaustion and their faces, when asleep, showing a grim picture of their past sufferings. Some are absorbed in magazines and newspapers, trying to catch up with the world. The writing-tables are always occupied. Some are scribbling away for dear life, pouring out pent-up excitement and emotion. Others sit, pen in hand, unable to find words, staring at the sheet of paper, putting down a few words, then throwing the paper away. There are always some noisy, cheerful groups, exchanging experiences or making plans for the future. But many just sit silent, staring into space, nibbling a bun, sipping a little tea, then getting up restlessly and going to another table.

We have tried all sorts of entertainment, for many of them ask if there is a show in the evening, but we find they are not yet in a state to take in anything. Community singing is no good, comedians are much too quick for them to take in, singers they like, but do not bother to applaud. So, after trial and error, we have now arranged for a series of small dance-bands who play morning and evening in the Canteen and a military band which plays in the barrack square in the afternoons. They just need a little music going on, old tunes of five years ago are best, and they hum and whistle a bit.

THEODORA FITZGIBBON
GI Bride

From the moment the Embassy sent me four labels, three for my luggage and one to tie on the lapel of my coat, with a covering letter enclosing my 'orders', everything promised to be unusual. I had become that unlikely person for me, a 'GI bride'. [. . .]

I arrived at Waterloo Station, labelled and with my luggage, on 14 March 1946. My grandmother had pressed five pounds into my hand and a bottle of whisky for the journey. A porter said to me: 'You a bride, miss?' which rather amused me as I had at that time been married for two years. He led me to a special train which was to take us all, not to the boat, but to an army camp at Tidworth on Salisbury Plain. I settled in the first compartment I came to, and watched the leave-takings of the other 'brides'. One fond mother produced a hot-water bottle which was disdainfully handed back with the message that 'where I'm going to everything's properly heated'. I wondered if it was.

The unheated train rattled slowly through the London suburbs. In Middlesex the first sign of fields appeared and I noticed a rather pretty farmhouse in the middle of a field, the small town about a mile away to the left. My reverie was disturbed by a dark girl, well wrapped in a travelling rug, sitting opposite me.

'My, I wouldn't like to live in that isolated spot,' she said in a very false American accent. I asked her where she was going to in America.

'Montana,' she replied calmly. I hadn't the heart to disillusion her.

It was dark when we arrived at Tidworth Camp. We were helped out of the bus by shadowy male figures. I heard the girl in front of me say, 'Thank you,' but as she came into the lamplight she wheeled round to me and cried:

'My mother would be furious with me if she knew I'd said thank you to a German.'

I saw then that our assistants were German prisoners. From then on the German prisoners looked after us entirely. In the bare room I shared with sixteen other 'brides', Fritz or Hans stood by while we made our beds and commiserated with us for the dust on the bare wooden boards. They cooked for us and served the food into our tin trays. We were frequently told over loudspeakers that we mustn't fraternize with them. My limited knowledge of German was a great nuisance as I found myself let in for many things. In this barrack room was a central old-fashioned coke stove around which we huddled in the evenings. I shared Grandmother's whisky with a chosen few.

It was all nightmarish. The beds were as hard as boards, the food uneatable, there were two baths only in an outhouse between two hundred of us. Also the American Army's passion for youth was a bit overwhelming: only one other girl apart from myself was in her middle twenties, all the others were teenagers, with the exception of one rather jolly old lady of about fifty, whom I took to be a relic of 1918.

We were not allowed out of the perimeter at all, and the Red Cross 'rest' room was built to hold about a quarter of us. The two public telephones it housed were beseiged at all hours by long queues of girls shouting inanities like 'and we had tinned peaches for dinner' down the mouthpiece. Most of the time you couldn't get through, and if you did you couldn't hear what was said at the other end because of the noise in the 'rest' room . . .

During the ten-day voyage I became an information bureau. Because I had been to America before I was expected to know in detail about all the cities and towns of every state. They seldom got my name right. Usually I was called Bedelia after the heroine of a current film; they knew it was long and ended with an 'a', that was all. I used to wonder and worry a little as to how some of them would make out, they had such odd ideas of what they were going to. One very pretty Welsh girl would spend long hours on her bunk gazing at her husband's photograph, which I thought omened well, until she confided that she had always hated tall men and her husband was six feet five inches. She wondered whether *it* was worth it; *it* being that she loved her busy home port of Cardiff and she was going to a box number in Iowa. There were large notices over the ship saying: *Orientation Meetings*, with an arrow afterwards. The lieutenant in charge of the meetings told me of the poor attendances. I inquired among the girls and found that most of them thought that if they went to the meetings they would come out resembling Geisha girls.

JANE GORDON
The End of the Black-Out

Nothing appeared to have changed, and I think we were still half consciously listening for an alert or the sound of a flying bomb or a rocket. Then one afternoon when we had finished extracting teeth in the operating theatre, I was cleaning the dental instruments in casualty and overhead on the roof workmen were moving about. I paid no particular attention until suddenly the tarpaulin was pulled off the glass part of our roof and the whole of casualty was flooded with sunshine. After so many years of darkness the effect of this unexpected daylight was like a miracle. Sister had just walked into casualty and I turned towards her. For a long moment she stood looking upwards at the sunlight streaming through the window – then her eyes met mine and her face wore the strangest expression.

CLARA MILBURN
The Return of a Prisoner-of-War Son

Wednesday 9th May 1945

A Day of Days!

This morning at 9.15 the telephone rang and a voice said: 'I've got a very nice telegram for you. You are Milburn, Burleigh, Balsall Common 29?'

'Yes,' I said.

The voice said: 'This is the telegram. "Arrived safely. Coming soon. Alan".'

I nearly leapt to the ceiling and rushed to the bottom of the stairs. 'We've got the right telegram at last!' I cried.

And then all three of us, Jack in bed, Kate nearby and myself all choky, shed a tear or two. We were living again, after five-and-a-half years!

At 11.15 a.m. the telephone rang again and it was a long-distance call. 'Is that Burleigh, Balsall Common?'

'Yes! Is that Alan?' I said.

'Yes.'

And then I said: 'Oh, bless you, my darling.' And off went Alan into a description of his leaving Germany and arriving here, ending by saying he might arrive late tonight or early tomorrow and would ring up again later, and so we said 'Goodbye'.

I wrote 19 postcards and one letter, had three or four long-distance telephone calls and about two dozen others during the day. I made two long-distance calls, and when I asked for a third the operator said: 'You're keeping me busy.'

'Yes,' I said, 'this is a thrilling day.'

'Something special?'

'Yes, my son has arrived in England after five years as a prisoner of war.'

'Exeter,' said the operator's voice, and then to me: 'Was he in Germany?'

'Yes.'

'He'll be glad to get home – there you are, call out, please. They're waiting.'

Such mateyness, it is amusing.

CONSTANCE GODDARD

The Whirlwind of War

1945

I sat up late that night for I could not have slept. My mind was running round in circles. I remembered the day war was declared, the day we worked in the hayfield on a Sunday and the whirlwind caught up the hay and carried it far and wide.

The whirlwind of war had caught up all our lives and tossed them into the air, they had been swept to and fro by eddying currents and dropped again in the same field. But was it the same field? The old landmarks had disappeared and the new ones were not yet clearly defined.

NOTES ON THE AUTHORS

MARGERY ALLINGHAM (1901–1966), detective novelist, helped organise evacuation and billeting in her Essex village, Tolleshunt D'Arcy. She wrote *The Oaken Heart* (1941) about her village in wartime for her American publisher, but it was more popular in England.

VERILY ANDERSON (b.1915), writer, joined the FANYs soon after Munich. She left a year into the war to marry and bring up a family, and lived in London during the blitz.

JOAN BRIGHT ASTLEY (b.1910) worked as a secretary and joined the War Office in 1939. From 1941 she was responsible for a special information centre in the War Cabinet Offices in London; she was also administrative officer for the British delegation at Teheran, Yalta and Potsdam.

ENID BARRAUD (b.1904) worked as a landgirl on a farm in East Anglia. After three and a half years she was dismissed, and her job given to Italian POWs.

ELIZABETH BOWEN (1899–1973), Anglo-Irish novelist, lived in London throughout the war. She worked for the Ministry of Information, and at night as an air-raid warden. Her novel *The Heat of the Day* (1949) is about wartime London.

KAY BOYLE (1902–1993), American novelist, poet, editor and translator, lived in the French Alps with her family until 1941, and helped Jews wanting to acquire US visas. On her return to America she worked for the war effort and wrote about conditions in Europe.

VERA BRITTAIN (1893–1970), writer and pacifist, worked tirelessly for pacifism during the war, lecturing and publishing, including her *Letters to Peace-Lovers*. Her 1944 pamphlet *Seed of Chaos* was almost the only public protest against the obliteration bombing of German cities.

281

MARY BROOKES (b.1918) married a merchant seaman in October 1939. He was reported 'missing, believed killed' in November 1940. In 1943 she was conscripted into the ATS, where she served in a clerical capacity.

BRYHER (Annie Winifred Ellerman, 1894–1983), novelist, poet and patron of the arts, came to London from Switzerland in 1940. She shared a flat in Lowndes Square with the Imagist poet H.D. (Hilda Doolittle). Her novel *Beowulf* (1956) is set in wartime London.

MAVIS BUNYAN (b.1923) worked for the Prudential, looked after her small daughter, and took a job as a bus conductress. She and her husband celebrated their golden wedding in 1992.

BARBARA CARTLAND (b.1901), best-selling romantic novelist, involved herself in a huge variety of charity and welfare work. She was Lady Welfare Officer and Librarian to all services in Bedfordshire.

PHYLLIS CASTLE (b.1909) worked for the BBC, joined the WAAFs but was deemed unsuitable; she then joined the Women's Land Army.

LENA K. CHIVERS, biographical information unobtainable.

CLEMENTINE CHURCHILL (1885–1977), married to the Prime Minister Winston Churchill, raised nearly seven million pounds for her Aid to Russia Fund. She went to Russia on a goodwill visit in April 1945.

DIANA COOPER (1892–1986), married to Duff Cooper, head of the Ministry of Information, helped in a YMCA canteen and became a keen dairy farmer in Sussex. She travelled with her husband, then Chancellor of the Duchy of Lancaster, on his missions to Asia, Australia and Algiers.

VIRGINIA COWLES (1910–1983), American journalist and war corres-pondent, reported for the *Sunday Times* on the war in Finland, Russia, Germany, Poland, Czechoslovakia, Paris and North Africa. She witnessed the entry of the German Army into Czechoslovakia, got arrested by the Gestapo and had to argue her way out.

MARGARET CRISP took up nursing in 1942, on hearing of the big allied raids over Cologne and Essen, and feeling that she wanted to 'help mend the ravages of war'.

AUDREY DEACON (b.1917) joined the WRNS in 1939 and was pro-moted to Acting First Officer, in charge of the Commander-in-Chief's

Cypher Office in Plymouth in 1944. She married in April 1943; her husband died in June 1944.

MARY DE BUNSEN (1910–1982) joined the Auxiliary Fire Service when war broke out, but left to test-fly Tiger Moth planes. She then joined the Air Transport Auxiliary, ferrying planes round the country.

E. M. DELAFIELD (Edmée Elizabeth Monica de la Pasture, 1890–1943), novelist and short story writer, lived in Devon during the war and lectured for the Ministry of Information. She was also involved with the work of the Women's Institutes. *The Provincial Lady in Wartime* (1940) is set in London in the first three months of the war.

SYBIL DOBBIE (1908–1973) did intelligence work before and during the war. She joined her parents on the besieged island of Malta, where her father was Governor, and worked as his private secretary.

BLANCHE E. C. DUGDALE (1880–1948) worked throughout the war at the Jewish Agency and Zionist Federation headquarters in London, and was the Zionist movement's principal liaison with the British Cabinet.

ELIZABETH, PRINCESS (b.1926) persuaded her parents to allow her to train as a driver in the ATS. She learned to drive and maintain staff cars, lorries and ambulances.

ELIZABETH, QUEEN (b.1900) refused to leave London during the blitz, even though Buckingham Palace was hit by bombs. She toured bombed-out areas in London and other cities, giving comfort to many.

GRACIE FIELDS (1898–1979), popular singer and comedienne, went to America at the beginning of the war with her husband, who would have been interned because of his Italian background. She raised huge sums in America for the British war effort, and toured widely entertaining British troops.

THEODORA FITZGIBBON (1916–1991), model, actress and cookery writer, left Paris in 1940 just ahead of the advancing Germans. She bicycled to Bordeaux on her own and caught one of the last boats back to England.

CELIA FREMLIN (b.1914), crime writer, worked for Mass Observation, first as a volunteer and then full-time. Called up in 1942, she was sent to a factory where she disguised her note-taking for Mass Observation as letter-writing.

BELLA FROMM, German diplomatic columnist on a Berlin newspaper, emigrated to New York in 1938. There she worked as a glovemaker, cook, waitress and typist. The Gestapo followed her to New York and she had the protection of two US bodyguards.

BERTA GEISSMAR (b.1892), German Jewish musicologist and personal assistant to the conductor Wilhelm Furtwangler. Forced to leave Germany in 1938, she was befriended by Sir Thomas Beecham and worked with the London Philharmonic Orchestra.

MARTHA GELLHORN (b.1908), distinguished American war correspondent and novelist, wrote for the American magazine *Collier's* during the war. She travelled widely and reported from Finland, China, England, Italy, France and Germany.

CONSTANCE FELICITY GODDARD ran a farm single-handedly in the Dales, where she took in an assortment of evacuees and helpers.

RUMER GODDEN (b.1907), novelist, children's writer and poet, struggled to provide a home for herself and her two young daughters in a remote part of India. She trained as an Auxiliary nurse in case the war should reach India.

MARGARET GOLDSMITH (b.1894 or 1897), American journalist, biographer and novelist, settled in Berlin then moved to London, where she worked as a literary agent.

JANE GORDON was a nurse in a children's hospital in Paddington. She was married to the writer Charles Graves.

JOYCE GRENFELL (1910–1979), writer, singer and entertainer, worked for ENSA. She and her accompanist Viola Tunnard toured military hospitals in the Mediterranean, the Middle East and India.

CHARLOTTE HALDANE (d.1969), journalist, was employed by the *Daily Sketch* to visit Moscow and report on the Soviet Union at war. She subsequently broke with the Communist Party.

MRS ROBERT HENREY (Madeleine, b.1906), columnist, novelist and short story writer, published a series of autobiographical accounts of her life in wartime London, including *A Village in Piccadilly* (1943) and *The Incredible City* (1944).

VERE HODGSON, welfare worker, was attached to a philanthropic and religious community in Holland Park, London. She worked at a night shelter for homeless women in Lambeth, and with families in Notting Hill. She wrote her diary when on fire-watch.

INEZ HOLDEN, documentary journalist and writer, had a variety of wartime jobs in aircraft and Royal Ordnance factories, Civil Defence and the Red Cross. She was sent to report on the Nuremberg trials.

DIANA HOPKINSON (b. 1912) worked for the Czech Refugee Trust. She married in 1939 and had a son; her husband was abroad in the Army for three years.

ELSPETH HUXLEY (b.1907), novelist, biographer and travel writer, worked for the BBC during the war. Starting in the news talks section (short morale-boosting talks after the news), she then became liaison officer with the Colonial Office, passing on and presenting news about the war efforts in remote cut-off colonies.

E. DOREEN IDLE, researched wartime conditions in West Ham on behalf of the Fabian Society and the Ethical Union. West Ham was particularly badly hit during the air raids on the London docks in September 1940.

STORM JAMESON (1891–1986), novelist, essayist and fervent anti-Fascist, was President of the English branch of PEN during the war, and worked vigorously on behalf of refugee writers. The name she used for her autobiography, Mary Hervey Russell, is adapted from her series of novels *The Mirror in Darkness*.

F. TENNYSON JESSE (1889–1958), novelist, playwright and criminologist, lived in St John's Wood, London, and collected the letters that she and her husband wrote to friends in America into two books.

SHIRLEY JOSEPH volunteered for the Land Army 'for the sake of the experience' and stayed for a year.

ZELMA KATIN (b. around 1900) married at twenty-two and could not find work for the next eighteen years, until she was called up for war work. She worked on the trams in Sheffield, earning the nickname 'The Red Conductress' for her socialist views.

MARGARET KENNEDY (1896–1967), novelist, took her three children to a Cornish village for the war, but travelled back and forth to London to visit her husband. Their home was destroyed by a bomb.

MARY KESSELL (b.1914), painter, mural decorator and illustrator, worked in Germany in 1945 as an official war artist.

FLAVIA KINGSCOTE was interned in Tuscany, Italy, during the spring and early summer of 1941, before being sent back to England.

RACHEL KNAPPETT worked as a landgirl in South West Lancashire.

LAURA KNIGHT (1877–1970), artist, was frequently commissioned by the War Artists Advisory Committee, often for portraits of women military medallists or for pictures of women doing war work on balloon sites and in factories. The picture she was commissioned to paint of the Nuremberg trials is in the Imperial War Museum, London.

MARGARET LANE (1907–1994), journalist, novelist and biographer, lived in Hampshire during the war.

MARGHANITA LASKI (1915–1988), novelist, journalist and broadcaster, had two children during the war. She also nursed, ran a dairy farm, worked in Intelligence and wrote her first novel.

NELLA LAST (1890–1968), a housewife and mother in the shipbuilding town of Barrow-in-Furness in Lancashire, joined the WVS and worked on mobile canteens. She started writing her diary for Mass Observation in September 1939 and continued for nearly thirty years.

LIVIA LAURENT, poet and translator, came to England from Germany as a girl. She was interned in July 1940, first in Holloway Jail and then on the Isle of Man. She was released in 1941.

ROSAMOND LEHMANN (1901–1990), novelist, translator and short story writer, took her two small children to live with her mother after her marriage failed. She became a reader for her brother John Lehmann, editor of the magazine *New Writing*, and contributed the short stories later collected in *The Gipsy's Baby* (1946).

SYLVIA LEITH-ROSS (1883–1980), expert on Nigeria, joined the British Committee for the French Red Cross and was sent to Paris in December 1939. Back in England she worked with refugees before returning to Nigeria in 1941 to assist the wartime colonial administration.

C.A. LEJEUNE (Caroline, 1897–1973) was film critic for *The Observer* during the war.

LORNA LEWIS drove a van for the Red Cross in France in June 1940. During the blitz she worked in London on a mobile canteen.

ROSE MACAULAY (1881–1958), novelist, travel writer, broadcaster and critic, joined the London Auxiliary Ambulance Service as a part-time driver. Her flat with all her books and papers was destroyed in the blitz; replacement copies of some of her favourite books were sent to her by complete strangers. She spent some of the war in Portugal, researching *They Went to Portugal* (1946).

BRENDA MCBRYDE (b.1918), nurse and writer, joined the Queen Alexandra's Imperial Nursing Service Reserve in 1943. She served in the invasion of Normandy in 1944, and subsequently in Belgium, Holland and Germany.

CICELY MCCALL, biographical information unobtainable.

CECILY MACKWORTH fled from Paris as the Germans entered in 1940. She worked for the Red Cross in France, before escaping to England via Spain and Portugal. She joined the Free French at their Headquarters in London, then lectured for the Army Bureau of Current Affairs in factories and hostels.

ETHEL MANNIN (1900–1984), novelist, essayist and pacifist, steadily produced a novel a year during the war. Her criticism of the Soviet Union, which she had visited in 1936, was not well received.

HILDE MARCHANT (1916–1970), star reporter on the *Daily Express*, travelled to France, Poland and Sweden, but specialised in home front reporting. Winston Churchill was so impressed by her report on the Coventry blitz that he asked for copies to be sent to British Embassies worldwide.

VERA LAUGHTON MATHEWS (1888–1959), Director of the WRNS, which she had joined the day it was formed in 1917. It was said she knew every one of her officers.

CLARA MILBURN (1883–1961), housewife and mother from Burleigh near Coventry, filled fifteen exercise books with her daily diary of 'Burleigh in Wartime'. She included letters, telegrams, maps and newspaper cuttings.

BETTY MILLER (1910–1965), novelist and biographer, moved round the country with her two young children and her husband, a major in the RAMC.

NAOMI MITCHISON (b.1897), novelist, traveller, socialist and feminist, moved to Carradale in the West of Scotland in 1937. Here she farmed and entered closely into the life and work of the community.

LILY MONTAGU (1873–1963), social worker and pioneer in the establishment of Liberal Judaism, ran the West Central Girls' Club in London, and was presiding Magistrate at Chelsea Juvenile Court.

DIANA MOSLEY (b.1910), married to Oswald Mosley, leader of the British Union of Fascists, was interned in Holloway Jail in 1940, under Defence Regulation 18b which gave the government the right to imprison anyone who was a member of the British Union. In 1941 she was allowed to share a house with her husband in the prison grounds; they were released in 1943.

ANNA NEAGLE (1904–1986), actress, toured Britain and Europe for ENSA. She was famous for her portrayal of wartime heroines.

ANNA NEY (Josephine Pasternak, 1900–1993), Russian poet and philosopher, left Moscow for Berlin in 1921, and moved to Oxford in 1938. The writer Boris Pasternak was her brother, and the painter Leonid her father.

JENNY NICHOLSON served as a Public Relations Officer in the WAAF. She wrote scripts for servicewomen on radio programmes such as the weekly 'Women At War' series, and 'In Town Tonight'.

BARBARA NIXON became an air raid warden in May 1940, and worked through the London blitz. She later became an ARP instructor and lecturer on Civil Defence.

KATE O'BRIEN (1897–1974), Irish novelist and playwright, lived in London during the war. *The Last of Summer* (1940) describes County Clare just before the outbreak of war.

LUCY OLBROMSKA, biographical information unobtainable.

EDITH OLIVIER (1879–1948), novelist and biographer, lived with her sister in the Dairy House at Wilton, Wiltshire. She was mayor of Wilton for several terms.

MOLLIE PANTER-DOWNES (b.1906), novelist and journalist, wrote her superb fortnightly *Letter from London* for the *New Yorker*, starting in

September 1939 and continuing throughout the war. Her novel *One Fine Day* (1946) is about the aftermath of war.

FRANCES PARTRIDGE (b.1900), diarist, pacifist and member of the Bloomsbury group, spent the war in the country at Ham Spray House in Wiltshire, with her husband Ralph (a conscientious objector), her young son and various guests.

POLLY PEABODY (b.1917) worked in an ambulance unit for the American Red Cross in Europe. She lived in occupied Paris, then escaped via Spain and Portugal to London, where she worked as a war correspondent in the blitz.

MARGERY PERHAM (1895–1982), expert on African affairs and colonial administration, was the first Fellow of Nuffield College Oxford in 1939.

BARBARA PYM (1913–1980), novelist, worked as a postal censor; in 1943 she joined the WRNS and served in England and Italy.

STELLA, DOWAGER MARCHIONESS OF READING (1894–1971), founder and chairman of the WVS (which became the WRVS in 1966), supervised the huge amount of administration involved in the WVS. She also spent much time touring the country to recruit, inspire and encourage individual members.

CONSTANCE REAVELEY, a lecturer in political philosophy, worked in various factories as machine operative, progress chaser and welfare officer.

NESCA ROBB (1906–1976), author and poet, worked in London as a temporary civil servant for the Women's Employment Federation, an employment register for professional women.

PAMELA RUFFONI (Pamela Moore) joined the Land Army in 1943. She was engaged and later married to a conscientious objector born of Italian parents.

DOROTHEA RUSSELL, army welfare worker, opened and ran the Tipperary Club for servicemen in Cairo in 1939. She started 'Music For All' in 1941.

VITA SACKVILLE-WEST (1892–1962), novelist, poet and gardening expert, spent the war at Sissinghurst Castle in Kent. She helped to organize the Women's Land Army in her area.

STELLA ST JOHN, vet and welfare worker, drove an ambulance voluntarily. She refused, however, to be directed compulsorily into war work, and was sent to prison for six weeks in 1943.

CYNTHIA SAUNDERS, biographical information unobtainable.

DOROTHY L. SAYERS (1893–1957), novelist and playwright, broadcast and lectured for the war effort. Between 1940 and 1943 she worked on the controversial but successful *Man Born To Be King*, a twelve-part dramatization of the life of Christ for BBC Children's Hour.

FLORENCE SHARP, biographical information unobtainable.

ETTA SHIBER, an American widow living in Paris, did welfare work with French soldiers. Imprisoned by the Gestapo for providing escape routes for British servicemen, she was exchanged for the German spy Johanna Hofmann.

CONSTANCE BABINGTON SMITH (b.1912), journalist and biographer, served with the WAAF and specialized in aerial reconnaissance. She started the aircraft interpretation section, vital for intelligence of enemy activity, including the new V weapons.

NAOMI ROYDE SMITH (1875–1964), novelist, biographer, playwright and literary critic, lived in Winchester during the war.

STEVIE SMITH (1902–1971), poet and novelist, was employed full-time as a secretary at Newnes, the publishers. She did much reviewing, as well as fire-watching.

FREYA STARK (1893–1993), traveller and writer, worked as a South Arabia (Middle East) expert for the Ministry of Information. In Egypt she founded the Pro-British Brothers and Sisters of Freedom in order to combat German influence. Besieged in the British embassy in Baghdad in 1941, she compiled daily news bulletins for the Embassy from foreign radio stations. She also travelled to America and India.

GERTRUDE STEIN (1874–1946), American author, lived with Alice B. Toklas in the French village of Culoz, throughout the German occupation. She returned to her Paris apartment in November 1944.

JAN STRUTHER (Joyce Maxtone Graham, 1901–1953) spent the war years with her children in America, where she lectured extensively for the benefit of British War Relief. Mrs Miniver first appeared on the Court page of *The Times* in a series of sketches of family life.

EDITH SUMMERSKILL (1901–1980), Labour MP, doctor and campaigner on women's issues, served on the 1942 government enquiry into the women's services. In 1945 she was under-secretary at the Ministry of Food.

MAVIS TATE (1893–1947), Conservative MP and champion of women's causes, visited factories to investigate the conditions of women workers. In 1945 she was the only woman in the party of MPs visiting German concentration camps, a visit which affected her deeply.

MARY TREVELYAN, founder and governor of international Students' House London, served on the YMCA Programme Staff with the Army in Belgium 1944–45. She worked on reconstruction surveys in Greece and the East.

EVELYN UNDERHILL (1875–1941), poet and writer on mysticism, joined the Anglican Pacifist Fellowship and wrote an uncompromising pamphlet 'The Church and War' (1940). She believed that 'the Church cannot acquiesce in war'.

HELEN WADDELL (1889–1965), medievalist scholar and poet, lived in London and worked for Constable's, the publisher. She was the assistant editor of the magazine the *Nineteenth Century*.

SYLVIA TOWNSEND WARNER (1893–1978), novelist, spent much of the war in Dorset with Valentine Ackland. She worked for the WVS and did much lecturing for the WEA, the Labour Party and the forces. She also learned rifle-shooting and grenade-throwing.

HILARY WAYNE joined the ATS with her daughter by lying about both their ages. Hilary was fifty-six but said she was forty-two; her daughter Hazel was fifteen but said she was eighteen. They both trained as cooks.

BEATRICE WEBB (1858–1943), socialist and co-founder of the Fabian Society, was living in retirement at Passfield Corner, Liphook. She continued to write her diary until a few days before her death.

MAUREEN WELLS (b.1921) worked as a billeting officer before volunteering for the WRNS. She joined a small group of Wren couriers, then became a stoker and served at invasion bases in the Portsmouth area.

REBECCA WEST (Cicily Isabel Fairfield, 1892–1983), novelist, essayist, critic and feminist, published *Black Lamb and Grey Falcon* in 1941, a major study of Yugoslavia. She superintended British broadcast talks to Yugoslavia, and went to Nuremberg to cover the war trials.

LESLIE WHATELEY (1899–1987), Director of the ATS 1943–46, battled hard to improve the public image of the ATS and the living conditions of its members.

WINIFRED WILLIAMS contributed a series of articles to *Time and Tide* on wartime life in the industrial north of England.

AMABEL WILLIAMS-ELLIS (1894–1984), author and journalist, married to the architect Clough Williams-Ellis, spent the war in North Wales. She took in evacuees and toured war factories to investigate women's working conditions. Her pamphlet 'Women in War Factories' was used by the Ministry of Information.

MARGERY WITHERS, biographical information unobtainable.

VIRGINIA WOOLF (1882–1941), novelist and critic, published her anti-war *Three Guineas* in 1938. The Woolfs' London house was severely damaged by bombs and they lived mainly at Rodmell near the Sussex coast, often disturbed by enemy planes and bombs.

SUSAN WOOLFITT (1907–1978) worked on narrow-boats for a year. Three-women crews managed pairs of boats, which carried cargo on England's extensive system of canals and waterways.

ESTHER TERRY WRIGHT married an RAF pilot and had to find 'forty different roofs in fourteen months' in order to keep up with him on his frequent postings. He was shot down in September 1940 and badly burnt, but back flying the next year.

ACKNOWLEDGEMENTS AND SOURCES

My thanks for help in compiling this anthology go especially to all those authors and their relatives who responded so generously and patiently to my requests and queries. I would also like to thank the staff at the London Library, the Roehampton Institute Library and the Imperial War Museum for their help, and Lynn Knight, Cathy Wells Cole and Nick Hartley for their invaluable advice and support.

Permission to reprint copyright material in this book is gratefully acknowledged. Apologies are offered to those copyright-holders whom it has proved impossible to locate.

Her Majesty The Queen: the text of the broadcast originally printed in the *Listener*, 17 October 1940, reprinted by gracious permission of Her Majesty the Queen.
Her Majesty Queen Elizabeth The Queen Mother: the text of the broadcast originally printed in the *Listener*, 14 August 1941, reprinted with the kind agreement of Her Majesty Queen Elizabeth The Queen Mother.
Margery Allingham: extracts from *The Oaken Heart*, copyright © Margery Allingham, Michael Joseph, 1941, reproduced by permission of Curtis Brown Ltd, London, on behalf of P. & M. Youngman Carter Ltd.
Verily Anderson: extracts from *Spam Tomorrow*, Rupert Hart-Davis, 1956, reprinted by permission of the author.
Joan Bright Astley: an extract from *The Inner Circle, A View of War at the Top*, Hutchinson, 1971.
E.M. Barraud: an extract from *Set my Hand upon the Plough*, Littlebury & Co Ltd, The Worcester Press, Worcester, 1945.
Elizabeth Bowen: 'Calico Windows' from *Soho Centenary*, Hutchinson, 1944, and 'London, 1940' from *Collected Impressions*, copyright © Elizabeth Bowen, Longmans, 1950, reprinted by permission of Curtis Brown Ltd, London.
Kay Boyle: an extract from *Primer for Combat*, Faber, 1943.
Vera Brittain: extracts from *England's Hour*, Macmillan, 1941, and from *Seed of Chaos: What Mass Bombing Really Means*, published for the Bombing Restriction Committee by New Vision Publishing Co, April 1944, reprinted by permission of Paul Berry, Literary Executor for Vera Brittain.
Mary Brookes: extracts from the Papers of Mrs M. Brookes, Department of Documents, the Imperial War Museum, reprinted by the generous permission of the author and the Trustees of the Imperial War Museum.
Bryher: extracts from *Days of Mars, A Memoir 1940–1948*, Calder & Boyars, 1972, reprinted by permission of Perdita Schaffner.

Mavis Bunyan: three letters, reprinted by the generous permission of the author.

Barbara Cartland: extracts from *The Years of Opportunity, 1939–1945*, Hutchinson, 1948, reprinted by permission of the author.

Phyllis Castle: extracts from 'A Week in the WAAFs' from *Leaves in the Storm, A Book of Diaries*, eds Stefan Schimanski and Henry Treece, Lindsay Drummond, 1947.

Lena Chivers: extracts from 'Night Duty', *Time and Tide*, 5 August 1944.

Clementine Churchill: an extract from *My Visit to Russia*, Hutchinson, 1945, reprinted by permission of the Lady Soames, DBE, Literary Executor for Clementine Churchill.

Diana Cooper: extracts from *Trumpets from the Steep*, Rupert Hart-Davis, 1960, reprinted by permission of the Viscount Norwich.

Virginia Cowles: an extract from *Looking for Trouble*, Hamish Hamilton, 1941, reprinted by permission of Harriet Crawley.

Margaret Crisp: an extract from *Utility Nurse*, Chaterson Ltd, London, 1947.

Audrey Deacon: extracts from the Papers of Mrs Audrey Deacon, Department of Documents, the Imperial War Museum, reprinted by the generous permission of the author and the Trustees of the Imperial War Museum.

Mary de Bunsen: extracts from 'A Hen among the Eagles', *Blackwood's Magazine*, April 1941, reprinted by permission of Raymond Salisbury-Jones.

E.M. Delafield: extracts from 'Notes on the Way', *Time and Tide*, 13 July 1940, reprinted by permission of the Peters Fraser & Dunlop Group Ltd.

Sybil Dobbie: an extract from *Grace Under Malta*, Lindsay Drummond, 1944, reprinted by permission of Jos Johnston.

Blanche E.C. Dugdale: 'All Ye That Pass By', the *Spectator*, 11 December 1942, reprinted by permission of Adam Fergusson, Literary Executor for Blanche E.C. Dugdale.

An Englishwoman: Letter reproduced in *War Letters from Britain*, eds Diana Forbes Robertson and Roger W. Strauss Jr, Jarrolds, London, 1942.

Ex-Landgirl: Letter to the *New Statesman and Nation*, 20 November 1943, reprinted by permission of Cover Stories.

Gracie Fields: an extract from the Papers of Gracie Fields, Department of Documents, the Imperial War Museum, reprinted by permission of Grace Orbell and the Trustees of the Imperial War Museum.

Theodora FitzGibbon: extracts from *With Love*, Century Publishing, 1982, reprinted by permission of David Higham Associates Ltd.

Celia Fremlin: an extract from *War Factory*, 1943, reprinted by Century Hutchinson, 1987, copyright © the Trustees of the Mass Observation Archive, University of Sussex, reprinted by permission of Curtis Brown Ltd.

Bella Fromm: an extract from 'Blood and Banquets', *Harper's Magazine*, October 1942.

Berta Geissmar: an extract from *The Baton and the Jackboot*, Hamish Hamilton, 1944.

Martha Gellhorn: 'Dachau' from *The Face of War*, Rupert Hart-Davis, 1959, reprinted by permission of Aitken & Stone Ltd.

Constance Goddard: an extract from *Come Wind, Come Weather*, Jonathan Cape, 1945.

Rumer Godden: extract from *Bengal Journey, A Story of the Part Played by Women in the Province 1939–1945*, copyright © Rumer Godden, 1945, published by

Longmans, 1945, reprinted by permission of Curtis Brown Ltd, London, on behalf of Rumer Godden.

Margaret Goldsmith: an extract from *Women at War*, Lindsay Drummond, 1943.

Jane Gordon: extracts from *Married to Charles*, William Heinemann Ltd, 1950, reprinted by permission of Reed International.

The Greenhill Knitting Circle: letter printed in *Dear Allies . . ., A Story of Women in Monklands and Besieged Leningrad* by Margaret Henderson, Monklands District Libraries, 1988, reprinted by permission of Monklands District Council.

Joyce Grenfell: extracts from *The Time of My Life* ed J. Roose-Evans, Hodder & Stoughton, 1989, copyright © Reginald Grenfell and James Roose Evans, reprinted by permission of Richard Scott Simon Ltd.

Charlotte Haldane: extracts from *Truth Will Out*, Weidenfeld & Nicolson, 1949.

Mrs Robert Henrey: an extract from *A Village in Piccadilly*, J.M. Dent & Sons, 1952, reprinted by permission of the author.

Vere Hodgson: extracts from *Few Eggs and No Oranges, A Diary Showing how Unimportant People in London and Birmingham Lived through the War Years 1939–1945*, Dobson Books Ltd, 1976, reprinted by permission of Dobson Books Ltd.

Inez Holden: an extract from *Night Shift*, published by John Lane, The Bodley Head, 1941, and an extract from 'Summer Journal' originally printed in *Leaves in the Storm, A Book of Diaries* eds Stefan Schimanski and Henry Treece, Lindsay Drummond, 1947, reprinted by permission of A.M. Heath on behalf of the author.

Diana Hopkinson: extract from the Papers of Captain and Mrs D.M. Hopkinson, Department of Documents, the Imperial War Museum, reprinted by permission of the author and the Trustees of the Imperial War Museum.

Elspeth Huxley: two extracts from *Atlantic Ordeal, The Story of Mary Cornish*, Chatto & Windus, 1941, and an extract from 'WAAFs in the Operation Room', the *Listener*, 16 July 1942, reprinted by permission of the author.

E. Doreen Idle: an extract from *War Over West Ham, A Study of Community Adjustment*, published by Faber & Faber Ltd, 1943, reprinted by permission of Faber & Faber Ltd.

Storm Jameson: extracts from 'City Without Children' originally printed in the *Atlantic Monthly*, November 1939, and an extract from *The Journal of Mary Hervey Russell* (despite the title this is autobiographical), Macmillan, 1945, reprinted by permission of the Peters Fraser & Dunlop Group Ltd.

F. Tennyson Jesse: extracts from *London Front, Letters Written to America, August 1939–July 1940*, Constable, 1940, and an extract (reproduced on page 251) from *While London Burns, Letters Written to America, July 1940–June 1941*, Constable, 1942, reprinted by permission of A.M. Heath on behalf of the Estate of F. Tennyson Jesse and Constable and Co Ltd.

Shirley Joseph: an extract from *If Their Mothers Only Knew, An Unofficial Account of Life in the Women's Land Army*, Faber & Faber Ltd, 1946, reprinted by permission of Faber & Faber Ltd.

Zelma Katin: extracts from *'Clippie', The Autobiography of a War Time Conductress*, John Gifford, 1944.

Margaret Kennedy: an extract from *Where Stands a Wingèd Sentry*, Yale University Press, 1941, reprinted by permission of Yale University Press.

Mary Kessell: an extract from 'German Diary by a War Artist August–October 1945', the *Cornhill Magazine*, April 1946–Autumn 1947.

Flavia Kingscote: an extract from *Balkan Exit*, Geoffrey Bles, 1942.

Rachel Knappett: an extract from *A Pullet on the Midden*, Michael Joseph, 1946.

Laura Knight: extracts from *The Magic of a Line, The Autobiography of Laura Knight, DBE, RA* copyright © Laura Knight, William Kimber, 1965, reprinted by permission of John Farquharson Ltd.

Margaret Lane: extracts from 'The Wreckage Wind', the *New Statesman and Nation*, 25 November 1944, reprinted by permission of Cover Stories.

Marghanita Laski: 'Our Auxiliary Women', the *Spectator*, 22 December 1939, reprinted by permission of David Higham Associates.

Nella Last: extracts from *Nella Last's War, A Mother's Diary 1939–1945* eds Richard Broad and Suzie Fleming, Falling Wall Press, Bristol, 1981, reprinted by permission of Falling Wall Press.

Livia Laurent: extracts from *A Tale of Internment*, George Allen & Unwin, 1942.

Rosamond Lehmann: extracts from 'A Charming Person', the *Spectator*, 10 November 1939, reprinted by permission of the Society of Authors as the Literary Representative of the Estate of Rosamond Lehmann.

Sylvia Leith-Ross: an extract from *Cocks in the Dawn*, Hutchinson, 1944.

C.A. Lejeune: extracts from *Chestnuts In Her Lap*, published by Phoenix House Ltd, 1947, reprinted by permission of Carcanet Press Ltd.

Lorna Lewis: extract from 'Food on Wheels', *Time and Tide*, 2 November 1940.

Rose Macaulay: an extract from 'Notes on the Way', *Time and Tide*, 5 October 1940, and 'Consolations of the War' the *Listener*, 16 January 1941, reprinted by permission of the Peters Fraser & Dunlop Group.

Brenda McBryde: extract from *A Nurse's War*, Chatto & Windus, 1979, reprinted by permission of the David Grossman Literary Agency Ltd on behalf of the author.

Cicely McCall: an extract from *Women's Institutes*, Collins, 1943.

Cecily Mackworth: extracts from *I Came Out Of France*, Routledge, 1941, reprinted by permission of International Thomson Publishing Services.

Ethel Mannin: extracts from *Brief Voices*, Hutchinson, 1959.

Hilde Marchant: extracts from *Women and Children Last*, Gollancz, 1941.

Vera Laughton Mathews: extracts from *Blue Tapestry*, Hollis & Carter, 1948.

Clara Milburn: extracts from *Mrs Milburn's Diaries, An Englishwoman's Day-To-Day Reflections 1939–1945*, Harrap, 1979, reprinted by permission of Peter Donnelly and Judy Milburn.

Betty Miller: an extract from 'Notes for an Unwritten Autobiography' *Modern Reading* No 13, 1945, reprinted by permission of Jonathan and Sarah Miller.

Naomi Mitchison: an extract from *Among You Taking Notes . . ., The Wartime Diary of Naomi Mitchison 1939–1945* ed D. Sheridan, Gollancz, 1985, reprinted by permission of David Higham Associates Ltd.

Lily Montagu: an extract from 'Club Letter No 26, May 1941' (to the members of the West Central Jewish Girls' Club), from *Lily H. Montagu, Prophet of a Living Judaism* by Eric Conrad, 1953, reproduced in *Sermons, Addresses, Letters and Prayers*, ed. Ellen Umansky, Edwin Mellen Press, New York, 1985, reprinted by permission of Eric Conrad, Literary Executor for Lily Montagu.

Diana Mosley: extracts from *A Life of Contrasts*, Hamish Hamilton, 1977, reprinted by permission of the author.

Anna Neagle: an extract from *There's Always Tomorrow*, W.H. Allen, 1974.

The New Statesman and Nation: Competition and Correspondence, December 1939, reprinted by permission of Cover Stories.

Anna Ney: extracts from a letter in *Time and Tide*, 24 April 1943, reprinted by permission of Helen Ramsay.

Jenny Nicholson: an extract from *Kiss the Girls Good-Bye*, Hutchinson, 1944.

Barbara Nixon: extracts from *Raiders Overhead, The Record of a London Warden*, Lindsay Drummond, 1943.

Kate O'Brien: 'Cheffie', *Time and Tide*, 19 October 1940, reprinted by permission of David Higham Associates Ltd.

Lucy Olbromska: an extract from 'Poland's Women Appeal to the Conscience of the World', *London Calling, July 1941*.

Edith Olivier: extract from *Night Thoughts of a Country Landlady*, Batsford, 1943, reprinted by permission of B.T. Batsford Ltd.

Mollie Panter-Downes: extracts from articles from the *New Yorker*, reprinted in *London War Notes 1939–1945*, ed William Shawn, Farrar, Straus & Giroux, New York, 1971, reprinted by permission of the author.

Frances Partridge: extracts from *A Pacifist's War*, The Hogarth Press, 1978, reprinted by permission of Random House UK Ltd.

Polly Peabody: extracts from *Occupied Territory*, The Cresset Press, 1941.

Margery Perham: an extract from 'The World and Dockland', the *Spectator*, 10 January 1941, reprinted by permission of the *Spectator*.

A Polish Refugee: extracts from 'How it Feels to be a Refugee', the *Listener*, 3 June 1943.

Barbara Pym: extracts from *A Very Private Eye, Diaries, Letters and Notebooks*, eds Hazel Holt and Hilary Pym, Macmillan, 1984, reprinted by permission of Macmillan London.

The Dowager Marchioness of Reading: extracts from the article 'Women's Voluntary Services' the *Fortnightly*, April 1945, reprinted by permission of the Trustees for the Estate of the Dowager Marchioness of Reading.

Constance Reaveley: an extract from 'The Machine and the Mind', the *Spectator*, 7 April 1944, reprinted by permission of the *Spectator*.

Nesca Robb: an extract from *An Ulsterwoman in England 1924–1941*, Cambridge University Press, 1942, reprinted by permission of Cambridge University Press.

Naomi Royde Smith: extracts from *Outside Information, Being a Diary of Rumours*, Macmillan, 1941, reprinted by permission of Macmillan London.

Pamela Ruffoni: an extract from the Papers of Mrs Pamela Ruffoni, Department of Documents, the Imperial War Museum, reprinted by permission of the Trustees of the Imperial War Museum.

Dorothea Russell: 'Music for All', *Convoy 5*, 1946.

Vita Sackville-West: 'Country Notes', the *New Statesman and Nation*, 23 September 1939, copyright © Vita Sackville-West, 1939, and extracts from the *Women's Land Army* copyright © Vita Sackville-West, 1944, Michael Joseph, 1944, reprinted by permission of Curtis Brown Ltd, London, on behalf of the Estate of Vita Sackville-West.

Stella St. John: an extract from *A Prisoner's Log, Holloway Prison in 1943*, the Howard League for Penal Reform, 1944, reprinted by permission of the Howard League for Penal Reform.

Cynthia Saunders: 'Tribunal Day' the *Spectator*, 17 November 1939, reprinted by permission of the *Spectator*.

Dorothy L. Sayers: extracts from 'Forgiveness and the Enemy', the *Fortnightly*, April 1941, reprinted by permission of David Higham Associates Ltd.

Florence Sharp: an extract from " 'Sparrow Starvers' of Soho", the *Listener*, 8 April 1943.

Etta Shiber: an extract from *Paris Underground*, George Harrap, 1944.

Stevie Smith: an extract from 'Mosaic', *Eve's Journal*, 1939, reprinted in *Me Again, the Uncollected Writings of Stevie Smith* copyright © James McGibbon, Virago Press, 1983, reprinted by permission of Virago Press Ltd.

Constance Babington Smith: an extract from *Evidence in Camera, The Story of Photographic Intelligence*, Chatto & Windus, 1957, reprinted by permission of the Peters Fraser & Dunlop Group Ltd.

Freya Stark: an extract (reproduced on p. 210) from *Dust in the Lion's Paw, Autobiography 1939–1946*, John Murray, 1961, reprinted by permission of John Murray (Publishers) Ltd, and an extract from *Letters, Vol 5 1943–1946* ed Lucy Moorhead, Michael Russell, 1978.

Gertrude Stein: extracts from *Wars I Have Seen*, Batsford, 1945, reprinted by permission of David Higham Associates Ltd.

Jan Struther: an extract from *Mrs Miniver* 1939, reprinted by Virago Press, 1989, reprinted by permission of Virago Press Ltd.

Edith Summerskill: extracts from 'Conscription and Women', the *Fortnightly*, March 1942, reprinted by permission of David Higham Associates Ltd.

Mavis Tate: an extract from 'More on Buchenwald', the *Spectator*, 4 May 1945, reprinted by permission of the *Spectator*.

Time and Tide: Correspondence on 'Women's War Service', September–October 1941, and Correspondence on 'Cigarettes – for Men Only', 5 July 1941.

Mary Trevelyan: extracts from *I'll Walk Beside You, Letters from Belgium September 1944-May 1945*, Longmans, 1946, reprinted by permission of David Higham Associates Ltd.

Evelyn Underhill: prayers from *A Service of Prayer for Use in War-Time*, Church Literature Association 1939.

Helen Waddell: an extract from a letter by Helen Waddell in *Helen Waddell, A Life* by D. Felicitas Corrigan, published by Gollancz, 1990, reprinted by permission of David Bolt Associates.

Sylvia Townsend Warner: extracts from Sylvia Townsend Warner's *Letters* ed W. Maxwell, Chatto & Windus, 1982, reprinted by permission of Susanna Pinney and William Maxwell.

Hilary Wayne: extracts from *Two Odd Soldiers*, George Allen & Unwin, 1946.

Beatrice Webb: extracts from *The Diary of Beatrice Webb, Vol IV, 1924–1943, The Wheel of Life*, eds Norman and Jeanne MacKenzie, Virago Press, 1985, reprinted by permission of Virago Press Ltd and the Trustees of the LSE.

Maureen Wells: extracts from *Entertaining Eric, Letters from the Home Front 1941–1944*, the Imperial War Museum, 1988, reprinted by permission of the author and the Trustees of the Imperial War Museum.

Rebecca West: 'If the Worst Comes to the Worst', *Time and Tide*, 8 June 1940, and an extract from 'Greenhouse with Cyclamens', 1946, collected in *A Train of Powder*, Macmillan, 1955, reprinted by permission of the Peters Fraser & Dunlop Group Ltd.

Leslie Whateley: an extract from *As Thoughts Survive*, Hutchinson, 1949.

Winifred Williams: an extract from 'Northern City at Noon', *Time and Tide*, 24 October 1942.

Amabel Williams-Ellis: an extract from *Women in War Factories*, Gollancz, 1943, and extracts from 'Hostels and Girls' originally printed in the *Spectator*, 24 July 1942, reprinted by permission of the Peters Fraser & Dunlop Group Ltd.

Margery Withers: an extract from 'Children Under Hitler', the *Listener*, 18 February 1943.

Virginia Woolf: 'Thoughts on Peace in an Air Raid' (originally written in August 1940 for an American symposium on current affairs concerning women), from *The Death of the Moth and Other Essays*, The Hogarth Press, 1942, and extracts from *The Diary of Virginia Woolf, Vol V 1936–1941*, ed A.O. Bell, The Hogarth Press, 1984, reprinted by permission of the Random Century Group on behalf of the Estate of Virginia Woolf.

Susan Woolfitt: extracts from *Idle Women*, 1947, reprinted M.&M. Baldwin, Cleobury, Mortimer, Shropshire, 1986, reprinted by permission of Harriet Graham and Adam Woolfitt.

A Wren: letter reproduced in *Blue Tapestry* by Vera Laughton Mathews, Hollis and Carter Ltd, London, 1948.

Esther Terry Wright: extract from *Pilot's Wife's Tale, the Diary of a Camp-Follower*, John Lane, The Bodley Head, 1942, reprinted by permission of the Random Century Group.

Every effort has been made to trace copyright holders in all the copyright material in this book. The editor regrets if there has been any oversight and suggests that the publisher is contacted in any such event.

SUGGESTIONS FOR FURTHER READING

Braybon, Gail and Summerfield, Penny, *Out of the Cage*, Pandora 1987.

Calder, Angus, *The People's War*, 1969, rpt Pimlico 1992.

Henderson, Margaret, *Dear Allies ... A Story of Women in Monklands and Besieged Leningrad*, Monklands District Libraries 1988.

Lumley, Joanna, *Forces Sweethearts*, Bloomsbury Publishing 1993.

McBryde, Brenda, *Quiet Heroines*, 1985, rpt Cakebreads Publications, Saffron Walden, Essex 1989.

Minns, Raynes, *Bombers and Mash*, Virago 1980.

Sebba, Anne, *Battling for News: The Rise of the Woman Reporter*, Hodder and Stoughton 1994.

Sheridan, Dorothy, ed., *Wartime Women*, Heinemann 1990.

Taylor, Eric, *Women Who Went to War 1938–1946*, Grafton Books 1989.

Waller, Jane and Vaughan-Rees, Michael, *Women in Wartime*, Macdonald Optima 1987.

Waller, Jane and Vaughan-Rees, Michael, *Women in Uniform 1939–1945*, Macmillan 1989.

Waller, Jane and Vaughan-Rees, Michael, *Blitz*, Macdonald Optima 1990.

Warner, Lavinia and Sandilands, John, *Women Beyond the Wire*, Michael Joseph 1982.